Experimental Houses Nicolas Pople

For my brother Michael, 12.19.1946 – 7.20.1951

Author's acknowledgements
With thanks to the best of my
teachers: Jon Corpe, David Dunster
and Peter Ahrends, and the support
and encouragement of my teaching
colleagues, Katherine Shonfield
and Jeremy Melvin.

First published in the United States in 2000
by Watson-Guptill Publications
a division of BPI Communications, Inc.
770 Broadway
New York, NY 10003
www.watsonguptill.com

Library of Congress Cataloging-in-Publication Data

Pople, Nicolas.
    Experimental houses/Nicolas Pople.
        p.—cm.
    Includes index.
    ISBN 0-8230-1649-8
        1. Architecture, Domestic--20th century. I. Title.

NA7110.P67 2000
728--dc21   00-042277

ISBN 0-8230-1649-8

This book was designed and produced
by Calmann & King Ltd, London

Designed by sans + baum

Printed in Hong Kong

First printing, 2000

1 2 3 4 5 6 7 8 9 / 07 06 05 04 03 02 01 00

Experimental Houses
Nicolas Pople

Watson-Guptill Publications
New York

Experimental Houses contents

Houses, for the vast majority of the world's population, are a mundane backdrop to everyday life. Most houses are not actually 'designed' in the normal sense of that term; they are produced using tested methods of construction and building forms that have evolved into traditions over time. More recently these traditions have been progressively replaced by a culturally and economically driven aesthetic in which both vernacular and designed elements co-exist, usually to the detriment of both.

The word vernacular needs definition in this context. It is used here to indicate a method of conceiving and constructing buildings in cultural environments in which houses are built using relatively uncomplicated construction techniques and without input from specialist designers. The relentless global destruction of indigenous cultures during the past two centuries has largely removed the symbolic and ritualistic overlays which used to exist in the vernacular tradition and replaced them in the economically suppressed parts of the world with a pragmatic and materialistically functional approach. In industrialized countries, the twentieth century saw housing being influenced increasingly by an aesthetic driven largely by the skill and management structures of the construction industry, with construction techniques defined by the economics of the world market. Architecture's own internal discourse in respect of the house as a type has remained somewhat marginalized, with experimentation being almost solely confined to either one-off houses for relatively wealthy clients and, in the twentieth century, the provision of social housing as well. The great mass of housing within these two polarities has remained noticeably distant from the immediate influence of architectural theory and practice.

Introduction

However, because houses are so integral to our relationship to property, and are carriers of both social traditions and aspirations, they provide rich material for reading the myths and realities which drive different cultural environments. This ability of the house to embody fundamental cultural values is perhaps the main reason why there are relatively so few experimental houses built in any one given historical period. Houses are, by their very nature, structures formed by essentially conservative values, ideas and processes.

The vernacular building tradition accommodated changes very slowly and was not driven by abstract concepts but by functional necessity. The function of houses used to incorporate not just the element of shelter but the reinforcement of religious and spiritual values, and the confirmation of existing social structures. A direct and unequivocal relationship existed between this complex range of functions and the form, organization, and building technology of vernacular houses themselves. This is no longer the case in most parts of the world.

In present day industrialized society, an entirely different set of relationships applies – most houses in this cultural context incorporate vestiges of designed elements and, being stripped of any sacred significance, require a reading which can reveal the myths, references and preoccupations which underlie their apparently innocent nature. One could cite here the dominance of the two- and three- bedroom house as a type (terrace, semi-detached or detached), for example, in spite of the fact that throughout Europe and North America by far the largest percentage of houses only have one or two people living in them: the implication is that many factors besides the requirements of space promote the dominance of this house type.[1]

To experiment is to test a hypothesis or demonstrate an assumed fact, not from the position of conjecture but from experience. The critical point about this definition is that experimental activity assumes pre-knowledge of a subject. It depends on an understanding of what constitutes its opposite: working within known parameters which define the limits of any activity or discipline. The gesture of the experimental is expansive, moving beyond the known and comprehensible but under controlled conditions and with a clear set of stated objectives in view. In this sense, the experimental is not necessarily the same as the radical, the unconventional or the bizarre, although these might indeed be the outcome of such activity.

Experimentation, then, is a conscious activity: it implies a shift in the state of consciousness by groups or individuals into an extreme condition in which new possibilities for the future are investigated. In order to do this it is necessary to work out of an established discipline with defined parameters and methodologies which act as a point of departure. The discipline in which the term 'experimental' is used most often is science, and it is instructive to look at one particular view of the relationship between experimentation and the acquisition of knowledge. The American scientific historian Thomas S. Kuhn, in his book *The Structure of Scientific Revolutions* (1962), says:

Philosophers of science have repeatedly demonstrated that more than one theoretical construction can always be placed upon a given collection of data. History of science indicates that, particularly in the early development of a new paradigm, it is not even very difficult to invent such alternatives. But that invention of alternatives is just what scientists seldom undertake except during the pre-paradigm stage of their sciences' development and at very special occasions during its subsequent evolution. So long as the tools a paradigm supplies continue to prove capable of solving the problems it defines, science moves fastest and penetrates most deeply through confident employment of those tools. The reason is clear. As in manufacture, so in science – retooling is an extravagance to be reserved for the occasion that demands it. The significance of crises is the indication they provide that an occasion for retooling has arrived.'[2]

Kuhn argues that crises are a necessary precondition for the emergence of new theories and that the decision to reject a paradigm is always followed by the decision to accept another. He has a tendency to see crises as external phenomena, but it is possible to see them also as shift in consciousness by individuals or groups in response to perceived external changes in the conditions of life. The crises which would produce a shift in architectural production are economic, social, political and cultural, but in addition there are the internal pressures of architecture's own discourse and evolution as an autonomous discipline. Relatively stable cultural environments do not tend to force or engender experiments in housing, and so in examining experimental houses as historical phenomena, we need to look at periods of dramatic change in both the outer world of events and the inner world of human consciousness.

At what historical point can we justifiably begin to discuss the concept of the experimental house? We would need to identify the equivalent of one of Kuhn's points of crisis which corresponds to a period in which houses ceased to function both as shelter in the vernacular tradition, and carriers of commonly held belief systems. In such a period we would need to identify examples of houses which manifest individuality, reflecting the fragmentation of cohesive cultural values and social and economic forms. This is difficult because of the reasons alluded to by Lewis Mumford in his book *The City in History* (1961): 'Human cultures do not die at a given moment, like biological organisms. Though they often seem to form a unified whole, their parts may have had an independent existence before they entered the whole, and by the same token may still be capable of continuing in existence after the whole in which they have flourished no longer functions.'[3] So we are not looking for a break at a precise point in time but for outward signs of a new historical tendency.

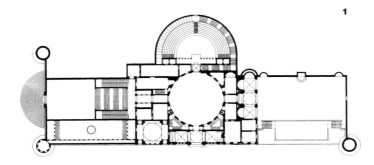

1

The last significant and clearly identifiable shift in human culture began in the first third of the fifteenth century. This can be stated with some certainty for a variety of reasons. The emergent trade-based economy and the resulting new class structure became a dominant force. As new towns were formed increasing numbers of the population became city-dwellers. While the abstract concepts of nature and science began to be understood, belief and faith – once central to all cultural activity – were marginalized. The work of artists began to be seen as the creation of an individual rather than a universally recognized world view. The method of depicting perspectival space was invented and at the same time semi-private internalized spaces such as courts, yards, colonnades and arcades were widely incorporated into towns and houses. As new forms of technology became widely available, human activity became less dependent on nature.

However, Lynn White Jr has pointed out in her book *Mediaeval Technology and Social Change* (1962): 'From the Neolithic Age until about two centuries ago, agriculture was fundamental to most human concerns. Before the late 1700s there was probably no settled community in which at least nine-tenths of the population were not directly engaged in tillage. Rulers and priests, craftsmen and merchants, scholars and artists, were a tiny minority of mankind standing on the shoulders of the peasants. Under such circumstances any lasting change in climate, soil fertility, technology or the other conditions affecting agriculture would necessarily modify the whole of society: population, wealth, political relationships, leisure and cultural expression.'[14]

In Europe, the transition from the Mediaeval to the Renaissance over the period 1250 to 1450, manifested itself in the built environment as if it were a mirror of these structural changes, with the falling away of previously important building types: the castle (hierarchy of social classes in specific and fixed economic relations) and the cathedral (an expression of collective belief in God and the dominance of the spiritual over the material). To provide new building types for emergent politically powerful classes, the Renaissance turned to the ancient world, but it did not so much rediscover antiquity as appropriate it for an entirely new set of symbolic representations.

One of the first major and latterly recognized individuals who encapsulates this trajectory is Filippo Brunelleschi (1377–1446). Such is his historical significance and achievement, that he is still sometimes referred to as the first 'architect' in the sense that we would understand today, in contrast to the collective role of the mediaeval master builders. Brunelleschi was trained as a goldsmith and studied ancient languages before becoming an architect, engineer and mathematician (he was one of the first accredited initiators of the use of scientific perspective). This apparent lack of specialization allowed him to avoid stereotypical roles and hence engage in complex projects which required interdisciplinary skills and original thinking, such as the building of the dome of Florence Cathedral (begun around 1418). Sigfried Giedion chose to start *Space, Time and Architecture* (1996) with Brunelleschi and his immediate successors: Leon Battista Alberti (1404–1472), Giorgio Martini (1439–1502) and Donato Bramante (1444–1514), sensing perhaps that they collectively foreshadowed the beginnings of a new cultural epoch, from which we have yet to emerge.

Raphael of Urbino (1483–1520) was one of Bramante's pupils who, although primarily remembered as a painter, undertook architectural commissions of which the unfinished Villa Madama outside Rome represents one of the most radical departures from established house design practice (1). First of all, the building is a new type – a suburban villa proper in which the emphasis is on the city, rather than the country, as the most important sustainer of cultural values. Its main axis of composition shows this by its alignment with the Tiber Bridge via a new road which acts to reinforce the symbolic and physical links to Rome. Secondly, the original design has as its other main organizing principle a large open but internalized courtyard sited at the junction of the main and cross axis. From this space, Raphael presents the visitor to the house with three distinct sets of relationships to the outside world: experience nature as raw via the amphitheatre, as panorama via the loggia, or as tame via the garden terrace further along the main axis. Thirdly, the architecture of the house was strongly influenced by the desire to create a 'Roman' villa as described by such writers as Pliny. In Raphael's own letter to the project initiator, Cardinal Giulio de Medici, he describes the as yet unbuilt villa in great detail as if giving a guided tour of the finished project, and in such a way as to paint a picture of the prospect of uninterrupted pleasure and contentment: 'The place will thus be most charming, not only because of the continuous sunshine, but also because of the view of Rome and the countryside, which, as your Excellency is aware, the clear glass will not obstruct at any point. It will really be a most pleasant place to winter for civilized discussions...'[5] The Madama is in part the outcome of Raphael's extensive surveys of ancient Rome, combining fragments of Roman buildings of all types. It is significant that it was the only contemporary building of which Andrea Palladio made measured drawings. But it is not just an exercise in applied archaeology; rather, it is an experiment in the application of historically established architectural forms to a new programme, building type and client social class, in an attempt to find a new way to resolve the relationship between the individual and natural forces (which in this cosmology would include spiritual ones).

The artistic movement that is often said to include this work is now termed Mannerism, a description not used widely until this century to distinguish the phase between the Renaissance and the Baroque. Raphael, who died tragically young at the age of 37, is less representative of this movement, however, than his pupil Giulio Romano, whose Palazzo del Té in Mantua is a better known example. Writing of this period in *The Social History of Art* (1962), Arnold Hauser draws the following conclusion: 'We are dealing here...with a completely self-conscious style, which bases its forms not so much on the particular object as on the art of the preceding epoch, and to a greater extent than was the case with any previous significant trend in art. From this point of view, Mannerism is the first modern style, the first concerned with a cultural problem and with regard to the relationship between tradition and innovation as a problem to be solved by rational means.'[6]

In the Baroque of the seventeenth century, the idealized sense of balance in the self-contained compositions of classicism gave way to more open, dynamic and sensual approaches. The other architectural characteristic is that the experience of the whole as a unity has primary importance over any question of the detail of the individual parts. The rise of the Baroque also corresponded with the shift of cultural influence away from Italy towards Northern Europe and in particular France. In 1665, King Louis XIV asked for papal permission to have his most favoured architect, Lorenzo Bernini, come to Paris to design a new Louvre Palace. Although a new housing type, the town mansion, was being developed in France, the influence of the absolute power of the monarch overshadowed this in the form of the royal château. Bernini's ideas were eventually rejected and the King embarked on a 50-year project to construct the Palace of Versailles, built outside Paris on a scale so vast that the resulting environment is an entirely formalized view of nature.

One hundred years later, the period leading up to the French Revolution of 1789–99 provided the context for the experimental work of the neoclassicists Claude Nicholas Ledoux (1736–1806) and Jean-Jacques Lequeu (1757–1825). Ledoux's own text accompanying the five-volume publication of his work states: 'The architect is the rival of nature, and out of it can form another nature... He can subject the whole world to the desire for newness that stimulates the chance movements of his imagination.'[7] Ledoux's work finally rejected the sensibilities of the Baroque, which by then represented a tradition, and tried to discover the elemental forms that he believed lay behind all architectural composition. His more extreme projects went far beyond what was technically possible at a time when it was still necessary to build in timber or load-bearing masonry and brickwork (2).

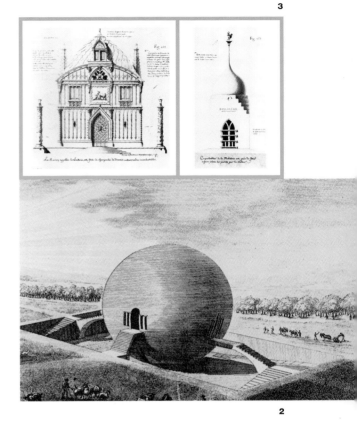

3

2

The Enlightenment provided impetus to the application of architectural ideas to building types previously the province of the vernacular. During the eighteenth century historians began to provide documented justification for an art historical method of analysis which linked particular styles to specific forms of culture and social organization. Architects like Ledoux revisited this history in an attempt to discover an imagined universal repertoire of forms, particularly in environments thought of as primitive. These were then appropriated, reconfigured and reapplied to the new context of social organization based on industrialization (as documented in Denis Diderot's *Encyclopédie* of 1751).[8] Lequeu's almost entirely unbuilt projects extended this range of references to include not just highly eclectic architectural ones, but those derived from anatomy and objects used in everyday life (3). In Lequeu's exquisite draughtsmanship we can see what Anthony Vidler called 'an internal exploration of a purely graphical discourse' in which the drawing itself became the purpose of the experiment.[9]

Box-or-Small-Bungalow-Residence.

Ground-plan

5

Similarly eccentric projects were proposed by other contemporary architects in the late eighteenth century, as in the work of Sir John Soane (1753–1837). Soane, like Lequeu, was someone born into relatively poor circumstances – his father was a bricklayer. Soane and Lequeu both trained under established masters; in Soane's case it was George Dance the Younger in London and in Lequeu's it was Jacques Germain Soufflot in Paris, and they both visited Italy as a result of scholarships. However, whereas Lequeu was left virtually without resources by the onset of the French Revolution, in 1790 Soane was bequeathed, in the will of his wife's uncle, property which produced a regular income from annual rents.

Most of Lequeu's architectural experiments remained private drawings made in one room off the rue St-Denis, while he earned his living as a government draughtsman. Soane was able to use his private income to build up his practice and at the same time construct his most extreme architectural experiment: his own house at 13 Lincoln's Inn Fields, London (4).

Soane had lived and worked in Number 12 on the site of a seventeenth-century town house which he had previously demolished. In 1808 he bought the freehold to Number 13 and built a new office and rooms to display his ever growing collection of antiquities. In 1813 Soane virtually rebuilt Number 13 and then continued to live and work there until his death, occupying a building that was a hybrid of house, office and museum. Soane's life spanned two centuries with very different characteristics: in his social life he was a man of the eighteenth century, living in a London as Boswell might have described it (dark and compact), but in his working life he was essentially of the nineteenth century, being upwardly mobile and part of the new professional classes. During the final 20 years of Soane's life, London's population increased by 20 per cent. Soane's house is a microcosm and manifests a most complex set of planning considerations involving hierarchy, spatial illusions and the manipulation of light and views. All this was achieved within the envelope of a standard London house overlooking a public square.

The plan expresses the idea of retreat from the city, both literal and symbolic, but this does not diminish the experience of culture in all its richness – rather it condenses and makes it part of the private realm. The only external element which distinguishes the house from its neighbours is the projecting two-storey front bay, only later enclosed, the cause of an acrimonious dispute with the local District Surveyor as an unauthorized deviation from the building line. This one-metre-deep space originally created an open balcony on the first floor: a semi-public space as an extension of the room behind in which the dual construct of the eighteenth- and nineteenth-century persona manifested itself in the transition between private and public realms.

Richard Norman Shaw (1831–1912), born six years before Soane's death, produced a number of experimental houses during the second half of the nineteenth century and provides a direct link to the present day. Like Soane, he was awarded a Royal Academy Travelling Scholarship, on which he explored Germany, France and Italy. Two years previously, at the age of 21, he had attended the funeral of the obsessive promoter of the Gothic Revival, Augustus Pugin, dead at the age of 40 from a combination of overwork and a turbulent emotional life. Shaw must have, at this moment, decided not to suffer or make a sacrifice of his talent and began to structure a career which was to last over 50 years.[10]

Whereas Pugin had passionately argued for a kind of morality in the production of architectural form, Shaw, although always at the forefront in the use of the latest technological innovations, was primarily interested in how buildings are experienced rather than the rigor of the laws of their conception. Hermann Muthesius said of him in *Das englische Haus* (1904–5): 'Shaw is the first in the history of nineteenth-century architecture to show this freedom from the trammels of style.'[11] The resultant aesthetic is an elegantly constructed fantasy about what English houses used to look like, unrestrained by any notions of historical authenticity or structural honesty. Shaw's clients, often introduced through his old Etonian partner Nesfield, were almost entirely members of the new monied classes. Cragside, for example, was built in 1869 for Sir William Armstrong, a Northumberland hydraulics engineer who amassed a fortune selling armaments during the Crimean War. The newly developed railway system in Britain rendered hitherto inaccessible sites a mere three or four hours from London, and Shaw's relaxed lack of design formality appealed to this new powerful class who were representatives of neither church nor state. Shaw embraced the new technologies of iron and concrete and the availability of electricity and coal gas, with the consequence that his domestic architecture exhibits the beginnings of what would later be called the free plan (Cragside, for example, was one of the first houses in the world to have electricity and Shaw's own London house had its own purpose-designed foul drainage system with wash-down toilets – a rarity at that time).

From around 1875, Shaw collaborated with William Lascelles, a building contractor who had developed a system for constructing small, inexpensive houses from concrete panels fixed onto timber frames (5). An example was shown in the grounds of the Paris Exhibition of 1878, and even in this small residence, Shaw's skill in handling the planning and elevational requirements are evident. Although semi-industrial in its conception, the house was picturesque, and within a mere 110 square metres (1,180 square feet) of floor space, Shaw managed to include two zones of occupancy (one for the family, one for a servant), a gun and boot room and a service yard.

One visitor to this exhibition was the young Belgian architect Victor Horta (1861–1947). In Paris Baron Georges Haussmann's boulevards, which cut through the mediaeval fabric of the city, would still have looked new and Charles Garnier's Opera House had only just been completed. The twin iron and glass Grandes Galeries for the fair were the work of Viollet-Le-Duc and Gustav Eiffel, and Horta was able to take back to Brussels this rich experience of the radical possibilities of building in these materials. Brussels was itself at that time a capital city with an active cultural life and relative prosperity, due to the success of Belgium's colonial activities.

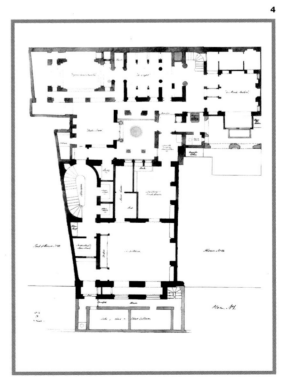

4

7

6

Shortly after opening his own office in 1890, Horta received a commission for a town house from Professor Tassel – a specialist in descriptive geometry, a freemason and a bachelor who was devoted to his grandmother. The programme of Hotel Tassel, which was to occupy an infill site 7.8 metres (25 feet 6 inches) wide, had to transform the typical arrangement of the bourgeois family in order to accommodate the complex combinations of privacy, entertainment and sociability, work and leisure, and the very specific family unit of Tassel, his grandmother, and several live-in servants (6). In Horta's work we can begin to see technology supplanting the accommodation previously required for servants. Hotel Tassel was heated by a coal-fired furnace in the basement providing a supply of ducted warm air to all the major rooms via grills. In addition, the rooms themselves were ventilated by extract grills working through stack effect with the lightwells acting as ventilation shafts. Several of the more experimental aspects of this system were later abandoned, probably at Professor Tassel's request, implying that it did not perform exactly as predicted. In this, one of his earliest houses, Horta set out to demonstrate his belief that materials and technologies previously used in industrial buildings could be applied to domestic architecture.

The plan and section are principally organized around two lightwells, one of which contains the main staircase. The major rooms, like the bureau and the saloon, look onto this top-lit internalized world which is the product of human thinking and making rather than of nature. In the highly articulated detailing, particularly at the junctions of different materials, we can see an attempt to invent an alternative nature and turn the products of industrialized processes into a plastic and artistic medium.

Experiments in glass as the ideal medium for the expression of the direction of new forms of architecture were given a theoretical justification by Bruno Taut (1880–1938), specifically through the exchange of letters which began between himself and his collaborators in 1919, later to be known as the Crystal Chain Letters. Taut's pseudonym was Glas, and among the 12 other contributors to the letters was Walter Gropius (1883–1969), pseudonym Mass, who was to become the first director of the Bauhaus in Weimar. Taut also founded the Arbeitsrat für Kunst (AFK) in Germany in 1918, which had the aim of unifying the arts within a projected vision of a new socialist state. Taut wrote in 1920: 'The architect will become an ethical and social creator. Through the design of the house, the inhabitants will be led to a better attitude in their social intercourse and their mutual relationships. Architecture will become a creator of new social forms'.[12]

In 1914 Taut collaborated with the writer Paul Scheerbart (1863–1915) for the design of a building at the Werkbund Exhibition in Cologne. Scheerbart's fantasy novels were highly influential to the participants of the Crystal Chain Letters, but the ideas which lay behind them were not so obvious, being deeply connected to the esoteric philosophy of the Theosophical Society and the teachings of the Austrian scientist and philosopher Rudolf Steiner (1861–1925). Steiner left the Theosophical Society in 1913 after profound disagreements with the direction it was taking, and went on to apply his insights into a whole range of practical activities, education, medicine, environmental work and art. His own architecture has not received much critical study, but his work at Dornach, Switzerland, from 1913 onwards must be seen as some of the most extreme experiments in architectural form of the twentieth century.

House de Jaager, built in parallel with the large adjacent meeting hall called the Goetheanum, provides residential accommodation combined with a large first-floor studio (7). Its highly sculptural forms have no obvious precedent but prefigure the language of the second Goetheanum which was begun in 1926 using *in situ* cast concrete after the first version in timber had been destroyed by fire in 1922, a mere nine years after its inception. Writing in 1914, Steiner's view of the purpose of such buildings appears to be the inspiration for Taut's statement six years later: 'Peace and harmony will flow into the hearts of men through these forms. Such buildings will be law givers. The forms of our buildings will be able to achieve what external institutions can never achieve...'[13]

Steiner's research led him to the conclusion that one of art's principal roles was to counter the trajectory of the dominance of technology and its consequent destruction of our relationship with the natural world. For him technology was not negative, but had to be worked with in a fully conscious way. It is significant that these experiments took place at the same time as the First World War: the first war in which killing was truly mechanized.

Social upheavals, driven by new ways of thinking, generate experiment; at no other period have so many socially driven experiments in housing been proposed than in Russia immediately after the Revolution of 1917. Architects were not just encouraged, but mandated to deal with the problem of mass housing from an entirely new perspective. El Lissitzky made clear this new agenda writing in *Russia: An Architecture for World Revolution* (1922): 'During this period the great challenges posed by the cultural revolution have taken deep root in the consciousness of our new generation of architects. It has become obvious to the architect that by virtue of his work he is taking an active part in the building of a new world. For us the work of an artist has no value 'as such': it does not represent an end in itself; it has no intrinsic beauty. The value of a work of art in our society is determined by its relationship to the community.'[14]

One of the most inventive examples, Housing Commune Type F, was characterized by living units in a 3:2 section in which the commonly shared facilities of dining rooms, recreation rooms and child-care facilities supplement the minimal, totally private space (8). The diminution of private space to a series of multi-purpose rooms for sleeping, washing and eating was given additional emphasis by the deliberate subversion of the party wall, which was no longer restrained by the limitations of defining property lines.

At the same time in the United States, the Viennese engineer and architect Rudolf Schindler (1887–1953) built a house for himself, his wife Pauline and another couple, in West Hollywood, Los Angeles (9). As originally conceived, the house provided individual rooms for each of the four adults in two wings, each with its own garden court, with a shared kitchen and guest room as a link. The roof of the single-storey structure originally had open sleeping porches which in the following years were enclosed. In a prophetic piece of forward planning, Schindler designed and built the house mainly using funds provided by his wife's father. At this time he was still employed by Frank Lloyd Wright to complete the difficult and complex construction of the Barnsdall (or Hollyhock) House. On the break-up of their marriage, Schindler continued to live and work in one wing of the house, but in 1937 Pauline returned to Los Angeles and occupied the other wing, which was by then vacated. They lived completely independent lives on either side of the shared guest room until Schindler's death; Pauline continued to occupy her own part of the house until her death in the 1980s.

The house is experimental not just from the point of view of its organization and provision of spaces; it also employed highly unusual forms of construction. The solid elements of the external walls were formed by casting 1.2 metre- (4 foot-) wide tapering slabs horizontally on the ground and then upending them when set. The narrow vertical slots between adjacent panels were direct-glazed and the walls facing the courts were fully glazed and set in Redwood frames with large opening sections to allow complete interpenetration of the internal and external spaces. Describing his own house Schindler said 'the traditional method by which structural members are covered onion-like, with layers of finishing materials...is abandoned'.[15] The idea that construction could be

made more expressive and at the same time more economical by removing these finishing layers and exposing everything was to become one of the main driving forces behind the Modernist aesthetic. Schindler went on to build over 150 houses in and around Los Angeles, often working alone and usually acting as architect, engineer and contractor, but he moderated his extreme position towards construction in his later work, probably as the result of numerous problems with the performance and durability of his earlier structures, even in the mild Californian climate.

Schindler's attitude to construction can be contrasted to that of his fellow Viennese Adolf Loos (1870–1933), who understood the necessity of layering the building envelope in order to accommodate the performance requirements of cold, damp Europe, and to allow for the hierarchy of skills normally employed in house building. The Czech-born Loos emigrated to set up practice in Vienna in 1896. Loos, like Schindler, had a close relationship with most of his clients. Claire, the 24-year-old daughter of Otto Beck, the man who effectively promoted Loos in his estranged homeland, would become his fourth and final wife when he was 59, in ill health, and entering the final phase of his career.

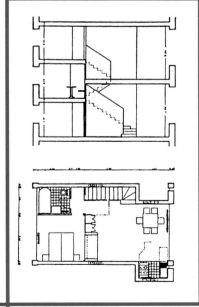

9

8

10

one metre (one yard) back from the extensively glazed garden façade. Every other one of the glazed units can be electrically lowered into a slot in the floor, opening the main living space to the landscape; an architectural tour-de-force which even now is rarely attempted in domestic buildings. Because of the section, however, these windows still deny physical access to the outside, unlike the Schindler House for example, and the landscape is treated as a framed backdrop to the highly controlled and ordered inner world of the house. Mies incorporated a sophisticated warm air heating system, filters and solar blinds in order to ensure environmental control. As a designer, he only experimented in so far as he could ensure predictable outcomes: the Tugendhat House was meticulously detailed throughout, with over 300 construction drawings being produced during the design and building process. All the junctions have flush or inverted (negative) joints, a system of construction which allows little room for error in either the manufacture of elements or the assembly on site. The resultant aesthetic is Mies' lasting legacy to following generations of modernists – for many of them, at times, an overdemanding burden. Unlike Schindler, Mies combined this approach with the use of highly worked and semi-precious materials such as onyx, thereby placing even more demands on himself, his assistants and his contractors.

Some of Mies van der Rohe's ideas had already been applied to mass housing at the Weissenhof Housing Settlement in Stuttgart in 1927 where he designed a three-storey steel-framed apartment block as part of a model housing scheme which he also masterplanned. Other innovative architects contributed their own projects by invitation: J.J. Oud, Mart Stam, Bruno Taut, Walter Gropius, Hans Scharoun, and Peter Behrens, for whom Mies had worked at the start of his career. The other major contributor was the Swiss-French architect Charles Edouard Jeanneret (1887–1965), better known as Le Corbusier.

Loos travelled as a young man in the United States, but unlike Schindler was never able to make a career there in spite of the fact that throughout his life he would continue to proclaim the supremacy of American and Anglo-Saxon culture. It was towards his country of birth that he turned at the end of his life in order to produce one of his most experimental of domestic projects, the Villa Müller (10). Built in a suburb of Prague in 1929, it was a mature attempt to demonstrate his concept of the 'Raumplan' in which the internal spatial complexities avoid rigid zoning both vertically and horizontally and are contained within a relatively simple envelope. The basis of the organization is a centrally placed meandering main stair off of which the principal rooms are arranged in a spiral at levels of 1.19-metre (4-foot) intervals, terminating at the horizontal plane of the bedroom floor. A secondary service stair and elevator maintain a hierarchical set of relationships between the main spaces and the service rooms. The clients were Frantisek Müller, a partner in one of Czechoslovakia's largest engineering firms, and Milanda Müller, and they were to occupy the house along with their daughter Eva, a governess, a chauffeur, a cook and three full-time servants.

Loos wrote: 'The artist, the architect, first senses the effect he wishes to produce and then envisions the space he wishes to create. The effect he wishes to bring to bear on the beholder (*beschauer*) – be it fear or horror in a prison, reverence in a church, respect for the power of the state in a government bureau, piety in a tomb, a sense of homeyness (*gemutlichkeit*) in a dwelling, gaiety in a tavern – this effect is evoked by the material and the form.'[16] This experiment in spatial organization generated by the house's layout and the programme of bourgeois family life with its specific class and gender roles, is rendered even more convincing by its lack of compromise in the integrity of the principle rooms and the completely understated manner of its execution.

Brno, the birthplace of Loos, provided the site for an equally radical experiment in house design at the same time, but with an entirely different emphasis. The German architect Ludwig Mies van der Rohe (1886–1969) was commissioned to design the Tugendhat House on a hillside site there in 1929 (11).

Mies' early work was strongly neoclassical and although the client, Grete Tugendhat, had seen his Perls House of 1911 in Berlin, she was not fully prepared for the stylistic evolution that had taken place over the intervening years. The site had a steep fall that allowed Mies to use the levels to create a free plan for the principal rooms with dramatic views across the south-facing garden to the distant Schloss. The house has a steel frame on a 5 by 4.6-metre (16 1/2 x 15-foot) grid, with freestanding columns, sheathed in cruciform chromium steel, and set approximately

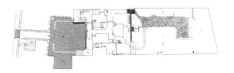

Le Corbusier had also worked for Behrens before leaving to undertake a study tour of Europe and Asia Minor. Later, he was to formulate what he termed the five points of architecture, essential characteristics which he believed should form the basis of all subsequent house design; the free column (*piloti*), the free plan (*plan libre*), the free façade, horizontally banded windows implying independence of skeleton and wall, and the roof garden. By 1928 Le Corbusier's office, by then based in Paris, was overwhelmed with work, due in part to his extraordinary success at self publicity and promotion. Le Corbusier was one of the first architects to use photography and publications to sell his skills and to advertise publicly his theoretical position through writing.

The office had been sustained by projects for private houses since around 1922, but because of either restricted budgets or tight sites, it was not until the offer of a commission from Madame Savoye for a country house outside Paris that the least compromised possibility existed to demonstrate the five principles (12). The commission, however, was not without its problems from the very beginning, with numerous design changes taking place between October 1928 and February 1929 in an attempt to reduce the contractor's unacceptably high tender price of 785,000 francs.[17]

While the Schindler, Müller and Tugendhat Houses all had garages which formed an important aspect of their organization, the Villa Savoye was conceived to make arrival by car one of the prime generators of its architectural conception. Arriving from Paris for the weekend, the owners would be dropped off by the main, centrally placed entrance under the cover of the living accommodation which was on the first floor and supported on *piloti*. The inset plan of the ground floor, which contains the garage, guest suite and servants' rooms, has its external envelope on the entrance side defined by the turning radius of a Grand Tourer. Unlike Mies' consistent application of the structural grid, Le Corbusier disrupts the column arrangement to accommodate both the parking requirements of three garaged cars, and the placement of the internal ramp which leads internally from the main entrance up to the first floor, and thereon externally to the roof terrace with its views south. The construction is in cast concrete with infill clinker blocks, the whole being rendered to create a uniform surface. The specially designed horizontally sliding sash windows were clearly influenced by contemporary car, train and ship design.

As a work of creative imagination it remains one the most powerful visions of the possibility of liberation from the dictates of nature, but it would appear that Madame Savoye never grew to love Le Corbusier's experiment in modern modes of living. Milanda Müller, however, remained in her own house at Prague for many years, living in just two rooms under the post-war Communist regime, until her death in 1968. The Tugendhats lived happily it seems in their Brno House until rising anti-semitism forced them to leave after eight years. Throughout the 1930s, however, Le Corbusier and Madame Savoye exchanged correspondence, some of it fairly acrimonious, about a whole series of problems she was experiencing with the house. Writing to her in 1937 concerning yet another round of repairs, seven years after completion at a final cost of 815,000 francs in spite of all efforts to make savings, Le Corbusier ends his letter with 'You know I must always remain a friend of my clients'.[18] It is a statement, not a request.

12

The design and construction of the Maison de Verre off rue St-Guillaume in Paris for Jean and Annie Dalsace was not the first project that Pierre Chareau (1883–1950) had undertaken for the couple, having previously renovated a small apartment for them in 1918 (13). This was the most complex project of Chareau's career, and he collaborated with Bernard Bigvoet. The site was a gift to Annie Dalsace from her father, and it contained a three-story 'hôtel particulier' flanked on two sides by party walls, with a court to the front and a garden to the rear. The plan was to demolish the entire building and replace it with a new house and office for Jean Dalsace's gynaecological practice, but this had to be severely modified in order to retain the existing second floor and the roof over it on account of an elderly tenant. Chareau proposed a solution, daring even using today's construction techniques, whereby this part of the building would be supported with a steel frame containing a new three-storey volume skinned mainly in semi-translucent glass bricks with distinct bands of metal-framed windows. The three levels thus created would contain the following accommodation: on the ground floor the gynaecological suite, accessed from the courtyard, on the first floor the living room (double height), dining room, kitchen and study and on the second floor the bedrooms.

Chareau built little, emigrating to the United States in 1940, apparently unwilling or unable to repeat such an architectural experiment. Because of the extreme difficulty in attempting an analysis of the formative ideas behind Chareau's modest output and personality, it was not until the 1960s that the Maison de Verre was 'discovered', since when it has been the subject of increasing exposure.

As with Carlo Scarpa, this work requires historical distance to allow a critical methodology to be applied fruitfully. For on most levels the Maison de Verre confronts us with a series of paradoxes. Constructionally, it is not particularly ordered, the structural grid shifting constantly to accommodate localized conditions. The circulation is deliberately contrived to blur the thresholds between public and private space, perhaps in a deliberate attempt to make the nature of the visits to the clinic ambiguous. And although the aesthetic is overtly about machine-made elements, Chareau worked in close collaboration with the metal workshops of Louis Dalbet, each component being meticulously hand crafted. Virtually no construction drawings of the house exist and most of the design work was done using mock-ups and prototypes as the construction on site actually progressed. The working relationship between Annie Dalsace, Chareau and Dalbet clearly transcended the conventionally accepted formal ones under a building contract. On 13th June 1932, Chareau wrote: 'Annie, You can share this letter with Jean. I'd like to tell you all about the work, that's my firm intention, and, as I continue, I'm held back by a kind of modest reticence that paralyzes me completely. On the one hand, I'm working out the pipes, drainage and heating system, such an essential but thankless task, while on the other, I grow quite excited and fancy I'm being of use. Out of all this there's one thing I'm certain of. I'm certain of love, and this certainty in itself is worth living for. Tell me I've battled like a lion for your house. Your house I'll cherish closest to my heart. (*Pour votre maison, je garde les premiers battements de mon coeur*).'[19]

One can read the Maison de Verre in two ways: either as an exercise in the total mechanization of the aesthetic of domestic existence by making an analogy with the mechanistic view of the human body (as foreseen in Marcel Duchamp's early paintings) or as an attempt, like Horta's, to render artistic and particular the universalizing and deadening tendencies of the industrialization of society.

The London-based designer Wells Coates (1895–1958) was less ambivalent about the process of industrialization. His design for his own apartment of 1935, the conversion of the attic of a London town house, is a highly concentrated compilation of his ideas about domestic interiors, embracing new technologies and social conventions (14).

On superficial examination, the apartment appears to be simply an obsessively ordered bachelor flat, influenced by Coates' fascination with yachts. In fact, it was his sole home and place of work for 20 years and was lived in by his daughter Laura for 12 years. In the 3.6 metre- (11 foot 9 inch-) high volume, with only one large window to the street, Coates used a highly inventive section to create two separate sleeping platforms, using the height over the storage spaces beneath to create walkways besides the beds. Tucked underneath the bed platforms are the bathroom, galley kitchen and clothes cupboard (which included a revolving rack to hold two complete changes of clothes). 'Space is saved,' wrote Coates, 'by not having to leave anything about.'[20] Practically all furniture was built-in; the only freestanding pieces being the dining table and chairs, and his own specially designed workstation. The influence of his formative years spent in Japan is clearly seen in this early experiment in what is now known as minimalism.

Wells Coates spent a considerable amount of time in the 1930s working on schemes for prefabricated houses to be produced by a company called Isokon, but these did not result in any built projects. However, the pressure to increase housing production after the end of the Second World War and the over capacity in Britain and America of aircraft and armaments factories, created an unprecedented series of experiments in this form of construction. But there is also evident here another distinct shift in consciousness: North American and European society was moving from seeing the built environment as one which was formed, to one that was assembled. The French semiologist Roland Barthes, writing about toys in 1957, made the pertinent observation that in this period we finally began to see ourselves not as creators but as users.[21]

F.R.S. Yorke, in his introduction to the section on experimental and prefabricated houses in *The Modern House* (1934), wrote with some degree of wishful thinking, 'The individual-architect-designed house is a luxury product; it is not possible, or even desirable, in an age of big population, that many such houses should be built. The homes of the people are mass-produced industrial products of the machine; in a lesser degree, admitted, as yet, than is desirable'.[22]

Experiments along these lines were more successful and more plentiful in the United States, as can be seen in the pre-war work of A. Lawrence Kocher and Albert Frey: the Aluminaire House of 1931 was a prototype for prefabricated mass housing. A more extreme version of this concept is Richard Buckminster Fuller's Dymaxion House, which comprised a 'mast' of duralumin tubes that supported the main living spaces arranged radially around it and suspended clear of the ground (15). Significantly, the first public exhibition of this house was as a model in the Marshall Field Department Store in Chicago in 1929, rather curiously in order to attract attention to a new range of French furniture. From this point the American department store became a regular site for promoting the modern house, and the house in this context could be seen as just another commodity. Driven by the early death of his daughter from ill health partially brought on by bad housing, Buckminster Fuller (1895–1983) devoted the rest of his long life promoting specifically applied technologies to improving human conditions.

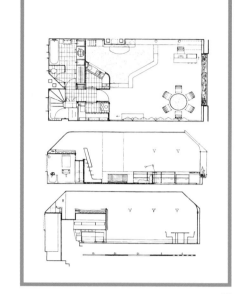

15 **16**

14

Whereas Fuller saw the house as a mass produced artefact, capable of being moved or replaced at regular intervals, British versions exhibited decidedly cottage-like appearances, forming part of an unbroken picturesque tradition that links to the vernacular via Shaw's experiments in concrete.

As part of a government-backed programme instigated by Winston Churchill, over 100 versions of small prefabricated houses were experimented with towards the end of the Second World War (16). Three types were developed further, the Aluminium, the Uni-Seco, and the Arcon, and they shared common features in having service cores and pre-made, road-transportable sections which were joined on site. A steel 'prefab', as they became known, was exhibited at London's Tate Gallery in 1944, and in 1945 an Aluminium was erected at the back of Selfridges Department Store in central London as part of a promotional exercise. Over 156,000 of these units were eventually built and proved to be popular, with their fitted kitchens, built-in wardrobes and sophisticated services (at this time in the United Kingdom 60 per cent of all low-income homes still did not have a bathroom and most did not have an inside toilet).

The Case Study House programme in the United States also had its origins in the austerity years of the Second World War, during which little domestic architecture was constructed. In January 1945 the magazine *Arts and Architecture*, under its editor John Entenza, instigated a programme of experimentation in house design by commissioning 8 different architects to design as many alternative houses. Such was the success of the programme that it was to endure for 29 years and result in 24 built examples.

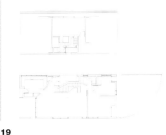

17   18   19

Of these examples, Charles and Ray Eames' (1907–78 and 1912–88) own house and studio at Pacific Palisades, California – begun in 1945 but not built until 1947 – is perhaps the most well known as well as being the most instructive to study (17). It would be a mistake to view this experiment as a prototype for social or mass housing; the cultural climate of the immediate post-war West Coast in any event was not suited to this (94 per cent of 1930s Los Angeles consisted of detached one-family houses). The aim of the project was to devise a low-cost construction system and the Eames approach was specifically technical. Most publications about the Eames House rarely show large scale plans because they are essentially uninteresting; it is the structure and its juxtaposition with the wooded landscape around it that now gives the house its iconic status. The steel fame is made of 100 mm- (4-inch) deep H-section columns supporting open lattice trusses spanning 6.1 metres (20 feet). The external walls between the columns are either standard production glazed sashes or painted panels.

It is reported by Esther McCoy in her book *Case Study Houses* (1962) that Charles and Ray Eames made a last-minute and fundamental change to the design after all the prefabricated steel had been delivered to the site.[23] A new arrangement was devised which entailed only one additional piece of steel being required and the result was the house that exists today. The Eames House, unlike the Maison de Verre, does not display any particular obsession with the finesse of detailing, which perhaps explains why it became the archetype for a whole generation of modernist architects for whom Chareau's approach with its non-repetitive details and intimate client-architect-contractor relationships, proved too difficult a model for either them or their accountants to endorse. The Eames House offered the attractive combination of radicalism and the possibility of commercial survival.

Even at the age of 86, Frank Lloyd Wright (1867–1959) remained an astute opportunist and, although if compared to the projects of Fuller and the Eames his work might appear anachronistic, it serves well to examine the trajectory that experimental houses took after a brief and uncritical relationship with the tenets of industrialization. As with all of Wright's work, it comes to us now so loaded with significance that any objective reading is virtually impossible. Wright first started working on his Usonion House projects in the early 1930s when his practice was near to bankruptcy, he had little work, and his private life was once more subject to very public scrutiny. The first prototype for his Usonian Houses was the Jacobs House of 1936, a low-cost single-storey timber building comprising very thin sandwich panels on drywall shallow foundations. Through numerous projects Wright developed these ideas and in 1953 he exhibited his latest conclusions in the form of an Exhibition Pavilion on 5th Avenue, New York (18). Wright's vision appears curiously out of place against the New York skyline and looks back to his ideal model of Broadacre City in which autonomous detached houses sit in one-acre plots, linked by a grid system of connecting roads. Later actual developments of this idea were to reveal that the serpent in this particular Garden of Eden would be the automobile. Wright's Conditions of Engagement, which clients for the Usonion Houses were required to sign, contained the clause: 'Dwelling houses on urban lots will not be accepted. Acreage is indispensable'.[24]

Experimentation at this point as viewed through this and numerous subsequent projects begins to enter the realm of self-parody. The belief in technological innovation and a programmatic social policy for architecture was a product of the 1920s and 1930s. By the 1960s a more circumspect attitude had become evident and projects became more mannered. Of the texts written then, and of the projects built, the pivotal work which highlights this shift is that of Robert Venturi (b.1925). His book *Complexity and Contradiction in Architecture* (1962) and the house he built for his own mother in Chestnut Hill, Pennsylvania (1962–4), take what Vincent Scully called the 'poverty of his time' and put its limitations to creative use.[25] This is one of the first serious examples of a house that attempts to marry so-called high art with a populist aesthetic, achieved with the absolute minimum of technological sophistication. In this sense Venturi returned to Norman Shaw's eminently workable position and threw out the holy cows of modernism: exposure, structural honesty, abstract ordering and the dream of technological progress. In its place was put a domestic architecture whereby the practitioners of which were only interested in the experience of form, surface and space, irrespective of how that experience was physically achieved.

In this (at that time) outrageous affront to modernist sensibilities, Venturi used his extensive knowledge of architectural history to set out to prove that his theoretical position was in fact the rule, not the exception, and that modernism itself was the aberration (19). The house displays various eccentric devices: a split pediment, a giant order staircase discharging into the living room, and a stair that leads nowhere in the attic (an echo of the anti-modernist staircase leading to Monsieur Hulot's apartment in the 1958 Jacques Tati film *Mon Oncle*).

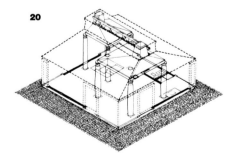

21

This form of resistance to modernist reductivism can also be seen in the work of Venturi's contemporary Charles Moore (b.1925). Moore's second house for himself at Orinda, California, of 1962 is simply one space (with the exception of the toilet cubicle) but in the interior, different areas of use are demarcated by the placement of two small 'temples' with ionic columns, set asymmetrically within the top-lit volume (20). One 'temple' encloses the open plunge-bath, while the other defines the living/dining area. Half of the external walls are large, horizontally sliding doors which when fully open invert this internalized world and turn it inside out. Like all the houses Moore built for himself, the Orinda house is diminutive and extremely modest.

Unlike Wells Coates' careful creation of private sleeping spaces within one volume at Yeoman's Row, Moore attempted no such trick and the plan subverts all conventional notions of privacy and hierarchy. Like Venturi, Moore used his intellect to attempt to bridge the gap between architectural convention and popular experience. Paradoxically, his own somewhat marginalized position helped him in this endeavour.

The United States remained fertile ground for these newly defined post-modern experiments during the 1960s and 1970s. Describing the conversion and extension of his own house in Santa Monica, California, in 1979, Frank Gehry (b.1929) wrote: 'I wasn't trying to make a big or precious statement about architecture, or trying to do an important work; I was trying to build a lot of ideas, and when I got caught in the game of the old house, it became serious... In using the rough carpentry and materials I wanted to prove you could make an art object out of anything'.[26] (21)

Gehry refers to artists such as Marcel Duchamp, Robert Rauschenberg and Donald Judd as influences, making it clear that his own house sits within a historical tradition of artistic activity in which the 'everyday' is metamorphosed into the exceptional simply by the application of ideas. This concept, and the disarmingly unambitious way Gehry describes it, directly contradicts a long history of received wisdom about architectural practice. However, such is the nature of our present cultural condition that, as the direct result of this project and its publication, Gehry has gone on to become one of the most successful international architects of the last quarter of the twentieth century.

The main characteristic of most recent experimental houses has been this overt desire to return architectural theory and practice to a place where it is accessible to the popular imagination, and not of a particular class interest group. Historically considered, experimental houses have had a tendency to be one-off, high-budget exercises for wealthy clients. At the other extreme, specifically in the twentieth century, mass housing has been used as a test bed for experimental forms of settlement pattern and the use of new materials and construction systems. For architects, the private house has played a critical role in developing ideas and careers. The media of photography, publishing and now television have been engaged in order to promote their ideas and work, and this has forced a more open debate about domestic architecture and its relation to the real conditions of the majority of its inhabitants. This new direction is in many ways positive, being both more democratic and inclusive, but it also presents a serious and not so immediately obvious problem.

Architects are still blurring the distinction between houses as a backdrop to everyday life, and houses as the 'designers' of everyday life; the danger now is that the dialectical relationship between object and experience will be rendered nonsensical by the dynamic of the everyday itself being 'designed'. The experimental proposal by Jeremy Till and Sarah Wigglesworth for their own house and office on an urban site in Islington, North London, serves to illustrate this phenomenon. (22)

The rigorous set of ideas which inform the physical realization of this house have been rehearsed in various publications for a number of years, and great care has been taken to make it clear that the 'everyday', as it is referred to here, should not be the subject of aesthetic focus. It has been rightly argued by both architects that canonic domestic architecture has inevitably emptied the domestic routine of any semblance of life as commonly experienced, by rendering it the subject of technical or formal abstractions. The tendency of recent architects such as Gehry to appropriate the world of everyday objects and render them part of a new aesthetic system has also been observed. Wigglesworth and Till have also noted architecture's continual tendency to exclude vast numbers of people from its remit by placing them beyond its margins, because of their gender, race or economic status.

20

However, this experimental house shows an inability to break free from the abstract obsessions of its own discipline and the cultural and economic basis of its production. This observation could be applied, to a greater or lesser extent, to any designed object which exists in the public realm. Roland Barthes, setting out the theoretical framework for his collected essays *Mythologies* (1972) made this point succinctly: 'Every object in the world can pass from a closed, silent existence to an oral state, open to appropriation by society, for there is no law, whether natural or not, which forbids talking about things'.[27]

The Till/Wigglesworth house appears to be experimental constructionally and environmentally. The office section is raised on fragments of wall made from cages of steel mesh packed with pieces of recycled concrete (as used in motorway retaining walls), while the office wall adjacent to a main railway line alongside is constructed of sandbags filled with loose mix sand and cement (the sacks will eventually rot to expose the cast forms inside). The walls of the house itself are straw bales infilled between timber trusses; these are then covered externally in a transparent rain screen of polycarbonate sheeting. Almost uniquely for an urban context, the house has a compost toilet and the five-storey bookstack acts as a thermal flue. Conceptually, we can see the house as consistent with Le Corbusier's five principles, including *piloti* and a roof garden, with planning on fairly conventional lines based on identifiable functions like entrance, working, living and sleeping. The spatial relationships are hierarchical and a combination of *raumplan* and *plan-libre*, allowing for certain social conventions; sleeping and reading are private, working and eating are not. However, the manner of presentation of these organizing principles has a stated intention. Sarah Wigglesworth writes: 'Whilst we may have introduced the everyday in distinction to high architecture, it is not our intention to get caught within the binary trap of remaining immersed in the ordinary. This would lead to the disavowal of architectural knowledge and creativity alike – knowledge because it is associated with the repressive structures of power and expertise, creativity because it is associated with uncritical genius. But this unequivocal disavowal leads to a disempowerment of user and architect alike. Instead, we suggest that the real productive potential for architects lies in an endless movement between engagement and retreat'.[28]

Now that this house has entered the public realm, however, certain areas of movement are curtailed and what it speaks of may not be so relevant to a populist theory of art. Its location, size and cost render it exclusive. It stresses through its form certain stereotypical attitudes with specific class positions – a multi-storey library signifies scholarship, a large studio predicts professional expansion while minimal bedrooms predict a stable number of occupants, and the conference-cum-dining space maintains its dominant role over social intercourse as if no other could be imagined (compare, for example, the dominant social space of the bath in Charles Moore's Orinda house or the Japanese-style 'snug' in Wells Coates' apartment).

No experimental house is free from this problem of speaking one thing and being understood as another. They are the exceptions to the rule and should no longer be seen as paradigms which might lead to generalized design solutions in domestic architecture; their strength is in their diversity. Until we have a coherent view of human culture, a collective will to achieve a democratic economic and political system, and an understanding of what an aesthetic liberated from class interest might look like, we should be cautious of the continual expansion of the designer universe. The historical trajectory of the experimental house mirrors the progressive emphasis on individualism and the increasing uncertainty about what represents commonly held belief systems and values. Ideas have extraordinary potential for instigating change, and our present cultural context demands that we intensify our faculties for understanding the deeper implications of these new paradigms for domestic life before treating any one of them as anything other than a particular response to a specific set of conditions.

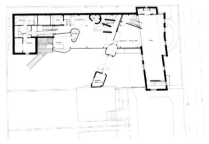

22

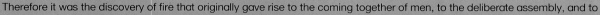

Therefore it was the discovery of fire that originally gave rise to the coming together of men, to the deliberate assembly, and to social intercourse. And so, as they kept coming together in greater numbers into one place, finding themselves naturally gifted beyond the other animals in not being obliged to walk with faces to the ground, but upright and gazing upon the splendour of the starry firmament, and also being able to do with ease whatever they chose with their hands and fingers, they began in that first assembly to construct shelters. Some made them of green boughs, others dug caves on mountain sides, and some, in imitation of the nests of swallows and the way they built, made refuge out of mud and twigs. Next, by observing the shelters of others and adding new details to their own inceptions, they constructed better and better kinds of huts as time went on.

Vitruvius: *The Ten Books on Architecture*

Vitruvius describes a process whereby the construction of shelters forms part of the historical development of cohesive social forms. There is ample evidence that human beings did not depend on built shelters in prehistory for survival and lived a semi-nomadic existence in small groups of hunter-gatherers. Shelter may very well have been for protection but there must have been a time when the forces of nature, in whatever form, did not present themselves as a threat. The construction of shelter primarily marks the beginning of a change in our relationship to the natural world and in our state of consciousness so that physical protection and comfort became synonymous with psychological well being. Shelter became a primal image of security.

In the first chapter of his book *The Poetics of Space* (1969), Gaston Bachelard writes: 'In the house itself, in the family sitting room, a dreamer of refuges dreams of a hut, of a nest, or of nooks and corners in which he would like to hide away, like an animal in a hole. In this way, he lives in a region that is beyond human images'.[1] Bachelard goes on to point out that the essence of the primitive hut is solitude and that it is an image of poverty transformed into something uniquely desirable.

In describing the construction of 'The Tower', the house that he built for himself by the shores of the lake at Bolligen, Carl Jung writes of a four-part house, built in stages over a period of thirty years. The first phase was planned as a primitive circular house centred around an open fire in the manner of certain forms of African hut. This was subsequently extended with a tower-like annexe, itself built in two phases, and finally a courtyard with a loggia. Jung, on completion of the various elements, came to realize that 'the small central section which crouched so low, so hidden, was myself'.[2]

While the shelter in this chapter is about revealing the house in its poetic essence by stripping it of its purely functional characteristics, by contrast, mobility is about the functional provision of shelter but with the richness and complexity of an entire house. Shelter offers the possibility of a house in which the detritus of the everyday is absent. Mobile houses offer the possibility of a return to nomadic existence with all the physical support of technology to mediate with a external world perceived to be hostile. In contemporary Western society where the biggest growth industry is tourism, the dream of mobility is clearly linked to this long sought for reconciliation between the two opposing views of nature: as both a source of pleasurable reverie and as a source of physical suffering.

Paradoxically, all the examples in this chapter are tinged by the exotic, even Shigeru Ban's emergency housing which reminds us, as Bertold Brecht pointed out, that it may require delicate and sensitive instruments for repairing a world that is unhinged. It reverses the tendency to see such houses as mechanistic and without any of the subtleties of the permanent ones they replace. The increasing need for quickly deployable emergency housing primarily results from rapidly expanding urban settlements and the correspondingly large numbers of people unhoused by natural or manmade disasters. In 1997, for example, over 4 million people (excluding those displaced by political actions and civil wars) were made homeless through famine, drought, earthquakes, high winds, floods, volcanic eruptions and landslides.[3]

Atelier van Lieshout's Master and Slave Unit mobile home might also serve as temporary or long-term housing but stresses mobility, flexibility and autonomy. The unit is a parody of both mobile home culture and the paraphernalia associated with suburban life: sheds, plastic garden furniture and crude extensions. This additive form of architecture does not seek to place value judgments on particular aesthetics but celebrates the indiscriminate couplings of apparently different value systems.

The Aura house, a minimal shelter created by F.O.B. Association, is an almost unique building type, the urban retreat for urban nomads for whom the city provides all needs except privacy. Whereas van Lieshout's project stresses services, the F.O.B.A. solution is to virtually dispense with them, providing only kitchen sinks and toilets, thereby accepting the multifarious options that a city provides for other basic necessities like eating and washing.

The form of F.O.B.A.'s Aura house is dictated by the context of the side walls, whereas in the extreme polarity of this condition, the Norwegian summer house designed by Carl-Viggo Hølmebakk, has a form defined by the position of existing pine trees on the coastal site. The plan becomes a residue of the interstitial spaces between trees and asserts the primacy of nature over any built intervention. The house is even capable of change in response to the future growth of the trees.

Níall McLaughlin's retreat for a photographer in the English countryside is a more finite structure but one which would come closer to Bachelard's definition of the primitive hut. Here the evoked dream is of a landscape transformed with the imposition of an architectural form which is both referential to nature, and yet clearly set apart from it. This particular project seeks a reconciliation between the oppositional characteristics of nature by insisting it is always viewed in the context of a consciously created form.

project **Master and Slave Unit mobile home**

location Otterlo, The Netherlands
designed 1995
architect **Atelier van Lieshout**

construction prototype for the Kroller-Muller Museum
approximate area 35m² (376 sq ft)
cost not available

In order to understand this and subsequent projects, it is necessary to be aware of the preoccupations of Joep van Lieshout's early work such as 'Operating Table', of 1984. The piece, in timber, wrought iron, copper and cement, is a cross between a butcher's block and a gynaecologicist's chair, and shows a disturbing fascination with the limits of scientific activity: that is the ultimate death of the patient in the cause of research. The writer J.G. Ballard has identified science as the ultimate pornography because it is the most extreme form of analytic activity in which the subject is removed from its context.[1] It is no coincidence that van Lieshout still seems to claim a strong association with the writings of Niccolo Machiavelli and the Marquis de Sade, both of whom were obsessed with systems in so far as they could be used for either the exercise of power or the ordering of debauchery under very precise circumstances.

Roland Barthes, in an essay on Sade says: 'The principle of Sadean eroticism is the saturation of every area of the body: one tries to employ (to occupy) every separate part',[2] and one can observe this phenomenon in all the Atelier's work. In the late 1980s van Lieshout began producing furniture as 'multiples'. These tables, chairs and shelving units were finished in bright polyester and based on his own system of standard measurements that allowed them to be combined and linked in a variety of ways. Shortly afterwards, in 1990, this was followed by the production of multiples for complete sets of sanitary-ware and kitchens. Van Lieshout started acting as a contractor and was able to provide an installation service to clients, thereby further compounding the ambiguity of the pieces as to whether they were art works or consumer durables. Present in all these pieces, and more overtly in his 1990 piece called 'Bed', is the implication that all the design moves are made with an erotic intention and that combinations of units are simply ways of suggesting a repertoire of sexual experiments.

The Master and Slave Unit embodies all these earlier ideas in one autonomous mobile living unit. The Master Unit is towable and self supporting, and based on a system of stretched-skinned wall panels screwed to a floor and ceiling platform, all of which are of polyurethane sandwich construction. By removing selected wall panels, a limited range of Slave Units can be 'coupled' to the Master Unit to achieve a wide range of combinations. The four principal Slave Units have identified functions – sleeping, kitchen, bathroom and dining/lounge, and each has its own particular visual references whose only common factor is that they deliberately try to avoid high art. The interiors are less synthetic and more a parody of caravan culture in which the complexity of a suburban domestic environment is compressed into a volume the size of a single garage.

The production of construction manuals for these and later similar mobiles suggests that Atelier van Lieshout see their work as part of the democratization and dissemination of art but through the personal engagement by individuals in modern processes of production. This and the Nietzschean emphasis on the individual ego, has the benefit of being an experiment with absolute clarity of intentions, one of which is a total lack of social idealism.

left The slave units have different forms and colours according to their functions.

above With its weatherboard cladding the dining/living room slave unit makes references to suburban garden sheds.

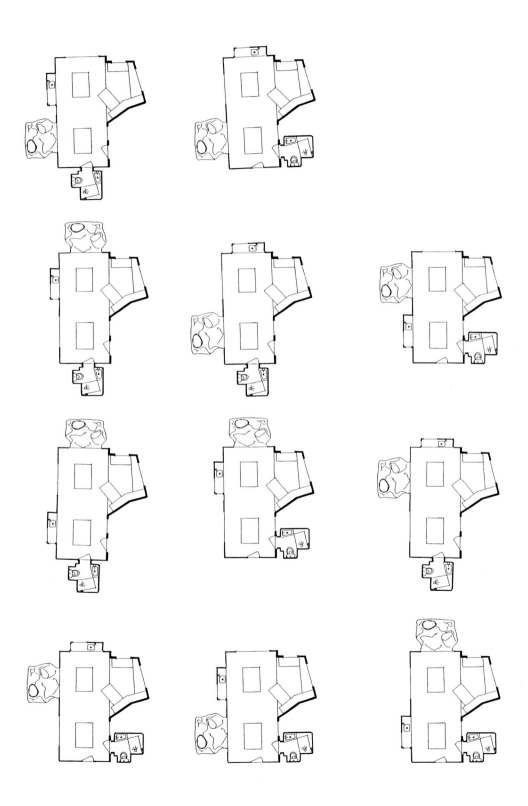

left Plans show the many ways in which the four slave units can be attached to the master unit.

above The interior is influenced by caravan and mobile home culture.

right The overtly vulgar bed unit is suitably suggestive of erotic possibilities.

project **Aura house**

location Tokyo
Japan
date commissioned 1994
architect F.O.B. Association

construction main contractor
area 122m² (1,313 sq ft)
cost undisclosed

In truly nomadic societies, architecture plays a secondary role to that of the organization of territory. The economic status of members of such societies is based on the value of their portable possessions, including their homes. Although increasingly rare, such ways of living are still to be found in north and central Africa, central and south-east Asia and parts of Australasia, and require that the landscape as found provides all the necessities to sustain life. In order to be easily transportable, the houses in these societies are normally frame structures covered in fabric or natural vegetation. In this project for an infill site in central Tokyo, F.O.B.A. conceived of the concentrated modern city as being a contemporary version of a landscape in which one moves constantly in order to survive. What would such a view mean in terms of the function of a house?

Even experimental houses rarely question the essentials of the normative lifestyles of the inhabitants of urban conurbations: the house is invariably seen as a vessel to contain and protect the functions of domestic life such as eating, bathing, sleeping and entertaining. The Aura house, however, has virtually no facilities to support these activities – there is a tiny kitchen with two sinks and space for a refrigerator, but no bathroom. The house has no insulation, although it does have electrical power from the city grid system. The clients for the house, like many of their contemporaries, often leave home early and return late. Eating regularly takes place in restaurants and for a hot bath there is the local *sento*. The internal spaces are only differentiated by the floor slabs and do not suggest any particular form of usage. There are no internal partitions but the location of the stairs allows for specific areas to be screened off with roll screens if necessary.

right A shelter for urban nomads, the Aura house redefines the function of dwelling by questioning assumptions about normative lifestyles.

The site itself is typical for a Japanese city where land values are high: a mere 3.5 metres (11 feet 6 inches) wide by 21.5 metres (70 feet 6 inches) deep with virtually no external private space. The two cast concrete side walls are in fact identical two-dimensional templates but one is reversed to produce a 'saddle' shaped geometry between the two. Eight cylindrical concrete beams at roof level provide structural bracing, their alignments being the product of the reversed profiles of the walls. The building envelope is formed by a stretched fibreglass single-skin membrane that is semi-translucent. While the traditional house in Japanese cities has a *tsubo-niwa* or courtyard garden, the Aura house is one volume that is filled with natural light by day and emits its own internal light by night, back-projecting the profiles of the inhabitants onto the fabric.

The primary function of this house is to provide a continuous internalized space emptied as far as possible of material content – a place to be still and concentrated. The technique for the production of such a space is the acceptance of the fragmentary nature of the modern city, and the primacy of architectural speculation over issues of context. Emphasis on context as a range of existing types and historically based styles, is in this view seen as incompatible with experimentation.

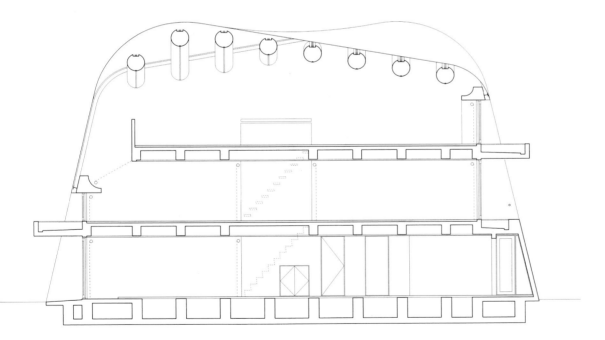

far left The second floor with, overhead, the cylindrical concrete beams bracing the side walls.

left A longitudinal section shows the reverse geometries of the side walls.

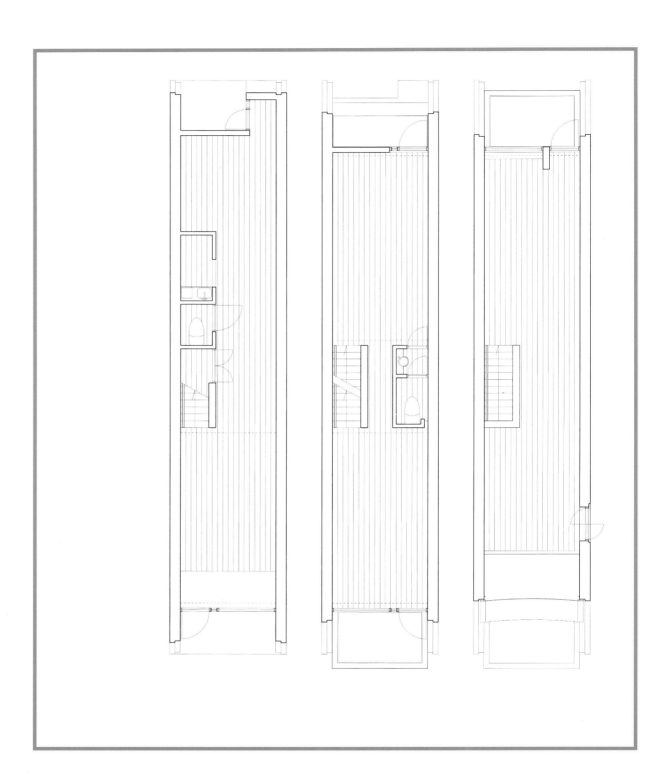

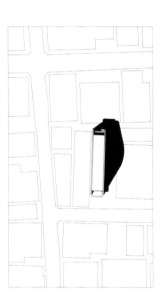

left From left: ground-, first- and second-floor plans do not imply any particular usage.

above The site, shown in this plan, is 3.5 metres (11 feet 6 inches) wide by 21.5 metres (70 feet 6 inches) deep.

right The fabric covering allows light to flood the house by day, and emits light by night, thereby projecting the profiles of the inhabitants.

project **photographer's retreat**

location Foxhall
Northamptonshire
UK

date commissioned 1997

architect Níall McLaughlin

construction Simon Storey
approximate area 30m² (320 sq ft)
cost £15,000

above The entrance end
of the retreat, with the
land once occupied
by a World War II air
base beyond.

above right Perforated galvanized
steel canopies are
held down by slender
steel rods, anchored
in the pond.

right When seen from the
surrounding fields,
the structure appears
to be buried in the
landscape.

From the time that Nicéphore Niépce created the first indistinct image of a laid dinner table around 1823, photography has maintained the character of authenticity: it never lies about the existence of something and confronts us with the irreducibility of the past. This authenticity has only recently been challenged; new techniques of digital manipulation have finally destroyed this unique quality of the photographic image to record what has been. Writing in the period between the two world wars, Walter Benjamin considered that the question was not whether photography was an art, but rather how its invention had fundamentally transformed the entire nature of both the production and consumption of art itself: 'When the age of mechanical reproduction separated art from its basis in cult, the semblance of its autonomy disappeared forever.'[1] Light, that most non-material and transformatory of phenomena, is frozen in time by photography as a trace.

This project for a retreat was born out of a shared fascination between architect Níall McLaughlin and the client – a photographer specializing in images of nature – with the possibilities of water as a means of modulating light. The client's house sits on a property in the relatively flat rural landscape of central England. At the edge of the garden there was a derelict pond which was renovated with filtration and oxygenation and the reintroduction of fish and plants.

The farmland beyond had been used during the Second World War as a US Air Force base for Consolidated B-24D bombers flying special operations over occupied Europe. These planes, known as Liberators, were less photogenic than the iconic B17 Flying Fortress but had greater range and load-carrying capacity and were therefore favoured for reconnaissance and long-range supply missions to resistance groups. Following the end of hostilities, the whole site was used as a nuclear missile base before it was eventually abandoned in the mid-1960s. The runway was broken up and used as rubble for a nearby section of Britain's first motorway, the M1. The design of the photographer's retreat, which was to be located over the edge of the pond, was based on the relationship between the photographer's work (which involves making close-up overhead photographs of insects) and wartime aerial intelligence photographs taken of enemy territory. Therefore, the building can be seen as a metaphor for both a camera lens and a reconnaissance plane hovering over the water to capture unsuspecting (and unwilling) subjects.

below The cockpit-like glazed lantern required many study models to finalize as construction drawings were not used.

top right A photograph of B-24D Liberators over central England from 1943. The plane's distinctive twin tail rudders are just visible.

right The entrance, to the far right of the plan, leads to the workspace, sauna and bed. The timber deck is on the left.

On the basis of a series of early drawings, Simon Storey (whose father had been a Spitfire pilot) agreed to construct the shack on condition that no construction drawings were produced. Client, architect, engineer and builder then worked with models and photographs to develop the design, which expanded slowly to encompass not just a place for experimental photographic work, but a sauna and a sleeping alcove for the family's use.

The small structure is built on a concrete raft which supports a thick blockwork wall facing the pond and the main house. A series of small frameless glazed openings in the rendered surface frame views of the pond from different heights and admit light into the linear interior so as to form part of the photographic process. The entrance door is at the lowest end of this wall, protected by the wing-like form of the roof, and is reached by crossing the surface of the water on stepping stones formed by the tops of submerged concrete drums. A similar detail gives direct outside entry to the sauna. At the other end of the structure is a timber deck which is in plan a virtual mirror image of the interior working space. Protected from the expansive landscape beyond by the existing vegetation, this deck provides an outside working space for further photographic compositions. Towards the open fields, with their fading traces of a violent past, the structure is protectively locked into the ground by the carefully articulated geometry of the roof, itself a composite of plywood, fibreglass, poly-carbonate and metal.

The roof canopies are made from perforated galvanized metal, and in contradiction of conventional practice are designed to flex and deflect in the strong local winds. Their ends are tensioned by slender steel rods which are secured under water. Light passing through the canopies is registered on the surface of the baffles underneath. At the apex of this composition of fragile elements is a glazed lantern; its reference both to aircraft cockpits and to the eye itself encompasses the building's role as mediator between natural and mechanical forms.

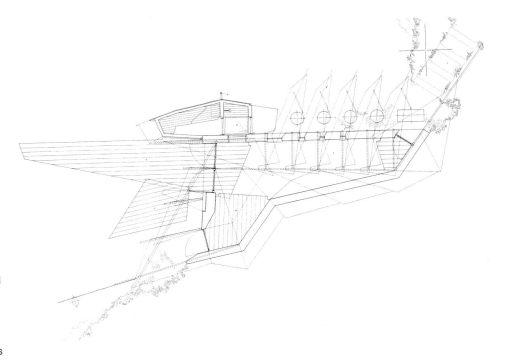

project **summer house**

location Risør
          Norway
date commissioned 1997
architect **Carl-Viggo Hølmebakk**

construction local carpenter and sub-contractors
area 60m² (645 sq ft)
cost undisclosed

During the period from 1907 to the time of the Stockholm Exhibition of 1930, Scandinavian architecture was dominated by influences from classicism and the vernacular tradition. That these two approaches were not seen as contradictory can be seen in Sigurd Lewerentz's Resurrection Chapel (1921–3) and Gunnar Asplund's Woodland Chapel (1918–21) both within sight of each other at Stockholm's Enskede Cemetery. The austere classicism of this period, and the return to an emphasis on construction and materials as the prime generators of form, allowed the subsequent transition to modernism to be more seamless than in any other cultural context. Hølmebakk shares with this earlier generation of Nordic architects an interest in primary forms – cylinders, cubes, and pyramids, with associations that go back to what is often referred to as the primitive. His well-publicized project for a small cylindrical tower to act as both garden shed and library revealed some time ago just how powerful is his ability to produce such conceptual compactness that it directly engages our imagination. The summer house, while still minimal, is a far more complex composition than the tower.

It is an integral part of Norwegian culture to have a *hutte* in uncultivated nature for use during the short summer months, but over the past 30 years these buildings have become less basic and therefore increasingly like conventional houses with all the trappings of modern domesticity. This particular summer house is located just 70 metres (230 feet) from the shore on the southern coastline in an area of small farms and other *hutte*. The dominant natural features of the site are the characteristic outcrops of rock and the mature pine trees. Hølmebakk developed a system for the foundations which comprised a matrix of oversized timber beams on concrete pillars that could be adjusted in position to avoid the root systems of the trees. Timber wedges, almost identical to those on 1000-year-old Norwegian stave churches, were used to level the beams once in place. The main structure of the house is a prefabricated laminated timber frame of columns and beams, joined to the base by steel shoes. The detailing of the envelope ensures that the frame and the external cladding of narrow strips of Norwegian larch are flush and read as pure planes of material separated only by precise joints. The roofs are at a shallow 5-degree pitch with a zinc covering, and are built to present the thinnest possible edge profile. Set at different heights, these roofs not only allow for a hierarchy of internal spaces with varying ceiling heights, but also avoid problematic junctions between opposing roof elements.

The plan incorporates and retains all the existing trees and is pulled apart to ensure that it is never more than one room deep and that views out are framed, often with multiple layers of foreground. The coherence of the plan is derived from the roofs, which impose an ordering system which is at once sympathetic to, and yet independent of nature. It is in this sense, rather than because of its obvious visual references, that this small but ambitious shelter reconnects with the essentials of classicism without regarding it simply as a historical style.

left The house is carefully wrapped around existing trees.

below The more open west side of the house with its timber deck and steps down from the kitchen door.

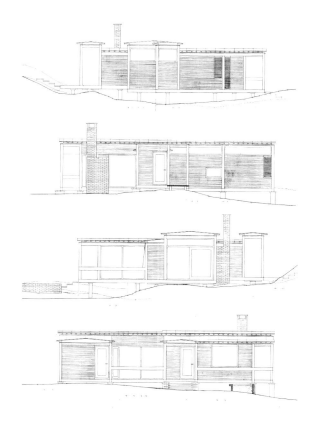

above Elevations, from top to bottom: north, east, south, west. The roofs and structural frame provide the main spatial ordering system in the house.

right The plan is designed to accommodate the trees on the site (represented in the drawing by dark circular shapes) and to allow space for future growth.

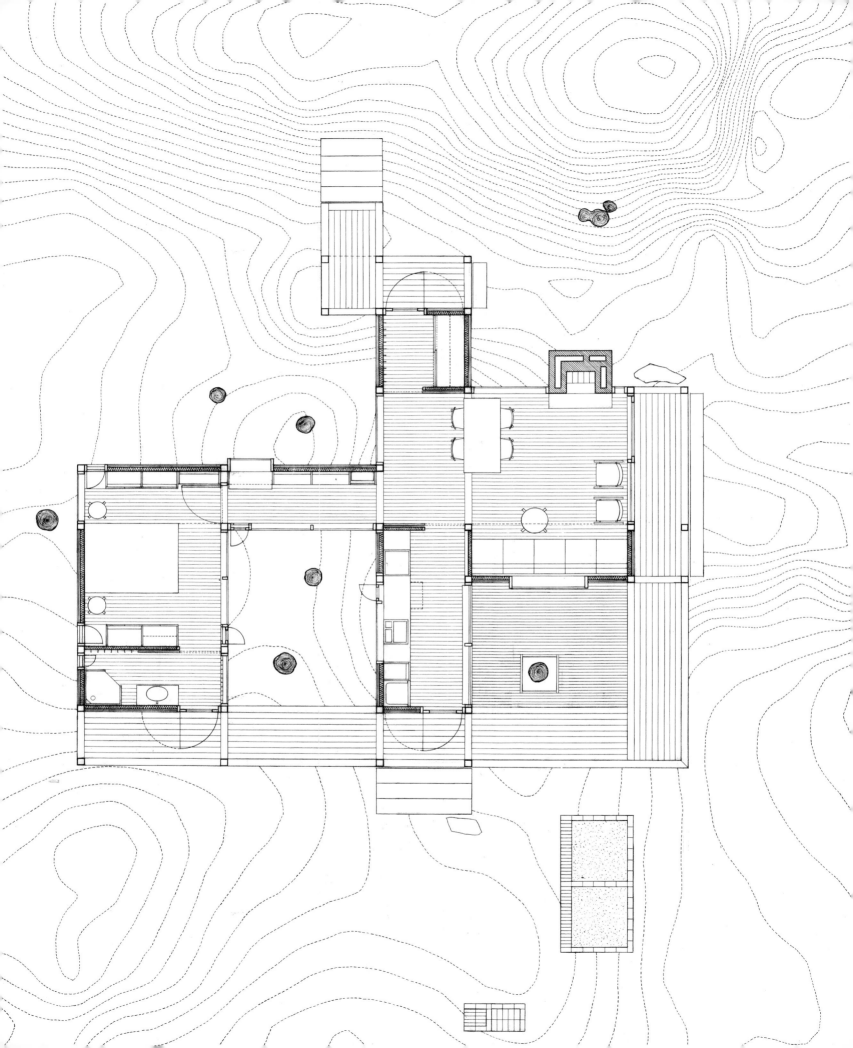

left Looking from the bedroom across to the kitchen wing, with the living room beyond.

project **paper log house for disaster relief**

location Kobe
Japan
date 1995
architect Shigeru Ban

construction prefabricated components self-assembled on site
area 16m² (172 sq ft)
cost ¥250,000

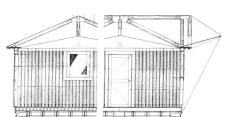

above The plan and part
elevations show the
placement of the tubes.

right An axonometric
diagram showing the
main construction
components.

far right top An interior of a shelter
with the occupant's
salvaged possessions
– privacy and space
are seen as key factors
in helping unhoused
disaster victims
maintain their dignity.

far right centre Foundations are made
of standard beer crates
filled with bagged sand.
The paper tubes are set
on plywood pegs.

far right bottom A row of shelters in use
at Kobe following the
earthquake of 1995.
Ban's own prototype
was used as reference.

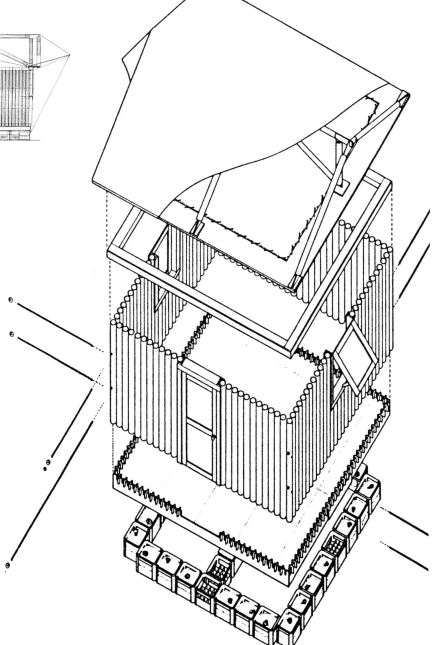

Early twentieth-century experiments with the possibilities for log houses were carried out by both Adolf Loos in 1913 and Rudolf Schindler in 1918. Inspiration for these projects came from the theme of the *Urhutte* envisaged by Gottfried Semper, which had a symbolic connection to the Greek temple and drew a strong connection between the original forms of both domestic and sacred architecture. The main connection between the ancient and modern in this work is the organizing principle of geometry, and in this respect Ban's work is a direct descendent of this design methodology.

Shigeru Ban first experimented with the use of paper logs – or, rather, paper tubes – in 1985 shortly after returning to Japan and after an architectural training at the Cooper Union in New York. Following a year working with Arata Isozaki, Ban's first solo commission was a design for the exhibition of the work of Emilio Ambasz; the paper tubes around which the exhibition fabric was wrapped when delivered caught his attention. He designed an exhibition of the work of Alvar Aalto for the Axis Gallery in Tokyo in 1986 using these leftover paper tubes as screens and platform supports. In order to investigate the possibilities of using paper tubes to create both building envelopes and to act as structural elements, research and testing was then carried out by Gengo Matsui's laboratory at Waseda University.

The first house Ban built using this technology was one for himself and his extended family. Designed in 1990, the first of what he terms the PTS Series, the house was not completed until 1995 because of lack of funds. In this experimental structure, which is based on a pure square of 10 by 10 metres (33 by 33 feet), 110 paper tubes of equal height create a series of external and internal spaces by conforming to geometry based on circles of different diameters. Ban both financed and allowed himself to be the subject of this experiment for both social and personal reasons.

Shortly after the Great Hanshin Earthquake of 17th January 1995, Ban travelled to Kobe and visited the ruins of the Catholic Church in the Nagata district, the place of worship for former Vietnamese boat people. As well as working to provide a temporary church built of paper tubes, Ban set about providing these already marginalized people with temporary housing in place of the inadequate tents that had been issued to them by the authorities. The same volunteers who built the church assembled over 20 paper log houses in a local park, using the prototype that was built by Ban himself as a model. Each house took about six hours to erect.

The foundations of the house comprise standard beer crates filled with sand. The 4 by 4 metre (13 by 13 foot) ply floor supports 108mm- (4¹/₂ inch-) diameter paper tubes tied together as wall panels, their junctions pre-sealed with double sided compressible tape. Each tube is slipped over a plywood plug and rows are held together by horizontal 6mm- (¹/₄ inch-) diameter steel rods. A semi-translucent double layer vinyl fabric roof is supported by a paper tube frame, and the gable ends can be opened to allow for rapid ventilation in Japan's hot summer climate. The door and glassless window frames are formed in plywood, the simple top-hung ply shutters providing both security and privacy. Ban's careful and compassionate work at Kobe, and his subsequent work for the United Nations High Commissioner for Refugees, has rightly gained him the description of 'ethical experimenter' and offers design standards to the disempowered that have been previously reserved only for the wealthy.

Let me tell you how his pavilion is made.

Marco Polo: *The Travels*

First, the tent in which he holds court is big enough to accommodate fully a thousand knights. Adjoining this is another tent which faces West and is occupied by the Great Khan himself. At the back of the great hall is a large and handsome chamber in which he sleeps. Let me tell you how these two halls and the chambers are constructed. Each hall has columns of spice wood very skillfully carved. On the outside they are covered with lion skins of great beauty, striped black and white and orange. They are so well designed that neither wind nor rain can harm them or do any mischief. Inside they are all of ermine and sable, which are the two finest and richest and costliest furs there are. The cords that hold up the halls and chambers are all of silk.

Although normally regarded as a product of the industrial age, the prefabrication of elements of domestic architecture is an extremely ancient activity. The world's oldest-known printed architectural treatise, the *Ying tsao fa shih*, (approximately twelfth century) from the Chinese Song Dynasty, systematically sets out the range of building elements necessary to build virtually all types of building. William the Conqueror, upon his successful invasion of Britain in 1066, is supposed to have brought a prefabricated timber castle with him to support his control of the immediate area around his landing place at Hastings. Many European mediaeval timber buildings have structural members reused from earlier frame systems with relatively standardized components.

The first portable prefabricated house to be built in an industrialized society was probably a tollhouse on the turnpike road between Birmingham and Bromwich in the English Midlands, dating from between 1790 and 1830. Its walls comprised cast iron plates which could be bolted together and it had a slate roof with elaborate iron finials. The extent to which it was demountable was demonstrated in 1870 when the structure was moved to Tipton Green in Staffordshire, where it remained until it was permanently dismantled in 1926.

Experiments in the prefabrication of houses like this one were rare, and it was not until the advent of production line techniques for commodities at the beginning of the twentieth century that prefabrication became a possibility on a mass scale. The drive towards prefabrication has to be seen in the context of the increasing commodification of all aspects of everyday experience which has dominated the twentieth century.

Because of the economics of the scale of production runs, the very restrictive lending arrangements for private houses, and the defining aspects of land values, historically, prefabricated houses have played no significant role in private sector housing in any country; they have not become generally accepted commodities within the market economy. In consequence, the largest scale programmes involving this form of production have been in the public sector to provide housing for low-income groups in which questions of consumer choice were never seriously asked. The provision of temporary prefabricated housing in Britain at the end of the Second World War is one such example, and it is significant that this particular

experiment was curtailed by the problem of high unit cost. The most commonly produced unit, the Aluminium Temporary, which had two bedrooms and was factory prefabricated in four sections, resulted in a unit cost of £1,365 in 1945[1], whereas at the same time the average build cost of a conventional 87 square metre (934 square foot) three-bedroom house was £1,242 (both figures excluding of land price, taxes and fees). The name temporary was a misnomer for this unit type for it was made out of high-specification materials, and many are still in existence today. The American TVA system, developed at the same time, proved more economical precisely because it incorporated simpler technologies and the resultant bungalows represented true temporaries, being extremely light, very compact in plan, and with very basic services and fittings. Short-life prefabricated houses incorporating simple technologies were similarly developed in Scandinavia, particularly in Sweden, where many were erected as self-build projects.

Throughout the 1950s and 60s systems of prefabricating large-scale building elements for mass housing were developed and utilized in an attempt to increase productivity and decrease construction time. One such application, the Larsen-Nielsen prefabricated system for concrete walls and floors came to prominence when in the early hours of 16th May 1968, the entire corner of a 22-storey tower block in East London called Ronan Point collapsed following a minor gas explosion in an apartment on the eighteenth floor. The causes were a combination of errors in erection procedures and the inherent inability of the system to contain progressive collapse.[2] Since that accident, hundreds of similar blocks have been demolished after being deemed unsafe; Ronan Point itself was finally taken down floor by floor from May 1986. These failures revealed a now obvious fact, which is that those complex and technically unforgiving construction systems in which large-scale elements were fabricated off-site, required on-site methodologies and inspection systems which the building industry was unable to deliver.

Subsequent refinement of these technologies and the industry's improved ability to correctly employ them, have once again meant that they represent an increasingly significant percentage of public housing provision in Europe, Scandinavia, the United States and Japan. The tendency appears to be towards smaller-scale prefabricated elements which allow design flexibility and diversity.

Kathan-Schranz-Strolz's apartments at Innsbruck incorporate prefabricated elements at relatively small scale and in such a way that any tendency towards repetition is alleviated by visual delicacy in the tradition of the best-designed machinery; this is the opposite of a reductive system.

The intelligent application of prefabricated modules to transform existing structures is shown in both Birds Portchmouth Russum's Pacemaker pod, and in Sills and Keim's housing at Rathenow. In both schemes the emphasis is on most of the servicing technology being placed in the module thereby setting up a distinct polarity between the old and the new in a reinterpretation of Louis Kahn's concept of servant and served spaces.

Another tendency, a legacy of the Eames approach, is to use low-cost basic components which have been designed for other applications like industrial or agricultural buildings. Lacaton and Vassal's house at Saint Pardoux La Rivière aims to achieve, through this device, the kind of neutrality claimed for nineteenth-century farm buildings. The paradox of this activity is that it attempts to return domestic architecture to vernacular building stripped of aesthetic pretensions: a literally and metaphorically fabricated state of innocence.

IKEA, entering a market in which the first-time private buyer or long-term leaseholder is the prime target, have opted for the maximum concentration of designed elements only where you see them, in the construction system of their mass produced units which will soon be available outside Scandinavia. Driven by consumer research and an expansive marketing strategy, IKEA's designers have dropped the main driving force behind twentieth-century thinking on the prefabrication of houses – technological innovation equates with progress – and gone for flat-packed veneered balloon frame, which any nineteenth-century carpenter would have understood.

project **apartment block in Innsbruck**

location Innsbruck
Austria
date commissioned 1996
architect **Kathan-Schranz-Strolz**

construction main contractor
area 1560m² (16,792 ft²) including basement storage
cost undisclosed

left Adjoining cantilevered conservatories on the building's south façade.

right Window bays looking out onto the street are glazed on the top and at the sides only for privacy.

following pages The sliding glazed screens of the conservatories form a constantly changing matrix.

This apartment block of 21 residential units for rental is intended as a prototype for part-prefabricated, economical housing which has the possibility of being contextually related to its local environment. Unlike most prefabricated schemes, which stress the primacy of technological innovation, the work of Armin Kathan, Martin Schranz and Erich Strolz draws its references from the traditional architectural elements of Innsbruck and the surrounding Tyrol: timber cladding, projecting bays and steeply pitched roofs. The technological innovation is underplayed and merely serves to support other, more carefully considered intentions.

The site lies between a major and minor road close to the university quarter of Innsbruck, an area of transition between the urban and the suburban. Reflecting this, a break in the street frontage has resulted in a disparity of scale between the adjacent buildings on either side of the site. The new building maintains both the eaves line of the taller buildings and the established street frontage. The units themselves are intended for those studying at the university, resulting in a specific requirement to reduce construction costs in order to allow for low rental charges in an area acutely short of cheap accommodation. The use of prefabricated façade elements combined with relatively inexpensive finishes was driven by this consideration: to reduce construction time and skilled labour input on site.

The façades comprise factory-made elements clad in oak on battens backed by 80mm (3 inches) of mineral fibre insulation, behind which is a hollow core frame unit faced on both sides in 25-mm (1-inch) particle board. Once in position on site these units, which are best understood as forming permanent shuttering, were filled with 150mm (6 inch) thick recycled concrete (this means selected concrete from demolition was used as aggregate). The concrete serves to enhance the structural, thermal and acoustic performance as well as enabling the six-storey building to comply with highly restrictive fire regulations. Internally, the building is more conventional with concrete floors and mainly solid load-bearing partitions.

On the main road side, which faces north, is a series of projecting bays which are glazed only on the top and sides, giving oblique views of the sky and the street but maintaining privacy for the bedroom/workrooms behind. On the south side, all but the ground floor and attic units have fully glazed cantilevered conservatories, which have large horizontally sliding single-glazed panels so that they can be opened to the outside air. Views from these sun spaces are afforded across the city to the distant Tyrolean mountains.

The apartments are arranged off a common elevator and staircase and within a simple volume. By using a strict planning grid around centrally placed service zones, a range of accommodation has been achieved from studios to three-bedroom duplexes with mezzanines and roof gardens. As well as low construction costs, energy use has been reduced through high levels of insulation, supplementary heating of living spaces via the conservatories, and the installation of solar panels on the roof for hot water provision during the summer months.

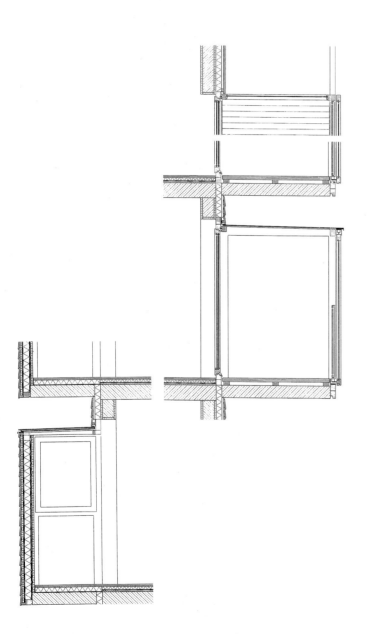

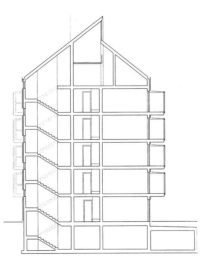

far left Contextual prefabrication: the building respects the scale and the form of the street.

bottom left The conservatories on the more open south elevation allow as much daylight as possible into the apartments, and there are solar panels on the roof.

left Detail sections of the bays: on the left a conservatory, and on the right a street-facing window.

above Section showing the street side on the left and the garden side on the right.

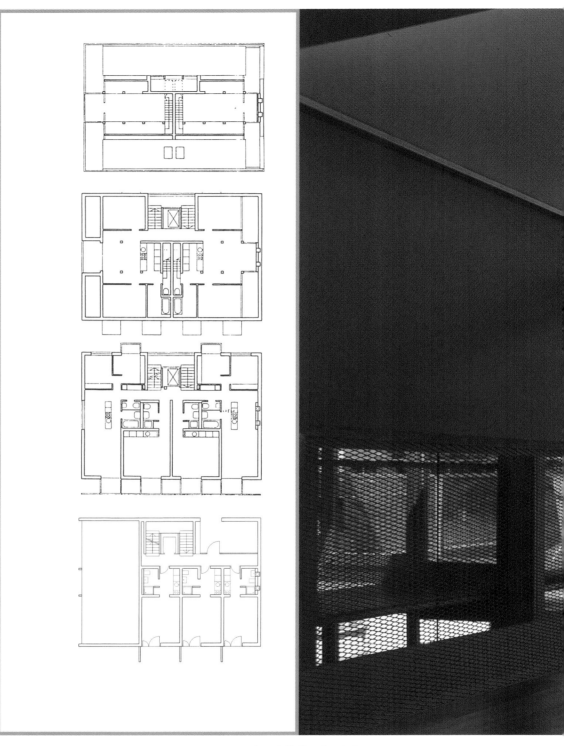

above left Plans, from bottom: ground floor with garages; typical apartments on the first/second/third floors; the fourth floor; and the mezzanine level.

above right Views of the distant Tyrol from the mezzanine in a fourth-floor apartment.

project **Pacemaker**

type integrated services module and flat-pack home

date completed 1998

architect **Birds Portchmouth Russum**

construction factory made units

area 145m² (1,560 sq ft) for three-bedroom version

estimated cost £97,500

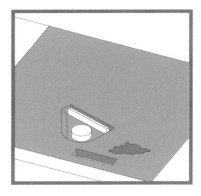 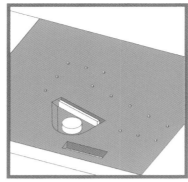 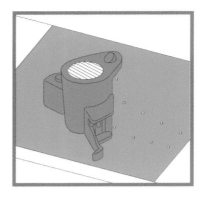 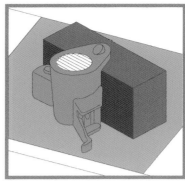

This project has its origins in the design of a prefabricated integrated services module in 1994 subsequently called the Pacemaker, later developed to be used in conjunction with a simple balloon-framed system for providing living and sleeping accommodation. The twentieth-century fascination with service cores is synonymous with the widespread installation of piped services, which have rendered our relationship to gas, electricity, water, sewage and communications systems totally passive. Conceptually, the service core establishes a strict hierarchy of spaces along the lines previously termed 'servant and served'. The principal rooms, in this particular view, are returned to the realm of free space in which the modernist preoccupation with absence can be given full expression. Earlier versions of the Pacemaker conceived of its use with redundant or dilapidated buildings, a poetic image that implies that these structures could remain ruinous and yet still offer all the benefits of a fully serviced home.

The Pacemaker contains all the complex service aspects seen as necessary for a contemporary house: washing, cooking, laundry, communications, heating and vertical circulation. The unit is transportable in four sections on a low loader, and its honeycombed, insulated GRP shell has the voids within its walls filled with concrete once on site, to give it thermal mass and further stability. The unit is designed to be mass produced in order to reduce unit costs and to improve the quality of the finishes and the technologies it contains.

The roof incorporates a solar collector which supplements the hot water provision, with the circular matrix allowing for all orientations on site. When incorporated into an existing structure or attached to a flat-pack unit, the Pacemaker provides heat through air circulated by fan heaters and linked to the honeycomb walls and integral flue. In winter, any solar gain during the day is utilized by drawing air through floor voids and storing the heat within the core walls. This is then used to heat blown air at night as outside temperatures fall. In summer, the walls of the Pacemaker module are cooled during the evenings allowing the circulated air during the following day to be cooler than the ambient outside temperature.

All the technology in the service module is integral including the kitchen unit and sanitary ware, which are formed in glass-reinforced plastic. The plan and section arrangement carefully minimizes the circulation space and exploits the possibilities offered by these specially formed elements to compact all the necessary functions into the most efficient of envelopes: the stair wraps around the circular bath and makes space underneath for a separate ground floor toilet cubicle. The kitchen itself is zoned in terms of temperature range, starting at hot by the cooker and ending with cold in the refrigeration room. Further demonstrating its ability to provide all possible services, the Pacemaker has the potential of four independent solid fuel fireplaces to serve any adjoining principal rooms, thereby connecting nineteenth- and twenty-first-century concepts of service provision.

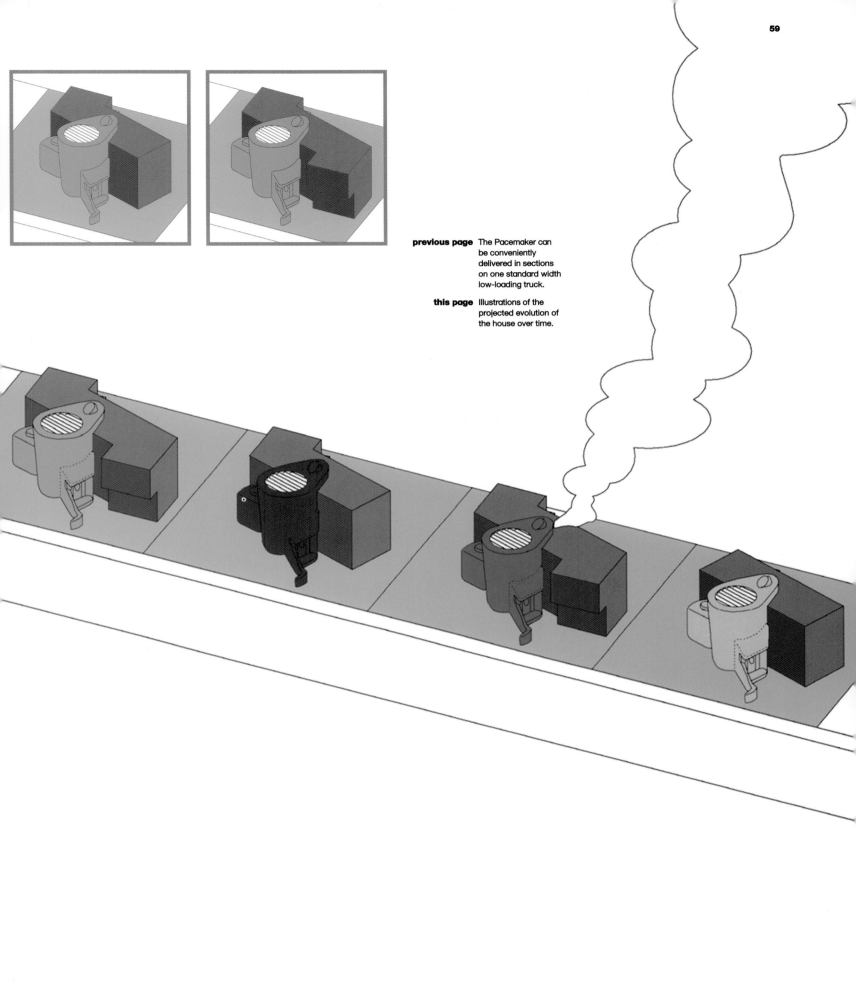

previous page The Pacemaker can be conveniently delivered in sections on one standard width low-loading truck.

this page Illustrations of the projected evolution of the house over time.

top right The fully extended
version with three to
four bedrooms and
a garage.

below and centre right From left to right:
ground- and first-floor
plans of a fully
extended version.

bottom right Pacemaker units
can also be used
with redundant or
unconverted buildings.

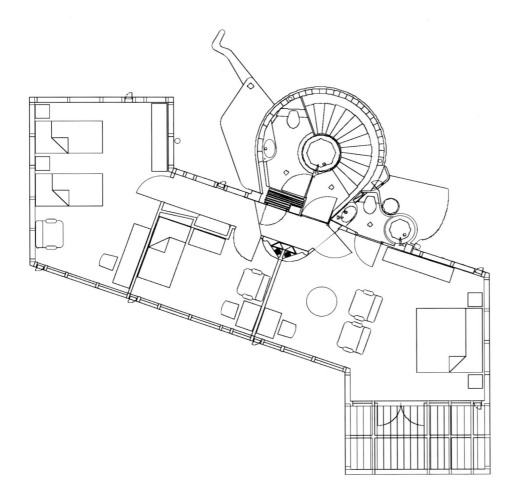

project **housing and commercial block**

location Rathenow
          Germany
date completed 1997
architect Klaus Sill and Jochen Keim

construction main contractor
area 900m² (9,688 sq ft)
cost undisclosed

Given that it is now over 100 years since François Hennebique prefabricated complete transportable houses in poured concrete, and that expectations for this style of manufacturing were high, it might appear surprising that factory-based production line systems for dwellings have not gained general acceptance. The intervening period spans the century that saw the commodification of almost the entire panoply of the products of the machine age. However, the brief period after the Second World War, in which there existed both the political will and the necessary economic circumstances for the proliferation of prefabricated buildings, also corresponded with the need for mass social housing, particularly in what was then known as the Eastern Bloc countries. The result was that unsophisticated derivatives of earlier experiments were used to house the economically underprivileged of war-torn Europe. In the United States, the cultural legacy of the nineteenth-century pioneers and the abundance of land combined to engender a rather different version of this concept: by 1948, 25 per cent of all new houses were prefabricated, but mostly single-storey standardized structures on privately owned plots. The characteristic of both these situations was the same: monotony. This was not the outcome envisaged by designers like Richard Buckminster Fuller, Jean Prouvé and Konrad Wachsmann.

It became clear that housing was no different from any other commodity subjected to factory-based systems of production in that the tendency was away from difference and inexorably towards similarity or repetition.

left A virtually complete prefabricated unit is lowered by crane into position on a precast concrete frame.

below An axonometric diagram showing the main components of a prefabricated unit.

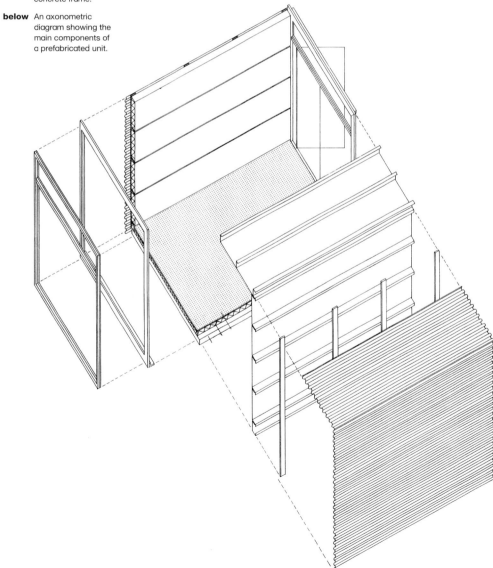

above The units were all installed in one working day.

right An interior of a top-floor apartment – a mezzanine level is located within the existing roof space.

far right The street elevation reveals nothing of the conversion behind the façade.

bottom right Section of the entire building: the apartments are on the top floor only.

Custom-designed prefabricated housing projects have subsequently remained a contradiction in terms, employing purpose-made systems often produced by specialist companies, but conceptually founded on the premise that they stand as representatives of a system of mass production. In addition there was, in the second half of the twentieth century, a significant slowing down in the development of all forms of mechanical, structural and materials engineering. The most rapid advances during this time have been made in electronic, communications and molecular technology: executives flying supersonic across the Atlantic are often in a machine designed 35 years ago and may well be carrying laptops with computing capacity in excess of that of the on-board management systems. The automobiles they pick up on arrival at the airport are based on mechanical systems that are even older.

It is no doubt for these sorts of reasons that the factory production of entire rooms or houses is now viewed as rather a product of the period of romantic speculation about the physical, rather than the virtual, world. What Keim and Sill have done is to breathe new life into this old preoccupation by using prefabricated units to upgrade an existing nineteenth-century building and emphasize the juxtaposition by giving the scheme a dynamic aesthetic polarity: the building in Rathenow is now known as the 'house with two faces'.

The division of different approaches is kept strictly between front and back. To the street the building appears to have been conventionally renovated, but to the rear 12 transportable prefabricated containers sit on a pre-cast concrete supporting frame. The lower two floors now serve as offices for a firm of engineers while above these are three multi-level units served by a separate stair and elevator. In the offices the containers provide service elements, while in the two larger living units they act as dining rooms. The aluminium-clad and steel-framed containers were fabricated in Flensburg 500 kilometres (310 miles) from the site but once delivered were craned into position in one working day, requiring only the installation of the under floor heating to render them usable. For reasons of vertical fire separation the containers have 110-mm (4-inch) reinforced concrete floor slabs as an integral part of their structure. Although the junctions between the two forms of construction are carefully articulated, the disparity is not so much between the nineteenth and twentieth centuries as between two different views of the physical act of assembling buildings, thereby confirming that virtually all carefully designed houses are prototypes and therefore unique.

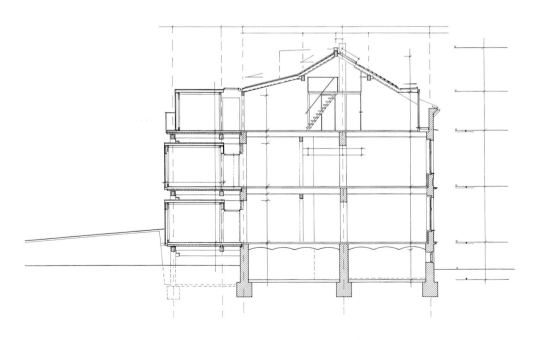

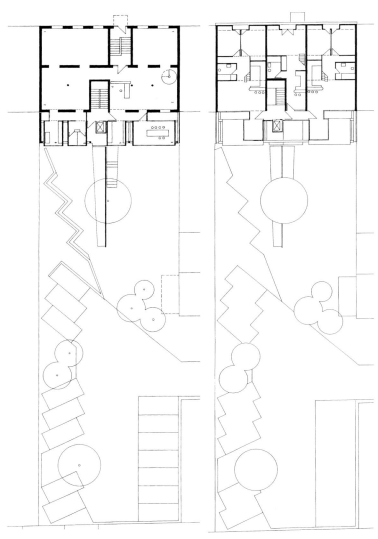

above left The ground-floor plan. Access to the apartments is via a ramp and an internal staircase, while prefabricated units provide service rooms for the offices.

above right Plan of the top floor with three apartments. The prefabricated units act as dining rooms.

right The rear elevation of the completed building, which is now known as 'the house with two faces'.

project **Masgonty house**

location Saint Pardoux La Rivière
France

date commissioned 1997

architect **Anne Lacaton and Jean Philippe Vassal**

construction main contractor
area area 242m² (2,605 sq ft) including garage
cost FF 754,150

One of the ironies of the case for prefabrication is that architects who promote it more often than not become better known for their ability to produce hand-crafted buildings. The reason they are allowed to continue to practise this duplicity is that the same architects continue to attract a relatively wealthy client base because in an age of mass production, the custom-made is a sign of status as well as being a safe investment. Many houses, however, are in one sense prototypes, and to produce a prototype that conceals the very human nature of its assembly is very expensive – as we know from extreme examples of design such as the Space Shuttle or the F117 Stealth Fighter.

The alternative trajectory for prefabrication has its origins in the twentieth century in the Eames House, but although this proved a more practical model to follow than Chareau's Maison de Verre, or Buckminster Fuller's Dymaxion House, it nevertheless proved a more difficult model to emulate well. The production of buildings in which the architecture has been designed out, leaving them in a fabricated state of innocence akin to the agricultural and industrial vernacular, is what seems to lie behind these minimalist intentions. Limited budgets and very restricted design briefs appear to be helpful in giving focus to this particular intention. The Masgonty house has both.

Lacaton and Vassal were asked to design this house for an older woman who required a home for herself but with capacity to accommodate regular weekend visits from her grandchildren – in effect two houses in one with very different requirements. The site is in the middle of the Dordogne countryside of meadows and fields, and is a narrow plot next to a minor road. The house has been conceived as a long, low single-storey building in two halves joined by a Plexiglas-roofed greenhouse. The constructional system and the plan are fully integrated and designed to use readily available standard components within the range normally found in agricultural buildings. The external walls comprise 200-mm (8-inch) blocks, rendered externally, and with full height openings to allow a regular sequence of fully glazed sliding aluminium door units set deep within the reveals. Sliding aluminium shutters are hung from continuous tracks under the eaves. The roof is clad in profiled aluminium sheeting, single sheets covering from ridge to eaves to avoid horizontal lap joints. Because the construction is lightweight, the foundations are shallow concrete strip footings which minimized the extent of the ground works.

Internally, the house is lined in plywood to avoid the need for wet trades such as plastering during the final stages of construction. This lining conceals a generous thickness of insulation which renders the house far more energy efficient than its appearance suggests. The details of the junctions of the various components are carefully worked out to avoid the need for sophisticated on-site skills and allow for the inevitable errors in the location of components – an attitude which takes a pragmatic view of the realities of constructing low budget domestic buildings.

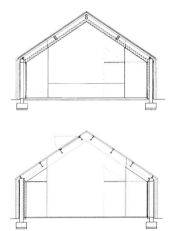

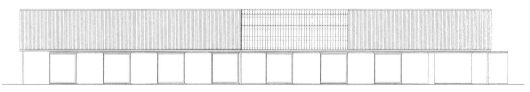

top Section through the main body of the house and underneath, a section through the Plexiglas greenhouse.

above Elevation of the house.

right The detailing comprises standard building components, which are easy to assemble.

above Aluminium shutters allow the house to be fully closed down when the occupants are away.

right Fabricated state of innocence: the building's aesthetic is taken from the local agricultural vernacular.

left The plan is rigorously ordered by the constructional system.

project **Bo Klok housing**

location Sweden
date in production 1999
architect Ahlström Arkitektbyrå for IKEA

construction main contractor
area variable
cost variable

Your new home
from around
3300 SEK per month

left A standard plan: both
floors of the two-storey
blocks are identical.
The top block has
access to the deck
via a common stair.

above The IKEA publicity
brochure stresses
economics over
aesthetics, promising
a new home for around
£250 ($500) a month.

Bo Klok® – Live Smart – is an idea from Skanska and IKEA. An idea to build houses more wisely and provide lower rents.
From around 3300 SEK per month.

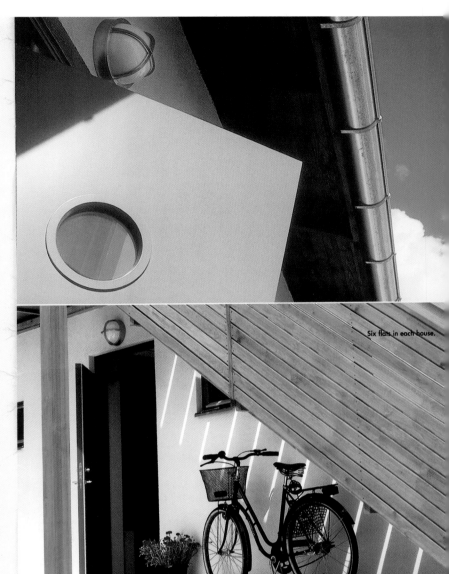

Six flats in each house.

Don't be surprised to find yourself standing at the entrance to your new home earlier than planned. Price is no longer an obstacle when looking for a personable home. They look like villas in the countryside but are in fact modern flats just a stones throw from town. You've never seen anything like Bo Klok before.
Welcome home.

Writing nearly one hundred years ago, the Berlin-born sociologist Georg Simmel observed, 'the fashions of the upper stratum of society are never identical with those of the lower; in fact, they are abandoned by the former as soon as the later prepares to appropriate them'.[1] Thus the appeal of IKEA to the mass markets of Europe and North America is due to the reinterpretation of design aesthetics derived from high art objects sampled from across the span of the twentieth century, and produced in sufficiently high quantities to make the resultant products more generally affordable. However, economies of scale and the need for wider markets inevitably force diversification in any successful company, and it is an obvious move for IKEA to make the transition from furnishing homes, to actually building the houses themselves. As with all their existing products, IKEA houses do not rely on innovative technology: instead they involve the application of simple timber framed construction, and a palette of commonly used building materials to the production of a building envelope that is composed of prefabricated elements and provides contemporary levels of thermal efficiency. Manufacturing costs are kept down by the standardization of components and their production in one factory. In addition, there are only two different housing units, both of which contain six apartments in L-shaped two-storey-high blocks. The apartments are relatively small at 48 square metres (517 square feet), 59 square metres (635 square feet) and 74 square metres (775 square feet), or one, two and three bedroom units respectively, and reflect IKEA's understanding that the housing market is increasingly dominated by the need for alternatives to accommodation designed for nuclear families comprising parents and children.

These houses are experimental primarily in the realm of economics and marketing, rather than technology and building construction, although all these aspects are interconnected. The main elements of the building comprise prefabricated timber wall panels and slender concrete floor planks. These, including the low-pitch roof trusses, can be erected on prepared foundations by two operatives using a crane in about three days. Completion of the rest of the envelope then follows rapidly, with the entire block fitted out and serviced in four months. The walls contain 290mm (11 inches) of insulation and are finished externally in either rough-sawn timber or plaster. The roof has 350mm (14 inches) of insulation and has the Roman profiled concrete roof tiles that are common throughout Scandinavia. The aesthetic is derived specifically from the early twentieth-century timber tradition of Sweden and Norway, which not only lends itself easily to the techniques of mass production, but is, within this social democratic context, relatively class neutral.

The plans of the units are strictly zoned in two bands with the service elements clustered at one end. Apart from this and the lack of a separate living room, they appear spatially retrogressive. Compositionally, from the scale of each block with its differential unit widths, to the first-floor access via a timber deck and the consistency of the window positions and sizes, the aim is clearly to allude to the local vernacular and hence signify a double meaning: as a resident one can be both fashionable and yet not part of an identifiable set of cultural values. This phenomenon allies with the two social tendencies that Simmel identified as essential to fashion: 'the need of union on the one hand and the need of isolation on the other'.

IKEA have so far completed nearly 1,000 individual apartments in seven cities and towns in Sweden and there are plans for similar developments in Norway, Poland and the United Kingdom. The sites are chosen carefully to be near good transport, social and retail infrastructures, to ensure that the finance package which goes with the sale or rental agreement is allied to a broader picture in terms of affordability. Since Buckminster Fuller's Dymaxion House was first exhibited at a department store in Chicago, it has taken over 70 years to arrive at the reality of a house and contents designed and supplied by one company as a packaged commodity. That the technology which supports this should differ little from that used in a prefabricated house unit by the company Skillings and Flint in 1861 is an ironic twist driven by the realities of monopoly capitalist economics and the marketing need to maintain the illusion of a craft base in a machine-made product.

top left Under construction: the two-storey building envelope takes three days to erect.

centre left The IKEA package includes a two-hour session with an interior design consultant.

bottom left The constructional section reveals a lack of technological innovation.

above The aim of the architecture is to be fashionable but classless.

The drawing room had about it some- thing extraordinarily intense, like the face of a wrinkled old lady. The walls were cracked, the ceiling stripped; and most bewildering of all in this bewildering house was the floor: it had simply caved in. Waxed, varnished, and polished though it was, it swayed like a ship's gangway. A strange house, evoking no neglect, no slackness, but rather an extraordinary respect. Each passing year had added something to its charm, to the complexity of its visage and its friendly atmosphere, as well as to the dangers encountered on the journey from the drawing-room to the dining-room.

Antoine de Saint-Exupéry: *Wind, Sand and Stars*

Although there are significant variations in the patterns of housing statistics in different countries, the overall picture is that in industrialized countries on average around 40 per cent of the population live in houses that are over 40 years old.[1] These are also the countries in which the population size is stable: in some cases it is even contracting slightly, which indicates that in these cultural environments it is not necessary to increase the size of the housing stock but to improve or replace that which already exists. In addition we have two phenomena to recognize. Firstly, there is the continuing availability of existing building stock in which the intended functions have ceased and the structures have become redundant under new economic circumstances. Secondly, industrialized countries produce artefacts which are deemed to have outlived their primary function within a very short space of time (say five to ten years) but which have not necessarily outlived their usefulness. Conversion in this chapter refers to the upgrading of existing structures, not necessarily houses, to create living units. Re-use is about the appropriation of the discarded products of industrialization to form the basis of new houses.

Stuart Brand, in *How Buildings Learn* (1994), documents the way in which buildings in general are made to perform tasks never originally envisaged for them.[2] Experience directly contradicts the early modernist dictum that form follows function, because function is not initially a precisely defining term, and subsequent to a building's erection is historically determined and therefore transient. Artefact appropriation is an extreme form of functional redefinition, and because it involves the transgressing of categories, has for a long time been the object of architectural fantasies in stories, for example the witch's house in Hansel and Gretel which is also a meal of bread, cake and sugar. References by early modernists to houses as machines also fuel an ongoing professional fantasy amongst designers about the desirability of living in warehouses, factories, water towers, windmills, lighthouses, barns and farm buildings. It is a revealing paradox that modernism as an architectural movement was responsible for a

historically unique engagement in mass housing as a design issue, but also gave rise to generations of architects, artists and designers whose ideal residence was precisely anything but a house. The ultimate apologist for the modernist literary project, William Burroughs, spent some time in the 1970s living in a windowless underground ex-YMCA dressing room.

There are sensible environmental reasons why conversion and re-use should take a dominant role in housing provision, but at the level of cultural value systems, it is easy to see the attraction of the illusion of neutrality and an external aesthetic at least that is not associated with a particular social class and its associated historical traditions.

Brookes, Stacey, Randall's conversion of a former factory in West London is a seriously concentrated material investment by a single client and is invisible from the street. This is very much in the tradition of the neutral container of a box of exotic tricks, but the interior takes this genre into the realm of the experimental by virtue of its obsessional attention to detail.

In the conversion and restoration that Enric Miralles and Benedetta Tagliabue carried out in the previously derelict Mercaders building in the historic city centre of Barcelona, the transformation was achieved through a layering of existing and new elements in a palimpsest of materials and details from different periods of the building's life. Miralles and Tagliabue were extremely adept at not exhibiting prejudices in favour of one particular period and the result is a powerful condemnation of the obsessively conservationist position in working with historic houses. Instead the architects posited the idea of an experimental architectural archaeology.

The work of Alex de Rijke for his mother and her home in Plymouth, England, has to deal with the restraints of a terraced Victorian house. Whereas Miralles and Tagliabue and Brookes, Stacey, Randall have felt the need to be precious about detailing, in this low-budget self-build (de Rijke and his relatives did much of the work themselves) the materials used are very ordinary and it is in their assembly and unexpected juxtapositions that the project becomes experimental. This particular way of working has its antecedents in the work of Rudolf Schindler and the way in which crude materials are alchemically transmuted into the exotic by the application of clear inventive ideas.

The hypothesis that an existing house can be, over time, turned into a total work of art is the basis of the work of sculptor Walter Pichler in Burgenland, Austria. Pichler's gradual accretion of structures around the grounds of an old farmhouse provide a place to live, work and exhibit. In this extreme project all space becomes the subject of ritual, and everyday images of domesticity are subsumed in an environment based on a highly refined set of obsessions.

As with de Rijke's work, Nicole Edmonds' creation of a small house at Findhorn, Scotland, out of a whiskey vat from a distillery is not reliant on complex technological solutions. Although the artefact's shape is potentially prescriptive, the final form of the house is inventively free of the restraints it might have imposed.

Michael Reynolds' Earthships also aim at form transformations but start from smaller recycled components like car tyres. Earthships not only disguise their source material but transform it from detritus by not aiming overtly at an abstractly conceived design aesthetic. This is the nearest the late twentieth century gets to Baroque.

Elemer Zalotay's own house near Bern, Switzerland, is an experiment in the creation of an architectural aesthetic out of carefully worked detritus. Here the methodology relies on juxtaposition, composition and scale to create a totally new series of compound surfaces which are experienced as more than the sum of their constituent parts.

Finally, Tony Wrench has built a round house in Pembrokeshire, Wales, that is not only the cheapest structure in this book (being almost entirely made from free materials), but more importantly a demonstration of the possibilities for experimental design without the use of specialist professional assistance.

project **Art house**

location London
UK
date commissioned 1999
architect **Brookes, Stacey, Randall**

construction main contractor with nominated specialist sub-contractors
area 450m² (4,844 sq ft)
cost undisclosed

The envelope for this conversion is a former textile factory that at one time served as the offices for the architects of the 1951 Festival of Britain, Powell and Moya. The three-storey building is on a backland site amid the gardens of surrounding residential properties and has very limited access to the street via a car-width entrance court. Two small private courts adjoin the building at ground level, one on the east side and the other on the west. There is no indication of the nature of this internal world until once inside the tiny entrance lobby, which gives a glimpse of the larger court beyond with its installation of a built-to-order water wall.

The anonymous client had already seen Brookes, Stacey, Randall's loft for Chris Lowe in the Clerkenwell district of London, and commissioned the architects to design a house as a London base for himself and his art collection. The brief, therefore, is not really about luxury but about a particular form of hedonism – pleasure based on the complete control of one's immediate environment and an unfaltering belief in sophisticated technology. Nothing, in this view, is more magical than matter.

The interior was completely demolished, the ground floor lowered and a new basement created. The internal space is most easily understood as comprising two 'bookends' of smaller-scale rooms stacked at either end of an open-plan main space which rises clear to the roof. This top-lit space has a mezzanine at first-floor level, a chimney of red polished Roman plaster suspended from the ceiling, and a straight-flight glass and stainless steel staircase that rises up through to the master bedroom in the corner. The sense of transparency is enhanced through the extensive use of both clear and sandblasted glass on the faces of the 'bookend' towers.

Each tower is virtually autonomous and has its own internal stair. Nearest the entrance is a stack of rooms exclusively for the use of the client: in the basement is a wine cellar which doubles as a utility room and above this an office five steps lower than the main space. Over this again, but only accessible via the secondary stair, is the principal bathroom, dominated by a custom-made freestanding stainless steel tub fed by a remote miniature version of a water cannon. The top room is the master bedroom and gains light both from an automated clear glass rooflight and the glazed backs of the storage units. At the other end of the house is another stack of rooms for guests over a ground floor gymnasium that is divided from the main space by glass screens.

The entire floor of the principal volume is covered in a matrix of French limestone slabs which continue flush out onto the two courtyards. Glass walls, cut into the existing brickwork, fold back to allow the courts to become extensions of the room. The other main materials used besides glass, stainless steel and stone are solid oak for doors and linings, leather for handrail cladding and slate for the bathroom floors. Virtually all the fittings are prototypes designed by the architects in response to the client's very specific requirements for cooking, entertaining, relaxing or working. The artwork is an incidental backdrop to these activities and reinforces the impression of preciousness and excess.

above View of the living space from the top of the glass stair. The mezzanine is to the left with a custom-made stainless steel bar.

right The custom conversion required a total rebuild inside the existing walls.

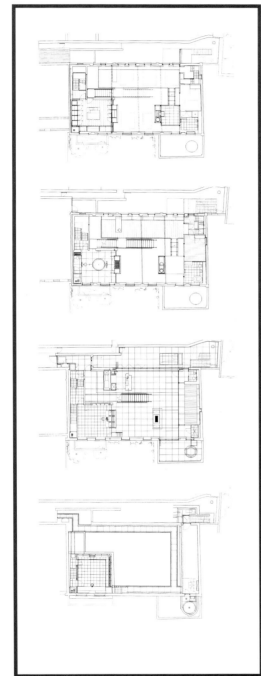

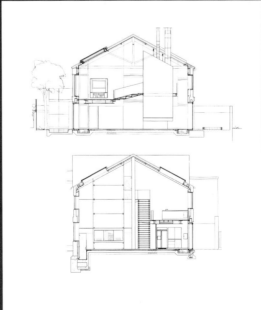

far left The interior fit-out is a detailed exercise in transparency.

left From bottom: basement, ground floor, first floor, second floor.

bottom left Two cross sections: the top view looks towards the guest 'book-end', while the bottom section looks towards the main bedroom/ bathroom 'bookend'.

below In the main bedroom glazed storage units overlook the living space below.

project **Mercaders building**

location Barcelona
Spain
date commissioned 1993
architect **Enric Miralles and Benedetta Tagliabue**

construction main contractor
approximate area 375m² (4,036 sq ft)
cost 3,260,000 PTA

right The stair in the building's entrance court leads to the apartment on the first floor.

centre right and far right The piano room and the study. The architects have retained some original floor tiles and left surviving wall painting visible, but have made no attempt at conventional restoration.

This conversion and renovation of the principal floor of the Mercaders building in the historic centre of Barcelona is a model for the alternative to conservation. What is the basis of the conservationist approach? It is the idea that there always exists a point of origin to which it is possible to return in order to recreate the authentic object. The alternative view is that most processes that modify buildings over time are irreversible and that the appropriate response is that of a progressive overwriting as with a palimpsest.

Miralles and Tagliabue's apartment for themselves adopts this second approach. By the time the space was acquired, the building was used as a warehouse and most of the internal partition walls had been removed and the ceiling decoration destroyed. Some original wall and floor tiles remained although the floors and ceilings were in a dangerous condition structurally. The main design decisions were to maintain the atmosphere of a dilapidated country house in the heart of the city and to concentrate on the floor surfaces as the organizing elements of the spaces. In reading the architects' published plans it is important to understand that the layering of old and new materials on the floor surfaces has equal importance to the location of the partitions. The plan as found was a virtually continuous space around four sides of the central court. The apartment is on the *piano nobile* and has its own access via an open stair within the court. The building has an enclosed wild garden to the north, and the rooms overlook the street to the south.

The original tiles have been relaid on top of the rebuilt floors but not aligned to the old original walls. Rather, they have been arranged like rugs between areas of oak block flooring, their geometry taking precedence over the partitions, thereby reinforcing the sense of continuous space. The new partitions are treated like curtains and specifically designed items of furniture further demarcate the individual spaces from each other. The large oak table that stands in the entrance hall is said to be representative of the whole house with its fixed centre section and complex array of folding flaps. The architects clearly enjoyed the possibilities of this experimental architectural archaeology, whereby a fundamentalist concept of authenticity is replaced by an inclusive and imaginative view of historical processes.

The consequences of this approach are eclectic and pluralist. Designer furniture sits alongside temporary ceiling props in the main living room, providing apparently permanent support for the distressed ceilings above. The gothic arches discovered in the living room are over-painted to abstract their forms and subvert their presence once again. Classic Danish light fittings by Poul Henningsen are suspended over the library area from a cobweb-like steel mobile. This theme of mobility is continued through the detailing of the specially made furniture in either steel rod or timber – very little is actually attached to the original fabric, but is layered onto, or peeled back from the surfaces in an intricate form of collage. Within this liberal aesthetic regime, the architects have given the overall composition a sense of coherence not through an obsessive need to control but by exercising extreme sensitivity.

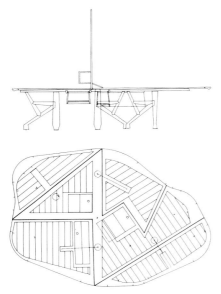

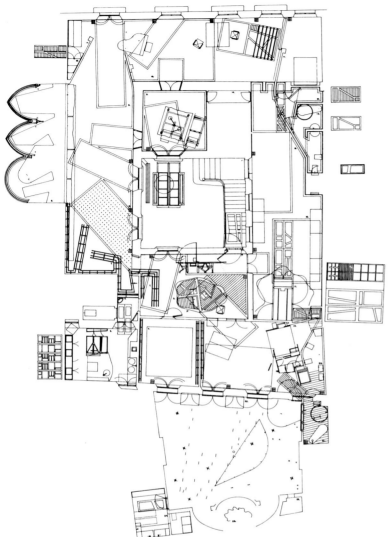

top left Sketches of the oak table in the entrance hall – a microcosm of the apartment.

left The entrance hall with the specially designed oak table.

above left In this drawing of the plan the floor texture and furniture have equal status with partitions. The edges show folded out selections from the wall elevations.

above The corridor linking the childrens' room and the main bedroom. Overpainting and complex juxtapositions distort the visual space.

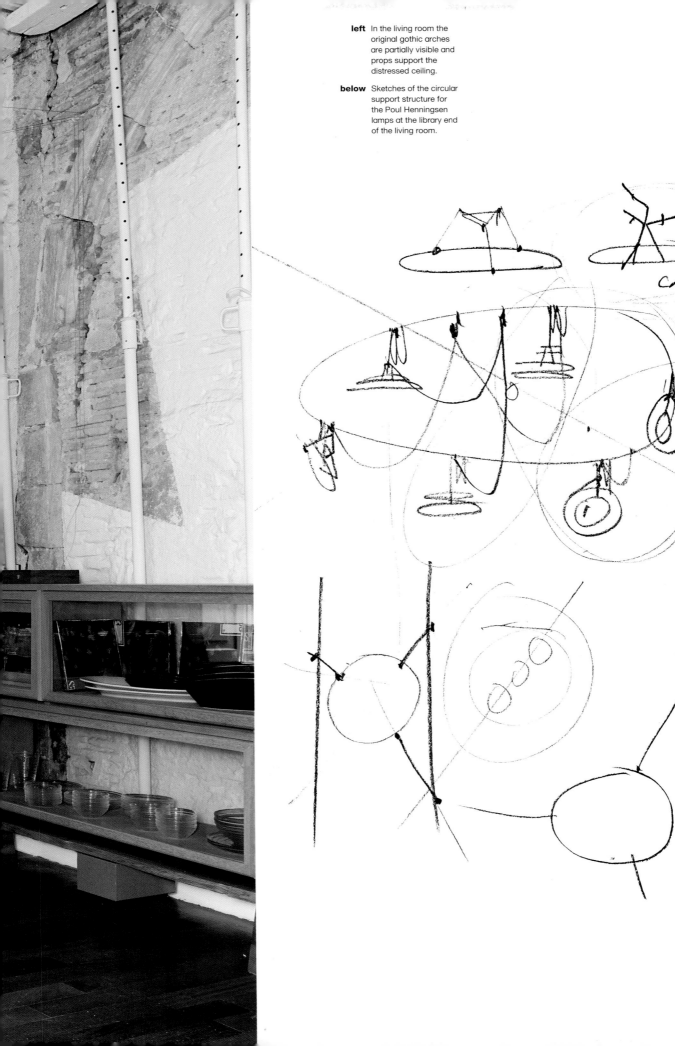

left In the living room the original gothic arches are partially visible and props support the distressed ceiling.

below Sketches of the circular support structure for the Poul Henningsen lamps at the library end of the living room.

project **architect's mother's house**

location Plymouth
UK
date 1992–5
architect **Alex de Rijke**

construction architect as contractor with family help
area 150m² (1,615 sq ft)
cost £35,000

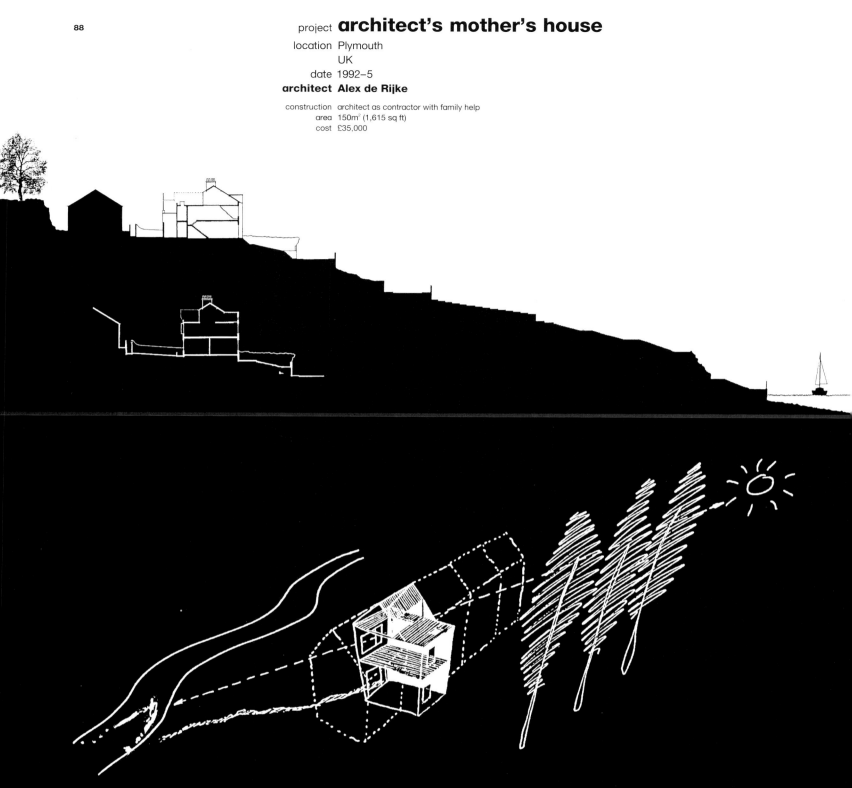

The main asset of the house is the spectacular view north of the River Tamar and the site of Isambard Kingdom Brunel's engineering masterpiece of 1859, the Royal Albert Bridge that links the counties of Devon and Cornwall. Prompted by this and the functional requirement for the house of accommodating regular visits from a large family of grown-up children, de Rijke's most important design move was to place the main living space on the first floor with its own mezzanine sleeping platform, and convert the existing ground floor rooms into what is effectively a self-contained apartment.

This project stands in marked contrast to the over-financed, one-off houses built for parents in the twentieth century by ambitious young architects anxious to kick start their careers. In the first place, the low budget required that de Rijke with his sister and two brothers did most of the construction work themselves during weekends and vacations. Secondly, the basis of the scheme was an unpromising and very ordinary nineteenth-century terraced house comprising four small dark rooms and a substandard rear extension that blocked out most of the sunlight.

The removal of part of the roof and all of the first floor internal partitions created a double-height space that enjoys maximum sunlight from the rear, and a new connection to the expansive views through the retained sash windows on the front façade. From the street, the conversion is invisible and to the rear one is aware that reconstruction has been kept to a minimum. What would have been the rear half of the unused roof space has been transformed into a roof deck, accessible from the mezzanine by a 'bridge' over the living space. This deck is covered in timber slats and screened by glazed panels made of standard off-the-shelf components. A large double-glazed unit allows sunlight to pass down through a void into the living room and kitchen below. The mezzanine, which has a view through a circular window in the existing gable, is constructed in timber and steel flich beams and stressed plywood to give back structural integrity lost by removing the existing ceiling. A new plywood stair, which leads up from the living room, is integrated into a bookshelf. The kitchen unit is made of plywood, with plan-chest like drawers and a worktop made of off-cuts, end grain up, planed into a smooth surface.

The existing two-storey rear extension now contains the new bathrooms which are detailed in plywood and mirror glass. A glass skylight doubles as an outdoor table for the roof terrace and affords a dramatic view of the sky from the bath, or conversely a dramatic view of the bather from the terrace. Certain original features of the house are intensified through the juxtaposition with these new elements, like the exposed corbelled brickwork of the chimneys in the roof space, or the renovated Victorian fireplaces and sash windows. Elsewhere, the detailing has the kind of relaxed invention only possible with self build, most obviously the length of 'found' silver birch tree which performs the task of a balustrade on the bridge between the mezzanine and the terrace. De Rijke's work on this house is not just a labour of love, but provides a powerful model for affordable domestic design solutions unfettered by the restrictions of either populist or high art aesthetics.

above left The first-floor living room looking up to the sleeping platform. The tree handrail was found on a walk.

above The sleeping platform with a circular window in the house's existing gable.

right From bottom: ground floor, first floor, and second floor with sun deck. The ground floor is a self-contained unit for guests.

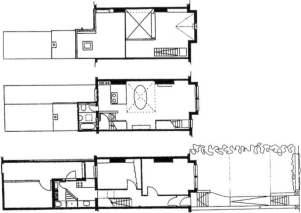

far left The stairs to the sleeping platform are integrated into a bookcase. Original features, such as the sash windows, have been retained.

left The sun deck has a built-in glass table that acts as a skylight for the bathroom below.

below The compact kitchen unit is made of plywood off-cuts.

project **farmhouse extensions**

location St Martin an der Raab
Burgenland
Austria
date 1972–present
designer Walter Pichler

construction self build and specialist sub-contractors
cost undisclosed

'If man is determined by his environment, he is not free', said the German artist Joseph Beuys. 'Freedom has to come not from the environment but from creativity'. The artist Walter Pichler began the gradual transformation of this farmhouse on the borders of Hungary and Slovenia in 1972, restoring the original buildings and gradually building new adjacent structures to house specific pieces of sculpture. Pichler's drawings are sold to finance the work, but the primary focus of his creative activity, the sculptures, are never put on the market – they have their home in St Martin and occasionally travel to appear at appropriate venues elsewhere. This situation has two significant consequences. Firstly, the sculptures are never truly finished and are worked on within an open time frame. Secondly, the individual pieces have a specific and unique relationship to their own particular houses – indeed the shelter often precedes the production of the piece to be contained, thereby acting as a formative force in its creation. At St Martin a symbiotic relationship exists between the present (banalities of everyday life), the past (as a given environment), and the future (as projects yet to be realized but already imagined). Pichler has established a set of social, economic and cultural parameters which allow him freedom to sculpt and build according to his own artistic principles.

left Pichler's drawing of the *Small Tower* with the *House for Torso and Skulls* on the left.

right The plan of the *Small Tower* with the *House for the Large Cross* on the right.

A narrow, undulating country road passes close by the compact complex of buildings on the north side. The original group of buildings comprised a traditional farm house with a west-facing courtyard and two outbuildings: one to the north-east for storage, and one for timber to the south-west. The farmhouse now contains Pichler's workshop and living spaces. Virtually unaltered throughout, the original kitchen has been preserved with its tiled stove and dining niche. In the workshop section, adjacent to the road, the table saw is overlooked by a guardian sculpture, rendering its use both functional and the subject of a private ritual. At the edge of this space, the two pieces called *Big Wagon* and *Small Wagon* (1962–90), await indefinitely their final short move by rail across a bridge to the *House for Wagons* (1973), a pitched-roof brick structure standing on eight square columns. To the south, across the end of the courtyard, stands the woodshed, and between it and the farmhouse is the skeletal *Glass House with Mobile Figure* (1982). Standing inside the fully glazed roof space at one end of a narrow timber gallery, the rake of the figure's outstretched arms matches the pitch of the rafters exactly. Small linked timber towers also stand on the west side, enclosures for two of Pichler's oldest sculptures, the *Houses for Steles*, permit only selected views from outside as in a shrine.

Up the gentle slope of the grounds on the east side of the farmhouse, aligned on the axis of the existing storage building, is the *House for Torso and Skulls* (1981), a pure white envelope with an exposed timber roof structure and narrow vertical slot windows, arranged geometrically. *House for the Large Cross* (1988), *Small Tower* (1989), and *House for the Ridge* complete the implied upper courtyard. All these new buildings make vernacular references in their form and detailing and yet are clearly the subject of intense thought and deliberation. Pichler's emphasis is threefold – first the need to create a unique and sympathetic setting for his creations, second a reworking of the archetypes of his chosen landscape, and third a regard for architecture's irreducible connection to abstract geometry.

That such working methods are transferable to other contexts has recently been the subject of a new architectural experiment by Pichler on the Greek island of Syros. Meanwhile, St Martin awaits the completion of its latest addition, the *House for the Two Troughs*, in which the sculpture and the building are indivisible.

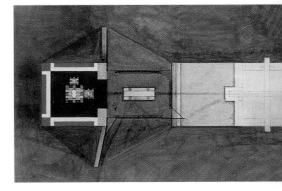

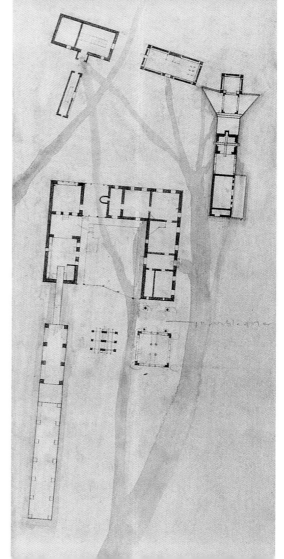

far left bottom The plan of the building complex: the original farmhouse is in the centre.

far left top From left to right: the *House for Wagons*, the *Houses for Steles* and the woodshed.

above Pichler's workshop with a model of the *House for the Two Troughs*, now under construction.

top left The *Glass House with Mobile Figure* is attached to the original wood store.

bottom left Interior of the *House for Torso and Skulls*.

above right View up the slope to the *House for Torso and Skulls*, with the *Small Tower* on the right.

project **Grania Oi**

location Findhorn
Moray
Scotland
UK
date commissioned 1994
architect Nicole Edmonds

construction The Findhorn Foundation/Philip Stewart
area 65m² (700 sq ft)
cost £52,000

above Living-room balcony
with storage underneath
(not shown in the plan).
The original barrel's
form does not dominate
the composition from
any viewpoint.

right The first-floor plan:
the sleeping platform
is over the bathroom,
and the main bedroom
is beneath the living
room/kitchen.

far right top View of the sleeping
platform and living
room with the balcony
beyond. The skylight
is directed towards
the sunset.

far right A section shows the
architect's inventive
use of levels to achieve
spatial complexity within
the small volume of
the barrel.

The Findhorn Community was founded as the result of the work of Eileen Caddy and her husband, who, from 1962 onwards, lived in a caravan and created a garden out of what was a rubbish dump next to the runway of the military airbase near the village of Findhorn on the Moray Firth. Out of this unlikely situation has grown a community which now has over 150 people committed to spiritual research and achieving an environmentally conscious, socially cohesive lifestyle. During the formative years community members occupied static vans in an adjacent caravan park, but during the last 25 years a number of permanent houses have been built by the Foundation for long-term residents.

Grania Oi is the most recent of a group of six barrel houses, the first of which was constructed by Roger Doudna in the 1970s as the first permanent house at Findhorn. The basis of the latest house is a single 6.8 metre- (22 foot-) diameter whiskey vat from a Speyside distillery. Whereas earlier barrel houses were single-storey, Nicole Edmonds decided to lift the barrels components onto a plinth and, in combination with excavation, effectively create a two-storey house with the Douglas fir base of the barrel as the main first floor.

However, the internal organization of the house is more complex than this simple description implies. In section, there are four levels: the lowest is the main bedroom, in a semi-basement, the next up being the entry level and bathroom with the cut-out third-of-a-circle of the barrel base as the floor. The main floor contains the kitchen and living area and 1.3 metres (4 feet) up from this again is a sleeping platform which occupies the space over the bathroom. This compact, interlocking series of spaces is linked by a spiral stair. The only addition to the circular plan form is the entrance lobby that, through its location, gives a strong connection between the rear of the house and an adjacent earth bank. Within a very small plot, this creates an entry sequence on one side of the house, and on the other a sheltered garden with a raised sundeck that has views across the woodland beyond.

The staves of the original barrel are used structurally and held together by an external galvanized steel band around its base. The barrel and the stone plinth are both lined to allow for extensive use of blown recycled newsprint as insulation, which, used in conjunction with air-permeable vapour barriers, produces a breathing wall construction. The roof is clad in titanium zinc and has a directional (south-west-facing but centrally placed) skylight which gives the sleeping platform an evening view of the sunset or a night-time glimpse of the moon. The external doors and windows are all made-to-order from surplus Douglas fir taken from the barrel and some have low emissivity glass to further reduce heat loss.

Findhorn has a 75-kilowatt windmill which supplements electricity supplied to all its houses from the National Grid. In addition, sewage is treated at its own environmental plant called the Living Machine. In this sensitive transformation of the redundant component of a semi-industrial process, Edmonds and her builder have neither destroyed the integrity of the original object nor let its form dominate the composition. This project is not a sentimental retreat from the practical realities of contemporary living, but a serious attempt, in the spirit of Eileen Caddy, to visualize hitherto unseen possibilities latent in our own culture's detritus.

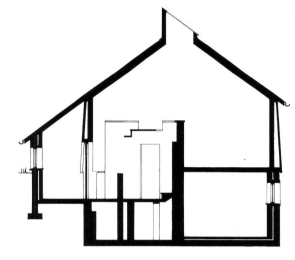

project **Nautilus Earthship**

location Taos
New Mexico
USA

designed 1994

architect **Michael Reynolds – Solar Survival**

construction self-build with specialist sub-contractors
area 130m² (14,000 sq ft)
cost variable

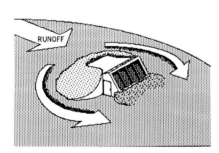

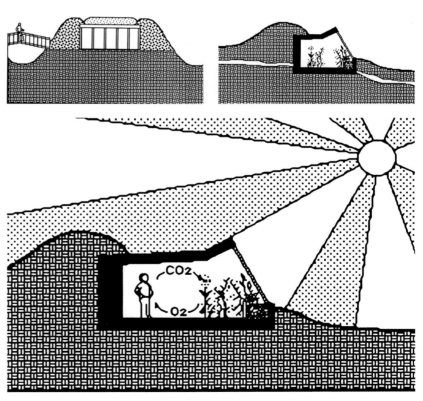

left As with all Earthships, the side of the house in shadow is partially buried.

right The basic principles of Earthship design as shown in Solar Survival self-build manuals.

above Extensive glazing to
the south maximizes
solar gain.

right The living room
with sleeping platform
and fireplace.

far right The plan is zoned
to exploit solar gain.
The large thermal
store is to the right.

There are primarily two differences between Earthships and other experimental houses. Firstly, Michael Reynolds clearly states in his Earthship manual that 'an Earthship is not a house', preferring to define it as a vessel concerned with self sufficiency rather than style or tradition. Secondly, Earthships are not one-off design exercises, but the product of a construction and servicing system which can be adapted to produce a variety of forms and configurations. After over 20 years of development, Solar Survival as a business is offering a range of client services, ranging from sets of construction drawings for self builders, to a full design service for custom-designed projects. Within the restrictions of the system there are essentially three types of Earthship, the hut being the most elementary. At the next level of sophistication is the vertical glass version designed for temperate climates, while the most complex is the sloped glass Earthship which provides more thermal mass and theoretically can cope with any climatic conditions.

In 1994 the Greater World Community was founded on a 630-acre site near Taos, as an extension to the work of Solar Survival, and the Nautilus is one of two rentable 'vessels' for use by visitors attending on-site courses. Located on the edge of a lava cliff and overlooking a small gorge, the building is completely autonomous and currently offers the experience of off-grid living for around $35 per person per night.

Irrespective of their complexity, Earthships all share the same basic common features. The primary material for the load-bearing external walls is used car tyres packed with earth and stacked rather in the manner of stonework. In the United States alone over 240 million car tyres are discarded every year (1999 statistic). Of these some 76 per cent are recycled but most of the rest end up in illegal landfill and it is both their abundance and their absence of value that is the attraction for Reynolds. Internal lightweight partitions comprise aluminium cans set horizontally in a sand and cement mix mortar. All walls are finished in a sand and clay render, applied to a sub-base of expanded metal lath. As with all other Earthships, the Nautilus has a large south-facing glazed solar wall and is partially buried on its other three sides. Heat from solar gain accumulates within the thermal mass of the earth walls formed by the tyres and evens out temperature variations. A thermal mass stack, centred in the earth mound behind the house, draws air through the building to aid ventilation.

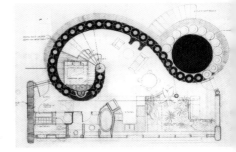

The plan of the house is carefully zoned with the internal garden, the kitchen and the bathrooms set out along the glazed southern wall, which is set at a 30-degree angle to the vertical to optimize heating potential from low winter sun angles. The living and sleeping spaces are set deeper within the plan and clustered around a large stove. Off-grid living means that the building is intended to encourage a lifestyle which requires little electricity – what is required being supplied by batteries charged by photovoltaic panels with a wind turbine working in tandem. Waste water is separated, with the grey water (from washing) receiving treatment within the building's own internal planters. The building is sited to allow rainwater to run off into cisterns for re-use after filtering. Finally, to complete this removal from materialistic values that Reynolds is seeking to achieve, there is no telephone.

project **architect's house**

location Ziegelried
near Bern
Switzerland
date 1984 to present
architect **Elemer Zalotay**

construction self-build and specialist sub-contractor
area not available
cost undisclosed

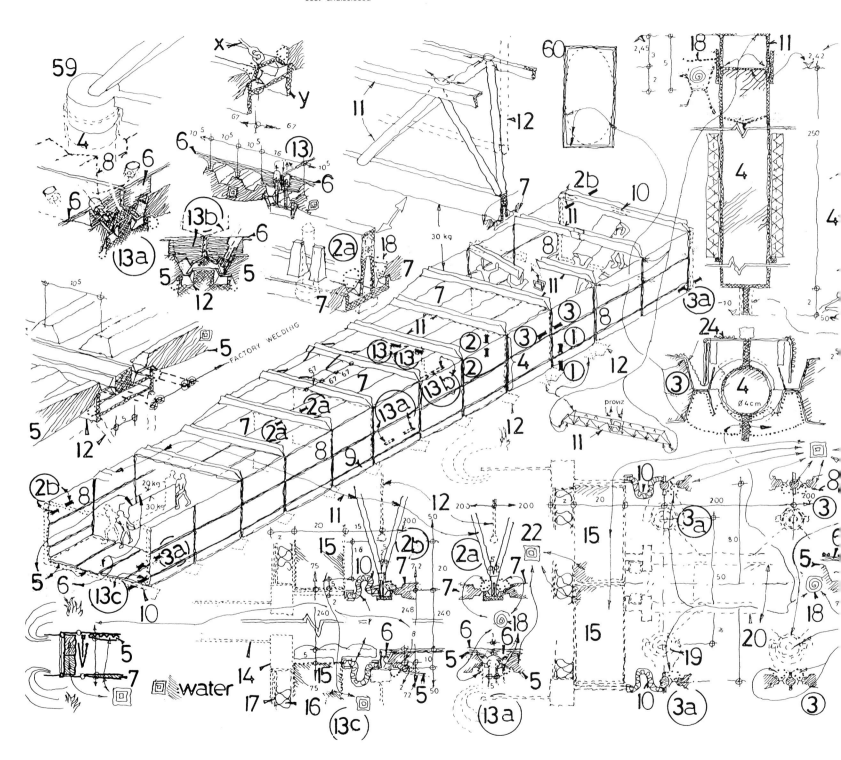

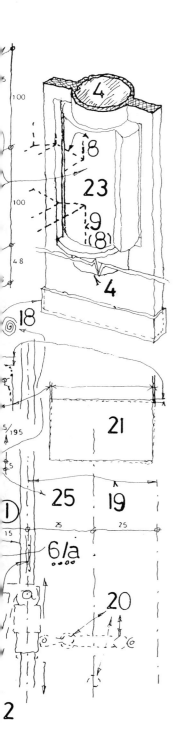

2

Elemer Zalotay's house in Ziegelried is a prototype for larger, as yet unbuilt, social housing projects. In literally hundreds of heavily annotated diagrams produced over the past 20 years, Zalotay has laid out the basis of multi-storey lightweight towers which allow self builders to use standard components to form shelters within engineered superstructures of concrete and steel containing pre-installed services and elevators. Behind this theoretical work is the attempt to balance the need for individual self expression against the reductivist logic of mass production.

This impulse towards individual freedom of expression is embodied in Zalotay's personal history: originally born in Hungary, his application to emigrate permanently to Switzerland was only finally approved in 1973 after he had served several terms of imprisonment as the result of confrontations with the Hungarian authorities. The construction of the house itself, on the edge of a conventional suburb, added to the architect's persecution. The delicate latticework of copper on the glazing is, in part, a series of repairs to panels broken by stones thrown by hostile neighbours. Previously published photographs of the house tend to give the impression that it is a rural retreat surrounded by trees but in fact it sits on a relatively small hillside plot overlooked by large detached houses.

Built on a slope with expansive views of the valley beyond, the house comprises one main living floor with a semi-basement wood store and workroom tucked underneath. Access is achieved via a complex timber bridge reached by walking up the adjoining bank at the side of the house. Underlying its visual complexity is a relatively simple framed structure infilled with glass or composite panels, this system being most clearly visible on the front elevation to the road. On the other three sides of the essentially square plan the external surfaces have been layered with rainscreen secondary glazing and a mosaic of applied reclaimed materials of extraordinary visual delicacy. The small suspended eight square elements which form a recurring motif on the facades are miniature versions of Zalotay's proposals for water-filled lightweight cladding panels intended for larger structures. The most obvious feature of the roof is the deck of profiled metal sheeting arranged in a series of shallow vaults on a planning grid. Stones, set in cement, are arranged on the roof like tiny cairns, creating the effect of a manufactured landscape (reminiscent of the late British filmmaker Derek Jarman's garden made from beach debris at his home in Dungeness, England). A spiral wooden stair allows access to this elevated world through a hole in the roof of the living room.

Although spatially unremarkable, the interior is an exercise in layering, suspension and pattern-making from found and transformed objects. In the most obsessive reworking of ordinary materials into surfaces of jewel-like intricacy, Zalotay has offered up a powerful counter movement to the repetitive tendencies of industrialized processes. The factors which allow this alternative vision to unfold are time and commitment, which explains why his work remains marginalized and problematic to reproduce.

right Zalotay is a trained engineer: under the layered surfaces of the envelope lies a rational structural frame made of standard components.

far right A collage showing an experimental prototype for as yet unbuilt multi-storey living towers in which designed and improvised elements co-exist.

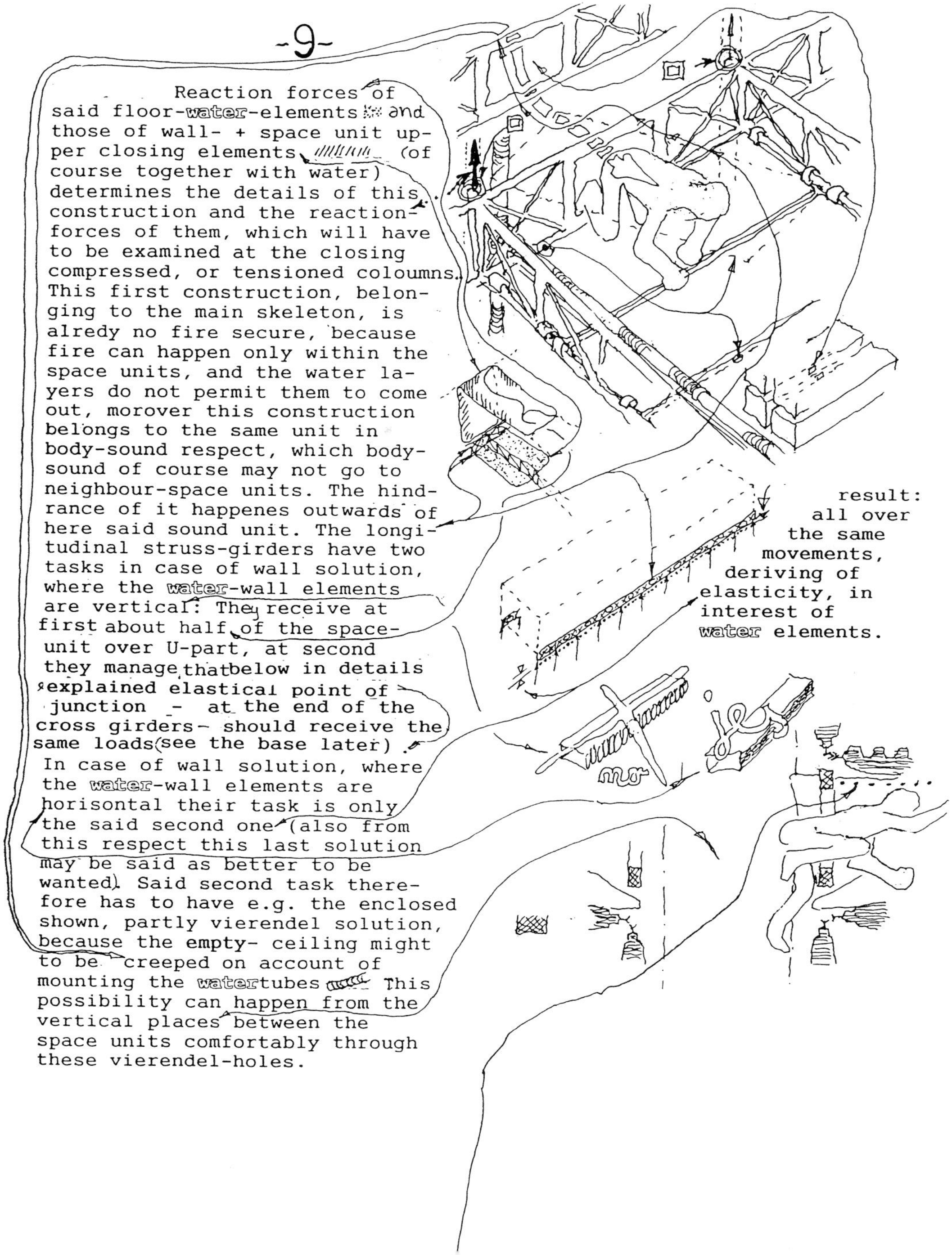

-9-

Reaction forces of said floor-water-elements and those of wall- + space unit upper closing elements ///////// (of course together with water) determines the details of this construction and the reaction-forces of them, which will have to be examined at the closing compressed, or tensioned coloumns. This first construction, belonging to the main skeleton, is alredy no fire secure, because fire can happen only within the space units, and the water layers do not permit them to come out, morover this construction belongs to the same unit in body-sound respect, which body-sound of course may not go to neighbour-space units. The hindrance of it happenes outwards of here said sound unit. The longitudinal struss-girders have two tasks in case of wall solution, where the water-wall elements are vertical: They receive at first about half of the space-unit over U-part, at second they manage thatbelow in details explained elastical point of junction - at the end of the cross girders- should receive the same loads(see the base later). In case of wall solution, where the water-wall elements are horisontal their task is only the said second one (also from this respect this last solution may be said as better to be wanted). Said second task therefore has to have e.g. the enclosed shown, partly vierendel solution, because the empty- ceiling might to be creeped on account of mounting the watertubes This possibility can happen from the vertical places between the space units comfortably through these vierendel-holes.

result:
all over
the same
movements,
deriving of
elasticity, in
interest of
water elements.

project **Round House**

location near Newport, Pembrokeshire
Wales
UK

date commissioned 1995

designer Tony Wrench

construction self-build with community help
area 110m² (1,184sq ft)
cost £2,500

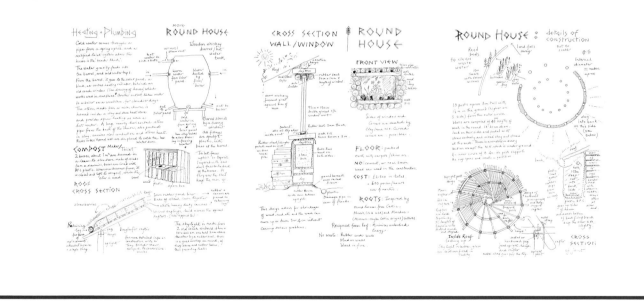

It is for its use of recycled components and available natural materials that this house is included in this chapter in spite of being more appropriately defined as 'ecological'. Tony Wrench's experimental structure confronts many assumptions usually made about both the provision of housing and the minimum essentials for domestic comfort. Still subject to enforcement action, this house does not conform to the local planning or building permit requirements in spite of its sensitive siting and the sophistication of its construction.

The house is situated on the edge of woodland, a short walk down a track from a series of farm buildings which have been occupied by a community of around 20 people since 1995. Wrench, who is a musician and a wood turner, built the house for himself and his partner with the help of friends and community members over a period of four months. The form is inspired by Celtic and indigenous North American culture, the structure comprising 13 timber posts set 1.5 metres (5 feet) into the ground in a circle which forms the outer framework, with an inner ring of 13 longer posts to help support the roof. The outer walls are mainly composed of 400mm- (16 inch-) long lengths of softwood, about 100mm (4 inches) in diameter, laid on their sides and then packed with straw in the voids. A mixture of clay and straw is applied to both inner and outer surfaces. Other sections of wall are infilled with standard sized straw bales faced in clay. All the windows are reclaimed double glazing units from a local glazier and these are cut into rebates in the supporting round wood posts: Wrench used a hand-held chainsaw for this detail, a trick which required considerable skill and ingenuity.

The roof has a geometry similar to a camera shutter with the aperture in the middle being a glazed circular roof light. Douglas fir rafters, again in the round, are covered in a mesh of coppice willow saplings and then overlaid with a canvas tarpaulin on top of which are bales of straw for insulation. The top of the roof, which is turfed and waterproofed with an underlay formed of a pond-liner, is now used for growing strawberries. The floor of the house is made of compacted earth and has no damp-proof membrane, but the central living area has a suspended timber deck to counteract this.

The house is not connected to the municipal water supply. Water is fed from a spring and is heated by a solar panel made from a recycled window and an old central heating radiator. A woodstove made from a milk churn provides space heating as well as additional hot water via a heat exchanger. Hot water is stored in a freestanding wooden whiskey barrel and the stove pipe is embedded in clay and stone to act as a heat sink. All electrical systems are at 12 volts and run off two old batteries which are recharged by a 200-watt photovoltaic panel built into the external wall. A lean-to timber structure houses a twin compartment compost toilet: when one is full it is closed and left to compost while the other is then used. Water from the kitchen and bath is filtered through two small reed beds which are integrated into the landscape.

The spaces within the house are demarcated by the posts and simple, hand-made shelves and storage units. There are no rooms as such but the functions of sleeping, cooking and bathing are kept to the outer perimeter leaving the central top-lit space free for relaxing and working.

far left Located on the edge of a wood and dug into the hill, the Round House appears to have grown out of the earth.

far left bottom Drawings of construction details and a notional plan document the house after it was completed. There were no drawings before actual construction.

below The interior – one large space ordered by the structure – questions many of the assumptions made about the domestic environment.

bottom Detail of a wall made up of logs and clay render.

The dimensions of the place in which I found myself were most unusual. The ceiling seemed extraordinarily high while the floor was so narrow that it would not have been possible for me to pass the policeman ahead if I had desired to do so. We went through another door at the top of the stairs and I found myself in a very surprising apartment. It was slightly wider than the other places and down the middle of it was a table about a foot in width, two yards in length and attached permanently to the floor by two metal legs. Then I saw that there was a small window set deeply in the left wall and that a cold breeze was blowing in through a gaping hole in the lower pane. I walked over and looked out. The lamplight was shining dimly on the foliage of the same tree and I knew that I was standing, not in Mathers' house, *but inside the walls of it*.

Flann O'Brien: *The Third Policeman*

There are essentially three reasons for the creation of infill sites, which by implication occur in urban areas or locations with local high densities of building: the demolition or destruction of a building or structure; the division of existing building land; and the development of plots previously considered unsuitable for buildings.

The impetus behind the present importance of infill sites is economic, and residential projects in this category tend to be in cities or towns with high land values and high densities of habitation. This is not, however, a purely modern phenomenon related to late capitalist market economies. The Greek city-state of the fifth century BC was typically 40 hectares (100 acres) with populations in excess of 5,000. During the Peloponnesian Wars, refugees from endemic plague camped on the Acropolis because Athens was so built-up and overcrowded.

Roman cities were larger, with typical populations of up to 50,000, but were planned within containing fortified walls which over time resulted again in high densities of building within the city. Rome itself, by the time of its enclosure by the Aurelian wall in 271–80 AD, covered some 1,305 hectares (3,224 acres), with a density of over 1,000 persons per hectare (2 acres). Today this number would only be exceeded in the densest parts of the most concentrated cities: Hong Kong, Moscow and Tokyo.[1]

The highest densities of population so far recorded historically in any city were in certain areas of Manhattan's Lower East Side at the end of the nineteenth century, where figures of 1,350 persons per hectare (2 acres) were reached, within the so-called Dumb-bell tenements.[2]

The historian Jules Lubbock has shown how London in particular has been subject to intense pressure since about 1550 to build on land within its own urban fabric and hence increase its density.[3] By the end of the nineteenth century architects such as Norman Shaw, Philip Webb, Charles Voysey and C.R. Ashbee were all designing spatially inventive houses for infill sites within existing terraces. Similar sites in Brussels received houses by Victor Horta and his contemporaries, these being more experimental in organization and construction than the British examples. In Barcelona, Antoni Gaudí applied the principles of organic form to the façade of the Palau Güell (1889), which fronts directly onto a narrow street and occupies a site of 16 by 20 metres (52 by 65 feet), ridiculously small for an entire palace. Early canonic Modern Movement houses were also often built on infill sites in contexts to which they were conceptually unsympathetic. Gerrit Rietveld's Schröder House (1924) in Utrecht forms the end of an earlier terrace of four houses. One of Le Corbusier's early Paris houses, Maison Planeix (1924–8), occupies a gap in a row of older and extremely modest buildings on a busy road. These extreme juxtapositions reach their apotheosis in the Maison de Verre (1933; see p.15), in which Pierre Chareau contrived to insert a house and a clinic both between and under existing buildings.

The economic pressure to infill has today produced the most inventive design solutions where land values are highest, most specifically in Japan. Kazuyo Sejima and Ryue Nishizawa have placed a two-storey house for six people on a site of just over 0.01 hectare (one fifth of an acre) in their Okayama project, a model which if reproduced on mass would create densities of 450 persons per hectare (2 acres), once allowance has been made for roads. The device used to deal with the extreme implications of such compression is a translucent plastic outer skin to veil the the inner world of the house from the outer world of the city. The veil does not imply a denial of the context but a very specific filtering of its influences.

Less physically restricted by its site, but subject to demanding building codes, the house for Toronto-based architectural archivist Robert Hill by Shim-Sutcliffe Architects sits on a small plot of similar size to its neighbours. The house is an exercise in exploring the limits of an indigenous local building form to suit the needs of a client who sought unconventional accommodation.

The response of Brandlhuber & Kniess to a site barely 2.6 metres (8 feet 6 inches) wide and 6 storeys high in a housing and commercial block in Cologne, Germany, is to take the existing party walls as prime generators of the proposal. The almost fully glazed infill panels, to the front and rear elevations, exaggerate the narrow constrictions of the site and reveal it for what it is: a gap between two buildings barely capable of habitation. The attempt to dematerialize the physical substance of the building in fact has the effect of drawing attention to it as an investigation of absences.

One of the rarely questioned parameters for designed housing is the imposed form based on assumptions about property rights. Party walls are invariably owned as physical objects in a precise division 50/50 either side of a notional centreline. This line generates a plane which extends vertically upwards and downwards thereby defining the plan form on all floors. In the Double House at Utrecht, de architectengroep and MVRDV has intentionally broken this organizational convention so that spaces on either side of the line have the possibility of being finger-jointed and overlapped in section at different levels. The normally restrained limits of the residential unit are by this means rendered malleable, fluid and dynamic, and the space within the two adjoining units can be collectively experienced.

Rick Joy's Convent Avenue studios in Tuscon, Arizona, is a cluster of residential units which makes a coherent semi-public space within an existing urban context. The opening up of private space to the city is a deliberate design move which contradicts the general tendency in the twentieth century to privatize public space. The gesture of this scheme is democratic and inclusive, accepting the concept of a hierarchy of external spaces such as road, street, alley, court, etc. – all of which offer different possibilities for social interaction. Seen in different manifestations through a historical continuum, the private house has been increasingly concerned over time with the provision of a private retreat from the public realm, in which the nuclear family is sheltered and nurtured. In this configuration, however, we see the private domain of the individual living unit, while retaining its autonomy, functioning at a more open level within the group, and the group acting as a semi-public social unit within the city.

project **S-house**

location Okayama Prefecture
Japan

date commissioned 1996

architect Kazuyo Sejima and Ryue Nishizawa

construction main contractor
area 142m² (1,528 sq ft)
cost not availible

left The S-house:
gift-wrapped
and surrounded
by conventional
dwellings.

If it still makes sense to discuss the fundamental differences between Eastern and Western philosophy, then it might be possible to say that in the West we have emphasized 'being' over 'non-being' and claimed meaning for what is said rather than what is unsaid. In one of those aphorisms in the *Tao Te Ching* which Western consciousness finds so difficult to comprehend, Lao Tzu says, 'Much speech leads inevitably to silence. Better to hold fast to the void'.[1] The centre of Tokyo is a kind of absence, a residence surrounded by moats and concealed by foliage, protecting an emperor who is rarely seen.

As with gifts in Japan, the S-house comes perfectly wrapped in an envelope that does not reveal anything about the value of what it contains. This outer box of profiled polycarbonate serves to filter the densely developed surroundings and allow the inner world of the house a degree of autonomy – there are, in fact, only two windows with views out in the entire envelope.

The organization of the house echoes Sejima's work with public housing at Gifu (see pp.156–61), in its careful delineation of private and semi-private spaces. The brief was to accommodate a family of six, including two children and two grandparents, on a corner site of barely 10 x 12 metres (33 x 39 feet) with other two-storey residences in very close proximity. Sejima's radical solution to these parameters was to conceive of the house as a box within a box, with the interstices at ground level as the circulation space. The inner box is a perfect square in plan, and contains the three bedrooms, a workroom and the bathroom. Over this is an open-plan living/dining room with a generous 3.1-metre (10-foot) ceiling height. Pivoted timber louvres separate this space from the upper part of the enclosing passage, and can be closed to control both light and temperature. On the ground level, the bedrooms can be isolated with folding timber screens, which when closed allow no natural light into the rooms and give total privacy. The narrow double-height space around the perimeter of the bedroom cluster also gives access to built in storage units: this and the double-entry bathroom suggests that Sejima sees this space as a place of incidental interaction between the three generations of family members.

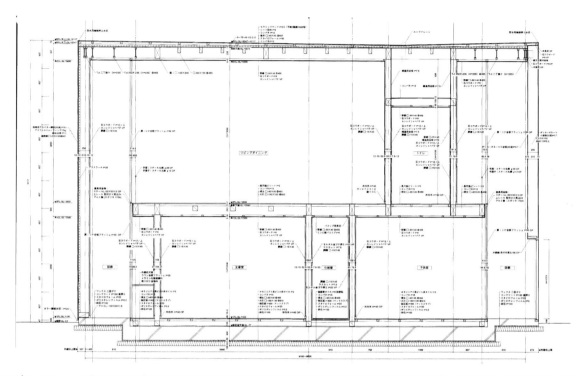

Constructionally, the house can be seen as deliberately insubstantial: 200mm- (7³/₄ inch-) deep timber posts support both an inner and outer layer of polycarbonate sheeting on the external envelope. Only on the party wall to the east is this substituted for profiled fibre cement sheet to achieve the necessary fire separation. There is no insulation as such in the walls and the roof has merely a 35-mm (1¹/₃-inch) thermal quilt to nominally reduce heat losses. Ventilation is achieved through low-level opening sashes in the outer envelope and there is also an access door to the small court to the south. The main structural elements are entirely of timber, with veneered plywood or plasterboard coated in vinyl resin as the main finishes.

On ascending the stair to the first floor, one arrives at the geometric centre of the plan in the living room – the supporting column here is offset to avoid obstructing the landing. The enclosing envelope follows the site boundary on the main entry side, thereby distorting the implied square geometry. There is not one single ordering system in this house that takes primacy over any other – rather one is constantly confronted with that which exists between things as the source of any possible meaning.

left The double-height circulation zone between the outer envelope and the inner 'box' of rooms on the ground floor.

top The construction section reveals the insubstantial nature of the envelope.

above The upper floor with timber louvres open (left) and closed (right).

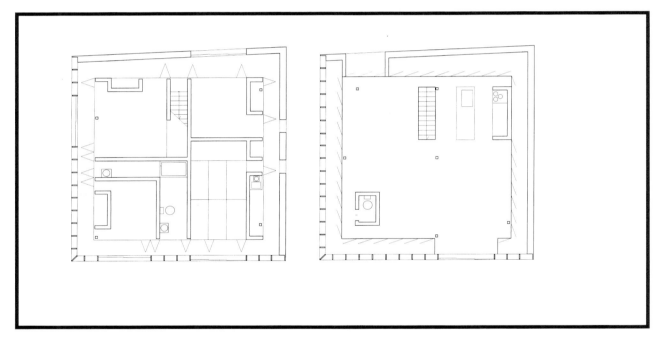

left Left to right:
ground-floor and
top-floor plans.

right The house almost
entirely occupies the
available site (shown in
the centre of this area
site plan). Lao Tzu says,
'better to hold fast to
the void.'

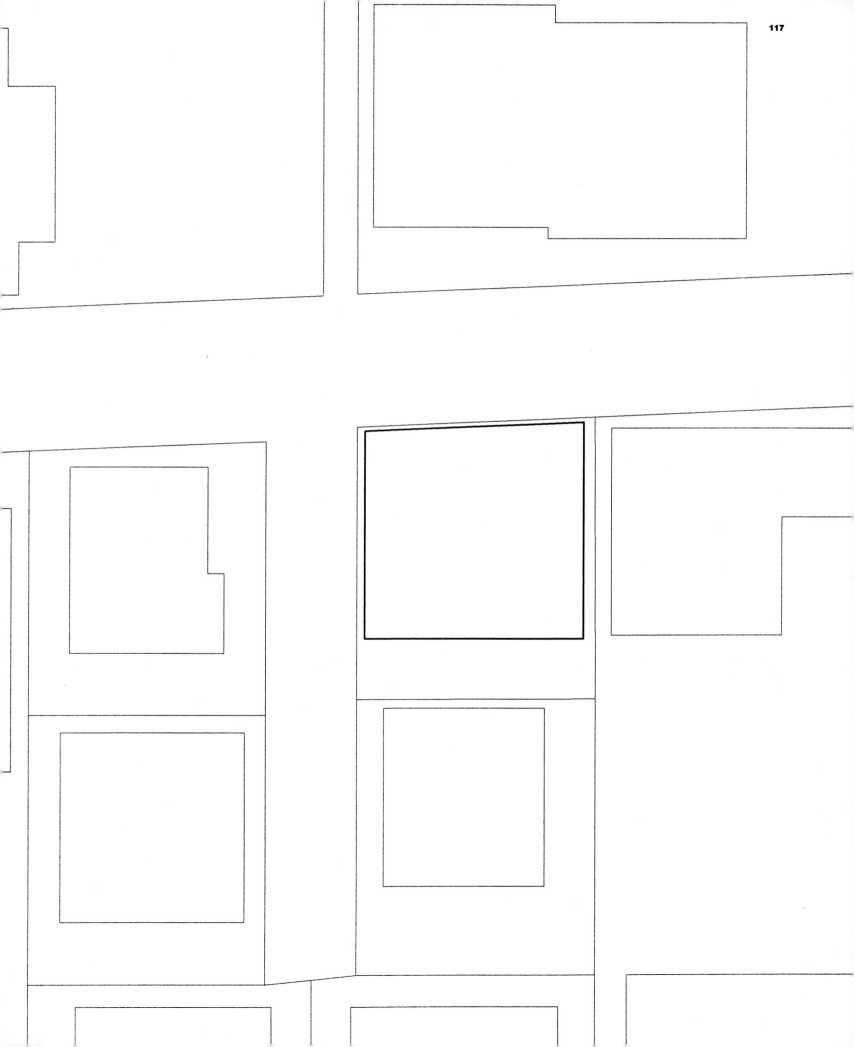

project **Craven Road house**

location Toronto
Canada
date commissioned 1995
architect Shim-Sutcliffe Architects

construction main contractor
area 102m² (1,098 sq ft)
cost CAN $65,000

below Section looking towards
the street façade.

right The street front
of the house
with the entrance
to the right.

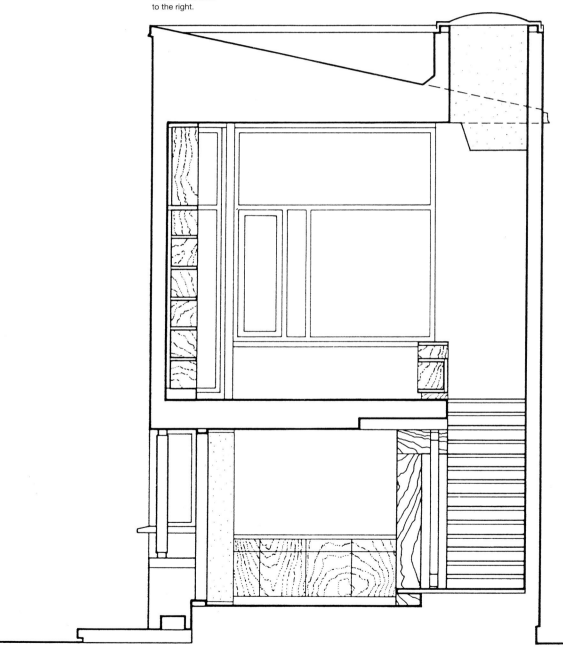

'I must show that the house is one of the greatest powers of integration for the thoughts, memories, and dreams, of mankind', wrote Gaston Bachelard in the *Poetics of Space* (1958).[1] In order to perform this task, for Bachelard at least, the house must possess the vertical polarity of cellar and attic, with the ground of everyday existence in between. In the cellar (the unconscious) we can confront our irrational fears, while in the attic (ego) we are in the space of the intellect and rationality. This tripartite division is essential for the organization of the oneiric house: the house of dream memory in which our thoughts can be concentrated. The two essential characteristics of verticality and compactness are both present in the Craven Road house.

The project was commissioned by architectural archivist and researcher Robert Hill and has been designed not only to provide living accommodation but to house his extensive library of architectural books. Outside of his daytime professional commitments, Hill is compiling a biographical index of late Canadian architects and their work, a task which entails a great deal of time working at home. The aim of the design solution, therefore, was to condense these diverse functions into an efficient and economic envelope which nevertheless contained internally an expansive range of spatial experiences. Unlike the character Peter Kien who, in Elias Canetti's novel *Auto da Fé* (1978), becomes physically incarcerated by his book collection,[2] Hill has the entire first floor of this diminutive house as a library and office which have both light and views in the manner of the traditional *piano nobile*. This floor has 3.6 metre- (12 foot-) high ceilings and made-to-order bookshelves in maple-veneered medium-density fibreboard on two enclosing walls in the library. It is painted entirely in white and has an open access stair which, being top-lit, also acts as a gallery. The low balustrade unit which divides it from the room is both a layout space and a double-sided storage unit for larger volumes. The office is designed to double-up as a guest bedroom and has its own en-suite shower room.

The ground floor, by contrast, is deliberately intimate with low ceilings and strong colours in terra cotta, red and mauve. These spaces, accessed directly from the entry porch, are for cooking, dining and entertaining, and must be traversed to proceed to the library above. The ground floor bedroom is one step up from the bottom stair landing, and looks east into the small rear garden. Under the kitchen area is a cellar. The architects describe the typological references as the cottage and the loft, both common throughout the city of Toronto. The exterior cladding, in both horizontal boarding and large ply panels, reflects this duality of scale and hence type.

The site itself is 7.5 metres (25 feet) wide and 27 metres (89 feet) deep – one of a row created by the progressive selling off of the rear portions of the gardens of larger adjoining houses to the east. The house is consequently set 0.5 metres (18 inches) from the boundary to the north, which is the minimum permitted under the city by-laws. Built in timber stud frame, it was one of the first houses in the city to be built under revised fire regulations which hitherto had required external walls in such locations to be stone or brick. In using an upgraded version of this construction, Brigitte Shim and Howard Sutcliffe have reconnected – in an entirely new way and in a dense urban context – with the shingle style tradition of the North American North-East.

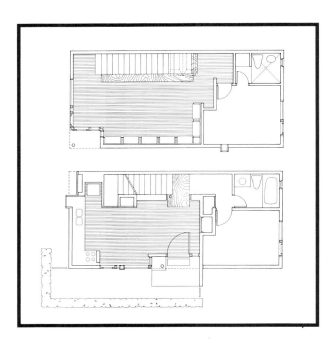

above From bottom: ground- and first-floor plans.

right The top-floor library looking towards the street. The balustrade acts as storage for larger volumes and a layout space.

far right Site plan showing the infill sites at the ends of the gardens of larger houses.

following pages The timber cladding operates at both large and small scale according to where it is on the elevation.

project **housing and commercial block**

location Cologne
Germany
date commissioned 1997
architect Brandlhuber & Kniess

construction main contractor with specialist sub-contractors
area units at 30m² (323 sq ft), 1 unit at 40m² (430 sq ft), commercial unit 120m² (1,292 sq ft)
cost DM 780,000

above At the rear of the building there is a slender steel access stair to the apartments.

top right A section of the building: the basement, ground and first floors are commercial spaces.

bottom right From bottom: plans of the ground floor, first floor, and fourth floor (the top three floors are a similar layout).

far right The 2.56 metre- (8 foot 5 inch-) wide flush glazed façade has timber doors and timber opening casement windows.

The main factors governing the development of this site were its dimensions of 2.56 metres (8 feet) in width and 32 metres (105 feet) in depth, and the 5-storey buildings adjoining it on either side. The narrow site fronts onto a street with commercial developments at ground floor level and to the rear there is a connection to a small courtyard. With such restrictions, all the design decisions, from the system of circulation to the specifics of the details, are directed towards overcoming the compressive presence of the two opposing party walls and transforming the redundant slot into habitable space.

The modernist fascination with the possibilities of narrow and deep housing units can be seen in such diverse examples as Le Corbusier's Unité Blocks in France in the 1950s and Atelier 5's housing at Berne, Switzerland, from 1961. Although representing completely different housing typologies, both these schemes make a strong connection between inside and outside space through the open ends of the unit, which are highly articulated glazed screens. The radical extension of this idea is that the party walls are ultimately so close together that the limits of the system are unavoidably confronted.

Brandlhuber & Kniess's solution to the problem of vertical circulation was to locate it, where possible, outside the building envelope. A straight flight stair, accessible from the street only via a secure door, passes right through the building and emerges onto a rear, first-floor open deck. From here a slender, steel external stair rises to the three living units above, taking advantage of the different depth of the adjoining blocks to help define its location. The ground-floor commercial unit occupies the entire depth of the site and has a small mezzanine which can be entered from the first floor. In order to save space, the 180mm- (7 inch-) deep concrete floor slabs are cut like shelves into the existing party walls. The main façade comprises fixed double-glazed units bolted at each corner back to a minimal steel frame, with opening timber casements for ventilation, and secondary means of escape to satisfy the local fire regulations. Setting this surface flush with the adjoining façades involved the rebating of the existing walls and the incorporation of a complex composite steel fire break glazing support into the set back edges of the new floor slabs.

Entry to the apartments is directly off the stair through solid larch doors, again detailed as flat planes of material. The space within each unit is divided in two by the service core. Sandblasted glass separates the shower cubicle from the toilet, and the core itself from the kitchen area, hence allowing light to filter into these otherwise windowless rooms. A single lighting track, set within the ceiling, runs front to back and aligns with the plane of the core. In the top unit there is a mezzanine which gives access to a timber roof deck via a horizontally sliding sheet of glass which also acts as a skylight.

In all the detailing, planes of different materials are clearly conceived to be experienced as if suspended in space by virtue of their clearly defined edges. The building itself is a space between two ordinary buildings in an unexceptional area, and hence the articulation of the joints between different materials at all scales has become the motif of the entire project; a meditation on the attraction of absence.

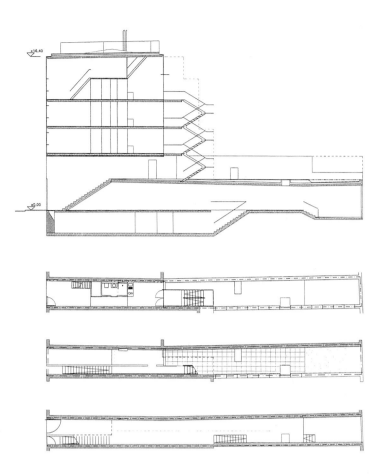

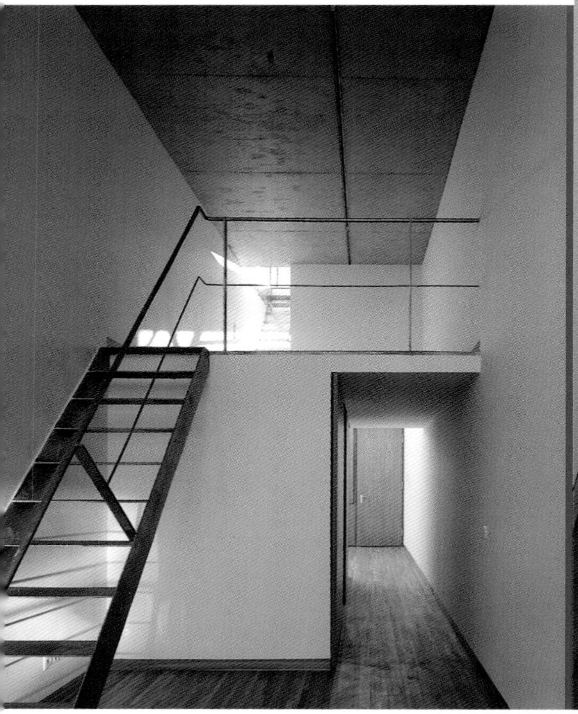

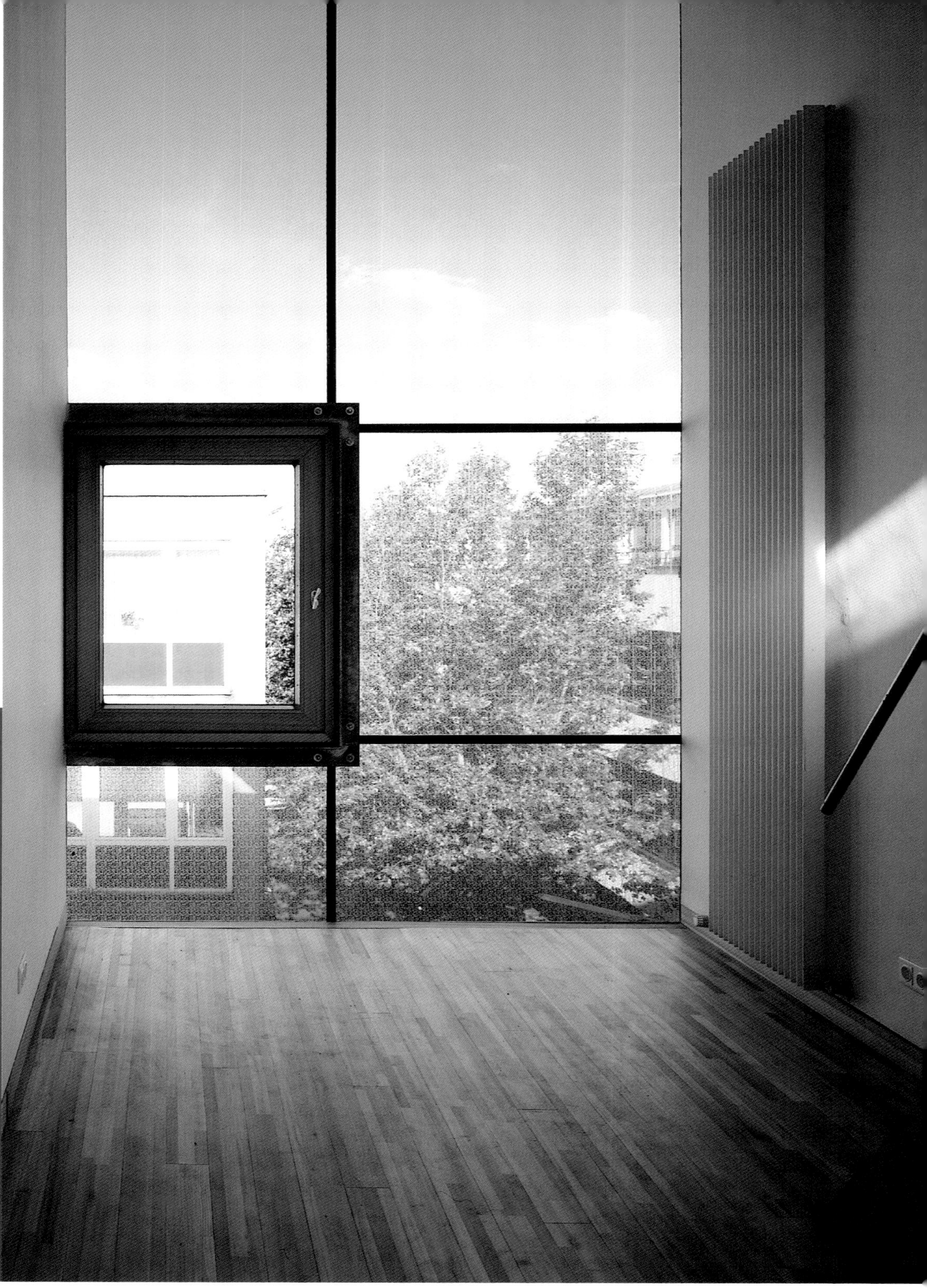

far left The fourth-floor apartment has a mezzanine with access to the roof deck.

left A typical living room.

below Shower rooms have sandblasted glass partitions (the kitchenette is not fitted in this picture).

left The timber roof deck provides an outdoor space for a range of urban lifestyles.

above The staircase leading to the roof with its sliding glazed skylight.

project **Double House (Villa KBWW)**

location Utrecht
The Netherlands
date commissioned 1997

architect **de architectengroep (Bjarne Mastenbroek with Floor Arons and Michiel Raaphorst)**

construction main contractor
total area 315m² (3390 sq ft)
cost undisclosed

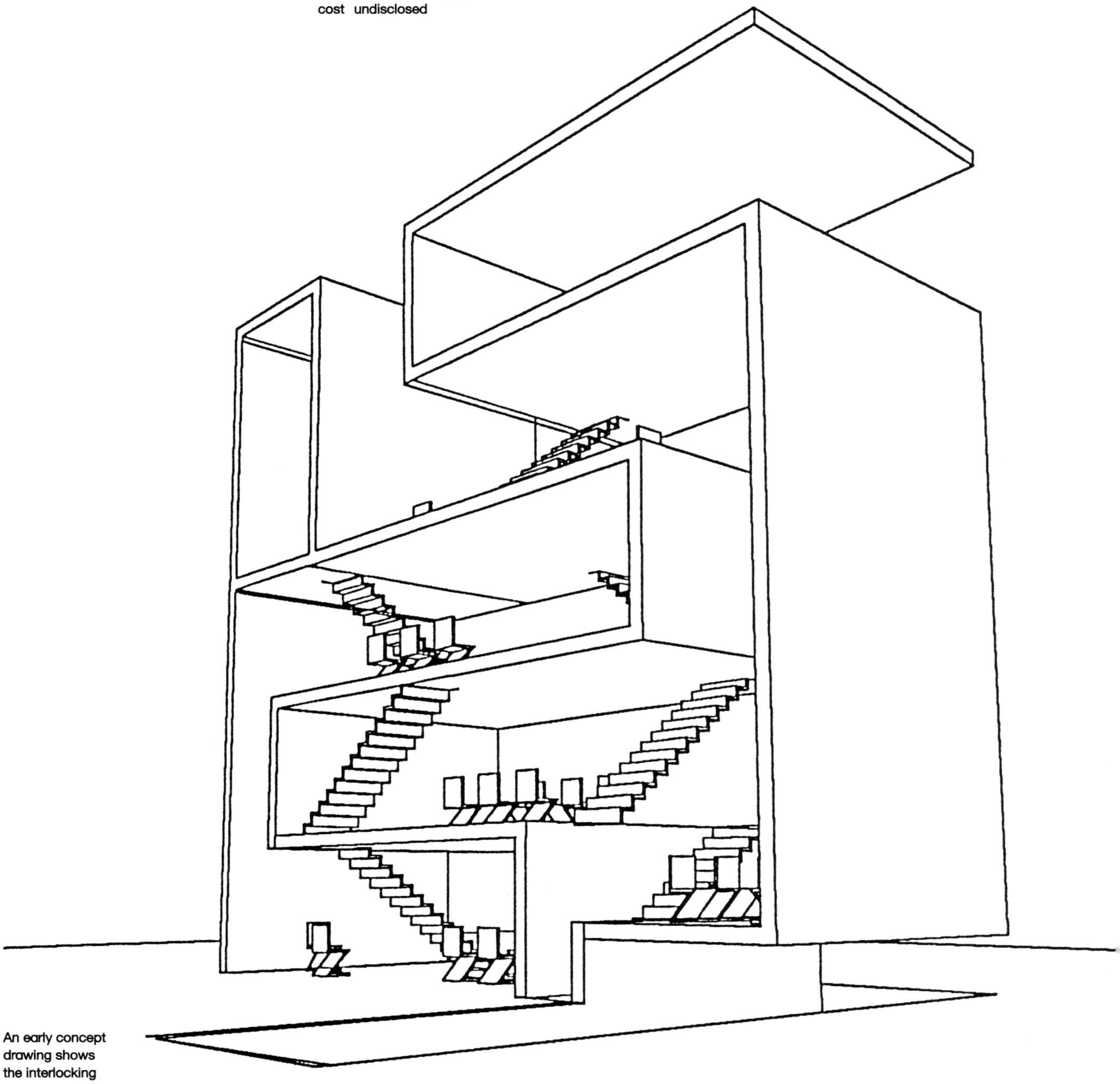

right An early concept
drawing shows
the interlocking
arrangement of
the two houses.

and MVRDV (Winy Maas, Jacob van Rijs and Nathalie de Vries with Mike Booth and Joost Glissenaar)

The spatial dynamic possibilities within the section of adjoining dwellings have been the subject of a continuous series of rather isolated experiments during the twentieth century. The so-called '3:2 section' was used in Russia immediately after the Revolution of 1917 and further developed in schemes by Hans Scharoun and the Ginsburg Group. Wells Coates used a similar section in his project for the Palace Gate Flats in central London in 1939. The post-war Unité blocks by Le Corbusier overlapped paired units in the cross section to allow two apartments to occupy three floors within a repetitive party wall system. A similar concept applied to an extremely shallow block was used by Ralph Erskine on his Byker Wall project in Newcastle, England, in the mid-1970s but in this scheme the overlap works laterally and there are no double-height spaces.

Although the Utrecht Double House is a villa typologically, it represents in many ways one of the most extreme forms of sectional interlocking between adjoining residences yet attempted. That such examples in private sector housing are rare is largely the result of the general mistrust within property law of ill defined edges to ownership and liability for maintenance. In this instance however, two families contrived to commission a single building in which their independence was maintained but the liberating nature of their combined needs would be built into the transverse section – a physical embodiment of both difference and tolerance.

The shallow suburban infill site required the depth of the building to be kept to a minimum in order to keep the garden as large as possible. This has resulted in a five-storey structure measuring a mere 7.5 metres (25 feet) from front to back. The street and garden façades, facing north and south respectively, are predominantly glazed to give both sunlight and extensive views of an adjoining nineteenth-century park. The complexity of the internal arrangement can be read on these façades by following the patterning of the infill panels set raised just above the glazing.

In terms of built floor area, one unit is approximately two-thirds of the size of the other, but they have similarly sized living spaces and equal access to the garden. The one consistent organizing principle in both units is that each has a stacked sequence of straight flight stairs linking all levels – otherwise the disposition of service elements and load-bearing internal walls defy modernist zoning practices. To overcome the structural implications of party wall offsets, the building has a steel frame whose bracing elements appear in the corners of the living spaces. In one of its more charming quirks, the soil stack in the larger unit runs horizontally in raised floors between vertical floor to floor drops inside partitions. The emphasis in this unit is on horizontality, its top floor being a master bedroom and workroom with potential access to a future roof garden. The smaller unit is more tower-like with the ground-floor kitchen and the third-floor living room being linked by a narrow two-and-one-half-storey height volume. Here, the top of the five floors is a shower room with its own terrace, perched at the apex of the less than 2 metre- (6 foot 6 inch-) wide chasm that contains the staircase.

In the developmental diagrams of the transverse section of the Double House, it is clear that the intention is that neither unit has dominance over the other, but rather that they should exist in a state of dynamic tension, reaffirming the primacy of the specific over the general and the necessity to balance rationality with intuition.

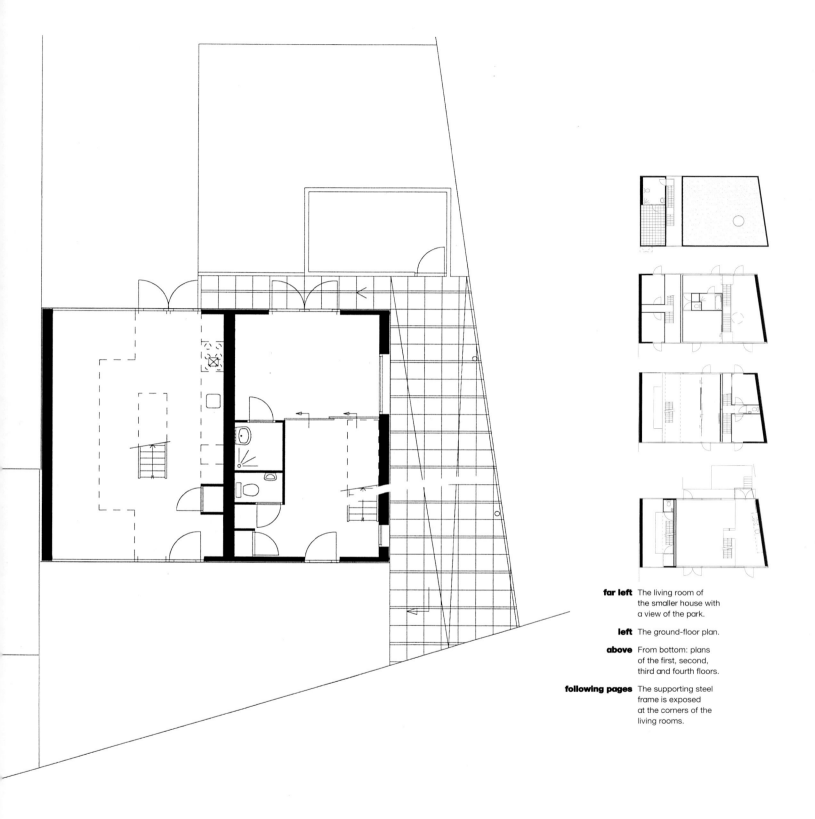

far left The living room of
the smaller house with
a view of the park.

left The ground-floor plan.

above From bottom: plans
of the first, second,
third and fourth floors.

following pages The supporting steel
frame is exposed
at the corners of the
living rooms.

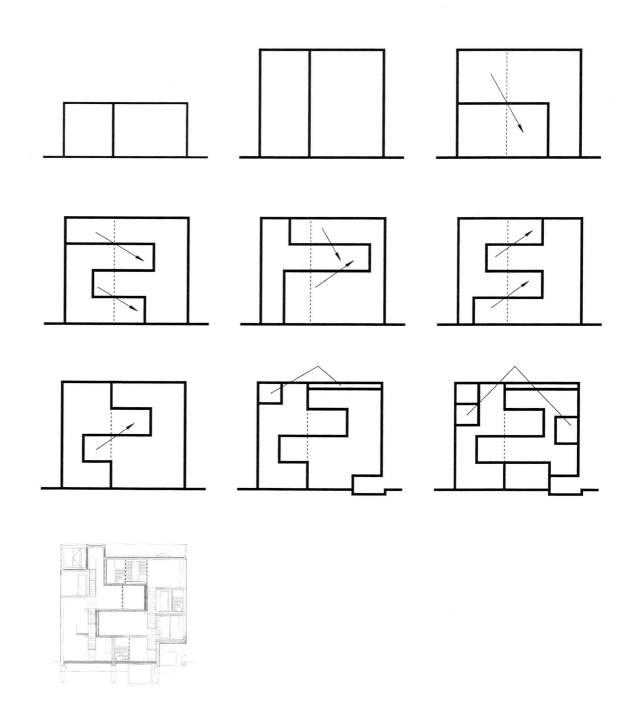

left Diagrams showing the evolution of the division of the two houses, starting with a conventional party wall and ending with a much more complex arrangement.

left bottom A lateral section of the completed house.

above The street view reveals the sectional organization and the shallow depth of the building.

right When seen from the garden elevation the boundaries of the two units are ambiguous.

project **Convent Avenue studios**

location Tucson
Arizona
USA
date commissioned 1995
architect **Rick Joy**

construction construction management with specialist sub-contractors
area 90m² (969 sq ft) each unit
approximate cost $90,000 per unit

Rick Joy acts as both architect and contractor on his projects, an arrangement that enables him, as with Rudolf Schindler earlier in California, to exercise very tight control over the construction process. Architectural students and recent graduates often work on his sites, which makes it more possible to produce experimental structures of a build quality far in excess of that normally achieved within standard budgets. Joy trained as a carpenter and during his later architectural studies in Arizona became interested in the houses and palaces of the Mesa Verde in New Mexico – buildings which Vincent Scully has referred to as a 'complex, highly evolved, and abstracted urbanism all slipped back into the earth as in some mad, modern science fiction dream'.[1]

Rammed earth is a building technology that uses no material or support other than itself. It is identical externally and internally, being one material with no layers – it thereby achieves an effect that modernists have often (and not always successfully) tried to achieve. Historically, its application is extremely diverse – about one fifth of the great Wall of China is rammed earth; the Romans used it; and as well as being common in South and Central America, it was introduced by Moors in Europe around 1000 AD. Building with rammed earth belongs to the vernacular tradition of the Tucson region and Joy has seen the potential for its present day application: allowing a large part of a building to be constructed simply with unskilled labour, and contrasting this with targeted areas for highly crafted elements.

In the Convent Avenue studios, the earth was cast monolithically into 450-mm (17¹/₂-inch) slip forms in 250-mm (9³/₄-inch) lifts. On each lift, the carefully combined soils from three different local sources were mixed with 3 per cent portland cement and then compacted to 50 per cent of their original volume before being exposed prior to the next lift taking place. The walls were pigmented red and set on cast concrete strip foundations. Joy has calculated that each house weighs around 180,000 kilogrammes (396,000 pounds).

The location of the infill site for this project is the Barrio Historico, just to the south of downtown Tucson. The long and narrow plot was left vacant for over 40 years, during which period all but one of the 7 original mud adobe houses on the site literally dissolved (mud technology is not the same as rammed earth and the walls are far more porous). The remaining house on the south-west corner was restored, and three new studio houses built in a settlement pattern that has created private courtyards and large north- and south-facing windows for each house.

The form of each house is abstracted from the common typology of the area and is a simple envelope for a large living space with a sleeping gallery over one end accessed by a slender steel stair. The monopitch roofs are structured in rough-sawn Douglas fir, while the kitchen cabinets and gallery balustrade storage units are in very precisely finished red birch veneer. Externally, this polarity of the elemental and the refined is taken into the landscaping with fences in weathered steel and the groundscape detailed in decomposed granite and rubble stone.

top right A sectional elevation of two studio houses with a courtyard in between them.

right A detail of the junction of two houses and the rammed earth construction of the walls.

far right The houses have elemental forms based on local vernacular building typologies.

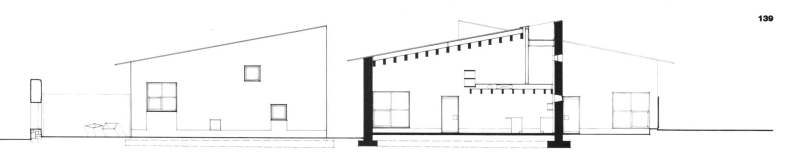

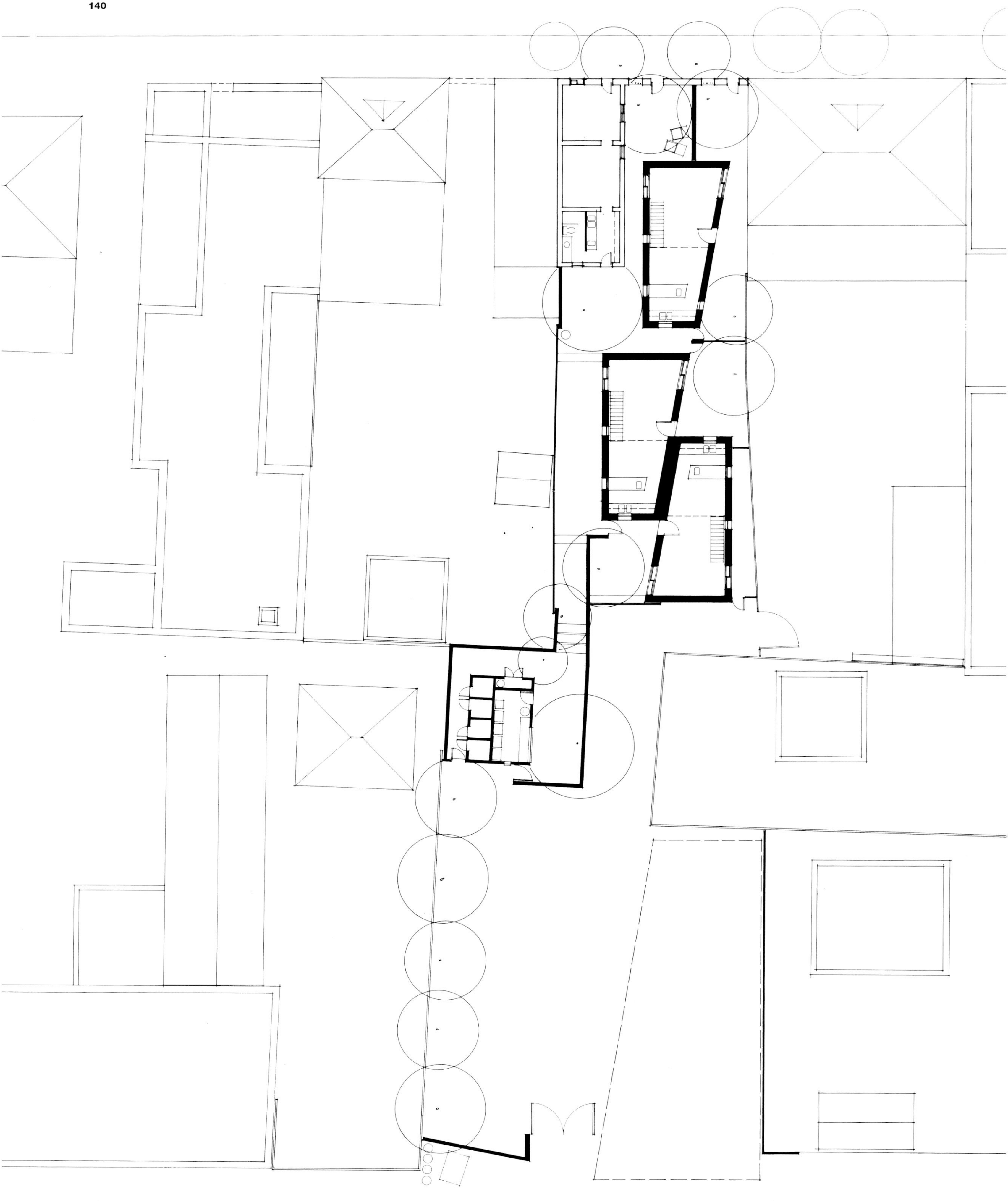

left The site plan shows how the arrangement of houses creates a series of courts and retains existing trees.

above On the sleeping platform refined joinery contrasts with the raw quality of the earth walls.

right Kitchens are tucked under the sleeping platforms.

left The main living space with its minimal steel stair.

above The eastern end of the site with the houses in the background.

J.G. Ballard: *High Rise*

The two thousand tenants formed a virtually homogeneous collection of well-to-do professional people – lawyers, doctors, tax consultants, senior academics and advertising executives, along with a smaller group of airline pilots, film-industry technicians and trios of air-hostesses sharing apartments. In short, they provided the perfect background into which Laing could merge invisibly. The high-rise was a huge machine designed to serve, not the collective body of tenants, but the individual resident in isolation. Its staff of air-conditioning conduits, elevators, garbage-disposal chutes and electrical switching systems provided a never-failing supply of care and attention that a century earlier would have needed an army of tireless servants.

Ballard's dystopian description of the eventual breakdown of social cohesion within a living complex is an ironic warning about the dangers of high density designer environments which ignore what he pointedly identifies as the collective body. The examples in this chapter, in some way or another, all address this issue: they are far more than the accretion of a number of closely packed individual living units.

A brief review of settlement patterns over the past three thousand years, regardless of geographical location or cultural context, shows that close proximity in clusters is the normal condition for living – we are essentially social beings. As a crude approximation, the greater the economic dependency, the greater the density of occupation. Isolation in comfort has only ever been achieved with the support of status and wealth.

In 1700, less than 10 per cent of the world's population lived in cities or towns but instead were in hamlets and villages of only several hundred persons. Only five cities in the world had populations of over 500,000.[1] Now, 300 years later, 50 percent of the world's population live in cities and the same percentage live on just 5 per cent of the earth's available land area. Over 400 cities have populations of over 1 million and they alone house 900 million people or 15 per cent of the world's total population. In Western industrialized nations city dwellers account for between 75 and 80 per cent of the population, but those regions with the lowest urban populations, like China, Central Africa, India and south-east Asia, are precisely those with the fastest urban growth.[2]

The questions of housing form, settlement pattern and sustainable urban environments are the critical ones for the twenty-first century. Experimental cluster houses offer the possibility of developing and testing models which might provide future workable typologies able to promote stronger social cohesion rather than fragmentation and isolation.

Szyszkowitz and Kowalski, in their Emscher Park housing project for a formerly polluted post-industrial site in Germany, use conventional unit types for reasons of economy but employ the device of numerous unit variations within a repetitive party wall rhythm. Here, spatial complexity is external with adjoining units of different height and block depth, and highly articulated semi-enclosed areas for balconies, porches and external access stairs. As with their earlier work in Austria, this approach is clearly intended to produce a series of incidental spaces at the interfaces of the public and private realms where community life can flourish unplanned.

The Hjulby Hegn project in Denmark, designed by Arkitektgruppen Aarhus, is a reversal of this arrangement to achieve the same ends. The units themselves are again unremarkable but are linked by an internal glazed street which provides a linear room as a shared extension to the individual living spaces. Like the Emscher Park project, the spatial and visual complexity comes from the close proximity of different kinds of units, in this case designed for different age groups and family structures. Denmark's progressive social attitudes are reflected in the unit plans, which although apparently conventional, do not imply conventional family occupation, rather that units might be used in combinations to suit extended groups of co-habitants.

The apartments at Ramat-Gan designed by Israeli architect Zvi Hecker gain their visual and spatial complexity through collage and geometry. This work has echoes of Islamic terraces and courts and is a reminder that geometry is a fundamental principle of all architecture and has a social dimension. The central circular space, into which all of the apartments look and which contains the primary circulation spaces, is a formal and richly decorated vessel for representing latent social possibilities.

Kazuyo Sejima at Gifu has applied to mass housing the ideas from her previous work on individual houses and produced, in terms of unit organization, probably the most experimental cluster housing project seen since the work of the Russian Constructivists. As can be discerned from close examination of the plans and section, the organization of the rooms, the circulation systems, and the placement of service elements has the effect of deconstructing the tyranny of the single family unit and replacing it with spaces which can be used individually or in series in a complex variety of permutations. In contrast to other projects in this chapter, the housing scheme at Gifu stresses the primacy of the individual over any collective social form. However, it would be a mistake to assume that the collective body is ignored – rather that Sejima refuses to articulate this function in a formal architectural space and prefers to see social interaction as arising spontaneously from the latent possibilities within the apartment building's organization.

With the work of the poets, artists and architects at the Open City, Valparaiso, Chile, the social form of organization becomes the prime generator of the built form. In this radical laboratory for environmental design, the role of the individual artist is redefined as an essential ingredient of a collective creative process, rather than an end in itself. The resultant buildings provide an important model for demonstrating the possibility that houses can, under very special circumstances, approach the phenomenon of a *gesamtkuntswerk* (total work of art).

project **Emscher Park housing**

location Gelsenkirchen
Germany
date commissioned 1997
architect **Szyszkowitz & Kowalski**

construction six main contractors responsible for different blocks
total area 12,700m² (136,700 sq ft)
cost DM 32 million

The idea that architecture would create new social forms, as put forward by Bruno Taut at the beginning of the twentieth century for example, was one in which an artistically conceived environment would form just one part of a progressive social policy based on democratic principles. The reality of much of the social housing that followed was that the architecture was seen as the sole carrier of the forces of change: the economic and social forms of organization remained unaltered. Rigid zoning policies disassembled the complex sets of interrelationships that had previously existed in cities, creating the planning equivalent of monoculture in farming.

Karla Kowalski and Michael Szyszkowitz had already demonstrated their experimental approach to the provision of social housing, when given an enlightened brief, in their work in Graz from the mid-1980s onwards. The common characteristic of these earlier projects is the provision of a number of unit types within a relatively simple system of regularly spaced party walls. This variety is expressed externally with standard constructional components being used to produce highly articulated surfaces and forms.

The recent conservative political climate in Graz has made it difficult for architects who built projects as part of the Model Steiermark housing scheme to continue to work there, but the large commission for the project at Emscher Park in the Ruhr came from a competition-winning entry from 1990. The brief was for 250 dwellings on a polluted industrial site between a residential area and an old railway yard: the ground was so contaminated with toxins and heavy metals that the soil had to be removed and replaced to a depth of up to 6 metres (20 feet). The competitors were encouraged to adopt an environmental strategy, and the competition requirements called for not only the inclusion of various social spaces but dwellings for both disabled and elderly people. In addition, although the majority of the units now built are for residential rental, some 42 are privately owned houses, and 720 square metres (7,750 square feet) of floor space has been allocated for business and retail use.

below left Perspective of a typical cranked block.

below Aerial view of the entire site, which is flanked by a residential area and a railway goods yard.

A representative part of the scheme, at the north end of the site near the specially built kindergarten, is a cranked two-storey block with one- and two-storey vertical projections, which in combination with external access stairs allows for a range of homes with from one to three bedrooms as either houses, apartments or multi-level units. Although the planning is conventionally three zones deep, with the service cores in the centre, the entrance side of the block varies in depth to produce a series of entrance courts and balconies.

The scale of the overall scheme is visually reduced by having three distinct landscaped areas around which the buildings are organized. These are linked by paths and by a new watercourse that is fed by rainwater from the buildings via high level aqueducts. Three earth mounds against the line of the railway tracks form part of a new linear park which contrasts with the urban emphasis given to the new buildings against the existing street on the opposite side of the site.

left A complex formal language is achieved using inventive changes of scale.

centre left Community facilities, such as the kindergarten, are an integral part of the scheme.

bottom left This typical landscaped area has a water course and high-level aquaducts carrying collected rainwater.

right Plans of a typical cranked block. From bottom: ground, first, second and third floors.

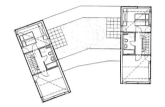

project **co-operative housing**

location Hjulby Hegn
Spørring
Denmark

date commissioned 1990

architect Arkitektgruppen Aarhus

construction main contractor
total area 2,336m² (25,144 sq ft)
cost undisclosed

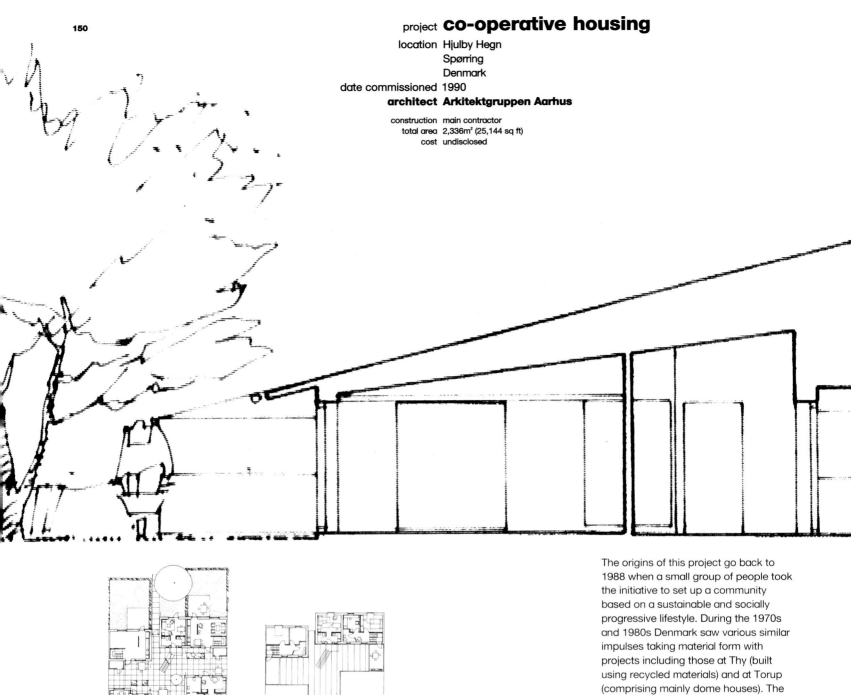

The origins of this project go back to 1988 when a small group of people took the initiative to set up a community based on a sustainable and socially progressive lifestyle. During the 1970s and 1980s Denmark saw various similar impulses taking material form with projects including those at Thy (built using recycled materials) and at Torup (comprising mainly dome houses). The project suffered initially from lack of realistic private funding and so a cooperative housing association was approached to provide a credible financial basis for the work. In Denmark, since the founding of the Federation of Non-profit Housing Societies in 1919, affiliated housing associations have provided an increasingly significant proportion of the country's public housing, to the extent that by the 1950s they accounted for 40 to 50 per cent of the new housing stock in all towns and cities.

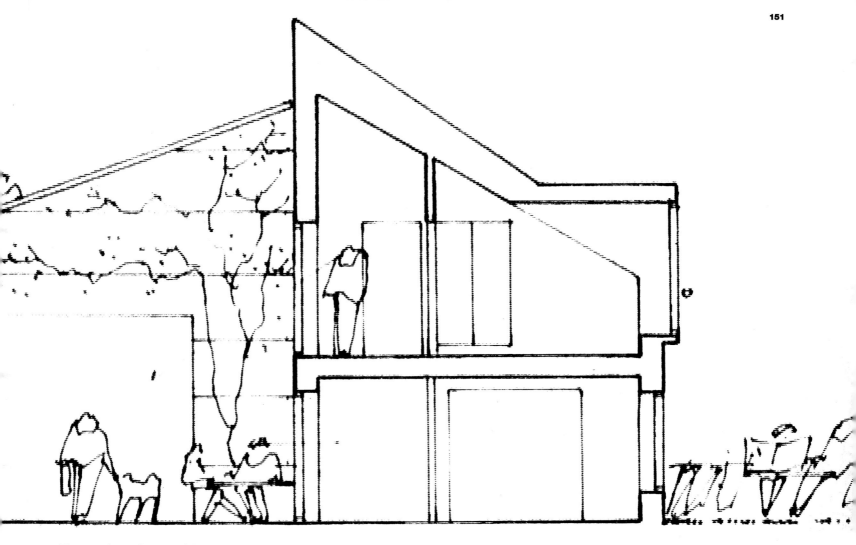

The experimental nature of the project comes from the overt attempt to embody utopian ideas in built form and in the dynamic process of setting the visionary against what is practically achievable in a particular set of circumstances. As originally envisaged, the scheme was to have been larger, with ecology and sustainability the main design considerations in terms of the construction technology employed. The complex of buildings was to be linked to agricultural production and to form an essentially autonomous village.

Because of the restrictions imposed by the funding arrangements, some of these features have not yet been realized – for example the heat reclamation system and the solar collectors. However, the design incorporates passive solar heating and rainwater collection systems, and the additional energy saving elements can be fitted at a later stage. Less easy to address subsequently are the economically driven design decisions which affect embodied energy and issues of toxicity.

The most obvious legacy of the project's original intentions is the settlement pattern and the organization of the individual units. At present there are 32 homes – 6 for the elderly, 6 for young people, and 20 for families – arranged in one- or two-storey terraces linearly linked by a fully glazed internal street. The section is the principal organizing feature and is designed to both maximize solar gain within the street to supplement unit heating, and to allow for a complex series of community spaces in a weather-protected environment. The locations of the different sorts of units are intended to encourage interaction between different age groups. Although the two-storey houses are on the north side of the terraces, they all have open south-facing roof terraces on bridges over the glazed street.

The planned expansion of the project is unlikely in the immediate future, but the development plan shows in total three such terraces arranged around a central garden, indicating that although the semi-rural location suggests otherwise, Hjulby Hegn provides a model for medium-density low-rise urban living.

far left The internal street provides social gathering spaces to supplement private accommodation.

bottom left The building form makes maximum use of solar gain to reduce energy demands.

top left From left: plans of the ground floor and first floor

above A cross section showing the glazed internal 'street', over which the two-storey units have south-facing terraces on bridges.

project **Spiral apartment building**

location Ramat-Gan
near Tel Aviv
Israel
date commissioned 1990
architect **Zvi Hecker with Gil Bernstein, Shmuel Groberman and Rina Hering**

construction main contractor
total area 1,115m² (12,000 sq ft)
cost $US 1.2 million

left A conceptual drawing of the organizing principles of the apartment block.

top The geometrical generation of the plan.

above Inspired by Giovanni Battista Piranesi (top) Hecker's own sketch (bottom) explores the intended spatial dynamic.

Having spent his childhood in Poland, and the years of the Second World War in Siberia and Samarkand, Zvi Hecker settled in Israel in 1950 at the age of 19, where he completed his training at the school of architecture in Haifa. While studying there he was taught by Alfred Neumann, both men discovering a shared interest in geometry. From 1959 to 1964 the practice of Hecker, Neumann and Sharon produced buildings based on triangular and polyhedric forms and patterns, such as the Bat Yam City Hall and the Mechanical Engineering building at Haifa's Technion University. In 1963 the firm constructed a condominium development just North of Tel Aviv known as the Dubiner House. This building is an early exercise in horizontal polyhedral geometry, and one of its apartments still serves as Hecker's own permanent home.

These experiments with form were taken one stage further in the conception of the Ramot Housing (not to be confused with Ramat-Gan) for an orthodox Jewish community on the hills to the north-east of Jerusalem. Here Hecker based the individual apartments on one of the five Platonic solids, the dodecahedron[1], but the practical realities of conventional *in situ* concrete column and slab construction did not produce true polyhedric interiors. This development of 720 apartments, eventually built in four stages (the last two not to Hecker's original plans), remains controversial in Israel mainly because of its scale rather than its crystalline aesthetic. Also controversial are Hecker's continual and sensitive references to Islamic motifs, which he maintains are an essential ingredient in the evolution of an architecture appropriate to Israel as it reconstructs its own cultural tradition. This is a country in which even flat roofs, the influence of the Bauhaus notwithstanding, can cause heated discussions because of their cultural associations. In criticism of the bifurcation of culture in Israeli society, he wrote in 1987: 'To my great regret, the spiritual sources behind Israeli art are largely remote from the heritage of our region'.[2]

The Spiral at Ramat-Gan is located just across the small access road from the Dubiner House, and is perched on the side of a hill with dramatic views. Its organizational geometry is based on twelve angle shifts in a plan of 22.5 degrees, with all but one of its nine apartments stacked in rotation, one per floor. The essentially semi-circular inner court thus created faces south-west back down the road, and has profiled metal-clad balconies which cantilever into the court on each level. The remaining wall surfaces are covered mainly in a mosaic of thin inexpensive stone, some of which Hecker himself helped to fix in position. Both the nature of the material and the manner of its application draw references that are much closer to the vernacular architecture of Arab villages and towns than to the imported Western suburban aesthetic that dominates most Jewish settlements in this landscape.

This project, along with the recently completed Palmach Centre in Tel Aviv and new work in Germany, suggests that Hecker's long struggle for the acceptance of his more democratic and humanistic vision of architecture is finally entering a new and constructive phase both in Israel and elsewhere.

155

left A view from the access road showing the entrance ramp.

right Hecker's earlier apartment building, Dubiner House, is just across the road.

below right A site plan and site sectional elevation showing the Spiral apartment building on the left and Dubiner House on the right.

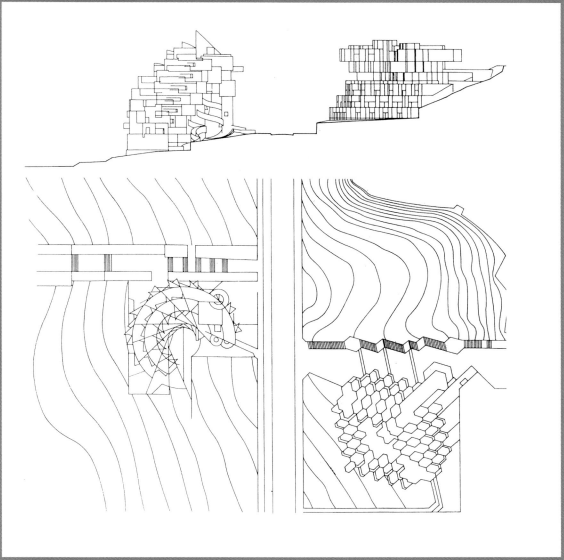

project **Kitagata apartments**
location Gifu Prefecture
Japan
design commissioned 1994
architect Kazuyo Sejima & Associates

construction main contractor
area variable
cost undisclosed

The narrator in Chris Marker's film *Sans Soleil* (1982) asks the rhetorical question, 'How can we understand history in an age dominated by the visual image?'[1] Much of Marker's footage was filmed in Japan, the site of the apotheosis of the urban condition as structured by capitalist economics. In responding to the design problem of mass housing, Sejima appears to be overtly non judgmental about our present cultural environment: 'I concede that I am indeed living in the present. But that is all the more reason why I don't believe in trying to deny or conceal that fact by creating oppositional architecture. I consider it anachronistic to take an impossible concept, present it as something of eternal importance, and completely base your architecture on it.'[2]

The reality of much housing, in Japan and in all industrialized countries, is that the nuclear family is often not the basic social unit that occupies dwellings. Sejima has made a study of standard public housing plans and has published the resultant *Metropolitan Housing Studies* with the aim of proposing new prototypes for collective housing in low, medium and high rise configurations. The main preoccupation of these proposals is to redefine the relationship between public and private space in the city, and to invent new unit plans and typologies that accept the need to develop the life of the individual, the family and the collective.

The project at Kitagata forms part of a larger development masterplanned by Arata Isozaki. Christine Hawley, Elizabeth Diller, Akiko Takahashi and Sejima were invited to design one block each on a suburban site surrounded by small houses, supermarkets and rice fields. In order to maintain the maximum possible amount of open groundscape, Sejima's solution was to propose an extremely shallow (7.3 metre/24 foot) nine-storey block on *piloti* which follows the perimeter of the site and which renders the external spaces as significant as the internal ones. The ground under the building is used mainly for parking bicycles and allows free access to the protected courtyard from all directions.

The structure of the apartment block is of reinforced concrete with loadbearing party walls consistently at approximately 2.8 metre (9 foot) centres. The plan of each floor is arranged in three zones: to the north are continuous public corridors served by elevators and externally mounted straight flight steel fire stairs, to the south are private passageways linking rooms within each dwelling unit. The rooms themselves sit between these two zones and are combined horizontally, vertically and diagonally to produce 30 variations of unit type. Each apartment has an open terrace which runs north/south right through the depth of the block, and these viewed externally appear as apparently random perforations of the building fabric.

The accepted conventions of privacy are inverted in the positioning of elements which serve the domestic routine – particularly those carried out in the past by women. The wash-hand basin in each apartment is in full view of the private court, while the laundry facilities are located on the open terrace. The dwelling entrance is via the kitchen/dining area which is here seen as the notional centre of all domestic activity. The bedrooms are internal rooms, separated from the private passageways by plywood flush doors like those on storage units, but these rooms also have direct access out to the public corridors allowing them to be used as individual living spaces independent of the apartment. This arrangement neither enforces nor discourages an individual or a collective lifestyle, but rather, as with the choice of materials and organizational principles, aims at complete neutrality. In revealing to the gaze of others the intimacies of domesticity, Sejima is clearly trying to liberate these activities from their historically acquired imagery and implied meanings.

left The building is on *piloti* to give free access to the large protected inner court.

above The access side of the block with external staircases.

left Apartment variations are achieved by using different combinations of rooms, sometimes on more than one floor.

above View of a kitchen/living room with the terrace to the left. The stair in the apartment leads to the bedrooms.

left This private corridor is equipped with a handbasin, inverting conventional concepts of privacy.

above The façade is modulated by the disposition of different apartment types.

right A diagram of the lateral section showing how extreme spatial complexity arises out of the overlay of two simple systems of organization: structure and circulation.

project **Open City**

location Valparaiso
Chile
date commissioned 1971–present
architect members of the Open City co-operative

construction self-build and specialist sub-contractors
area not applicable
cost not applicable

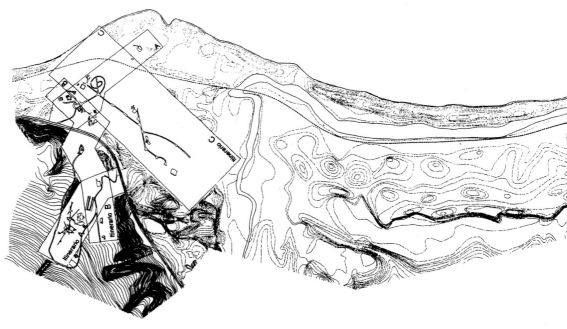

left The Puntilla complex, comprising a gallery and *hospederia* (house as a place of hospitality).

above The site plan shows how buildings are scattered in clusters amongst the sand dunes.

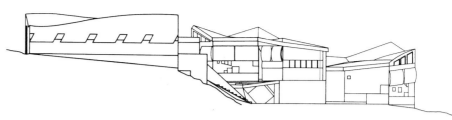

left The Puntilla complex: the buildings are made mainly of wood, canvas, metal and local bricks.

right Elevation of the Puntilla complex.

The Open City was born out of a meeting in 1950 between the architect Alberto Cruz and the poet Godofredo Iommi, both aged 33. Inspired by such diverse sources as the architecture of Le Corbusier – then working on Ronchamp and Chandigarh – and the poet Arthur Rimbaud – who, through his writing, sought the spiritual liberation of mankind from the confines of the past – they conceived of the possibility of creating an architecture based on poetic acts. Behind this aspiration lay their shared belief that it is possible to develop a form of science that is based on intuition; that science does not have a monopoly on reason and logic just as art does not have an undisputed claim on the creative imagination. Other poets who provided inspiration included the German Romantics Friedrich Hölderlin and Novalis, and the French Symbolists Charles Baudelaire and Stephane Mallarmé, all of whom imply in their work that modernity is a new state of consciousness requiring entirely new creative methodologies. The essential idea that emerged was that form could be generated from a phenomenological point of view rather than a purely materialistic one.

In 1952 Cruz and Iommi accepted teaching posts at the Catholic University of Valparaiso on the condition that they came as part of a larger collective group of architects, poets and artists. From this point on their faculty became more concerned with research than with the education of future professionals. A practical home for this research was established in the late 1960s through the collective purchase of a large area of land beyond Vino del Mar, to the north of the coastal port of Valparaiso. Comprising sand dunes and grass plateaus, the site is traversed by the coastal road and a railway line serving the local copper mine, but is primarily dominated by the proximity of the Pacific Ocean. Forming a co-operative, the residents of the Open City are connected to the university, and are mainly faculty members who have undertaken to use their own lives as a vehicle for artistic research, rather than making propositions for society in general.

The Open City is therefore both a home and a place of experimentation for all the members of the co-operative. Over the years some 30 or so structures have been erected in a dispersed settlement pattern within the landscape. The organizing principle is the series of public spaces called agoras after the meeting spaces in Classical Greek cities. Of these, the unfinished structure known as the Palace of the Dawn and Dusk is the largest, but should not be thought of as the City's centre since all the agoras are seen as forming part of a continuum.

The places of residence are called *hospederias*, each combining the role of a house with specific communal functions such as studios, workshops or rooms for visitors. Residents do not own their houses and all building projects, including the *hospederias*, are jointly funded by the co-operative, with the result that the structures are mainly built out of inexpensive and locally available materials: wood, profiled metal, handmade bricks and canvas. Within this restricted palette the formal language that has evolved over the past 20 years is extremely complex and rich. These buildings have the remarkable quality of creating presence from the apparently insubstantial and transitory. The context of the constantly changing forms of the sand dunes supports this impression.

As a working methodology, the collective design processes that have generated the physical form of the Open City, and the social experiment which has allowed its realization, stand in direct contradiction to the context of most architectural experiments, bounded as they are by the conventions of the commissioning system and the diversity of the main players' objectives.

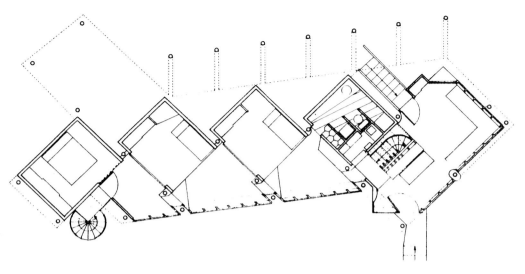

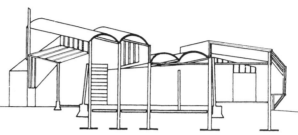

above left A smaller *hospederia*, which has been added to over time.

above right A section through a typical *hospederia*.

far left An interior of a *hospederia*.

far left top A plan of the Hospederia Entrada, at the entrance to the city.

below The agora of the Palace of Dawn and Dusk was created out of a collective poetic act.

At times I feel as if I am spread out over the landscape and inside things, and am myself living in every tree, in the splashing of the waves, in the clouds and the animals that come and go, in the procession of the seasons. There is nothing in the Tower that has not grown into its own form over the decades, nothing with which I am not linked.

I have done without electricity, and tend the fireplace and stove myself. Evenings, I light old lamps. There is no running water, and I pump the water from the well. I chop the wood and cook the food. Here the torment of creation is lessened: creativity and play are close together.

Carl Gustav Jung: *The Tower* from *Memories, Dreams, Reflections*

Experimental houses are the designed responses to the perceived inability of established housing form, organization and technology to deal adequately with new cultural, political and economic contexts. During the twentieth century, the predominant shifts in these contexts have been newly available technologies and new social forms which effect habitation patterns. In affluent industrialized countries the gradual diminishing of dependence on domestic labour and the corresponding dependency on machines has allowed the domestic space to transform from a space of labour and production to one more connected with leisure and consumption. This, combined with higher expectations about comfort levels, has had an obvious environmental impact; since 1970 the energy consumed in houses by domestic appliances in these countries has doubled. The average US citizen has an energy consumption of three times that of the average European and some 10 to 20 times that of the average Chinese or Central African.[1] This extraordinary disparity is the result of a range of factors, many of which are directly linked with housing. For example, figures compiled by the United Nations for the year 1996 reveal that the average size of a house in the United States is twice that of one in Western Europe and over three times the size of the average dwelling in Russia.

Buildings themselves, the largest proportion of which are houses, now account for approximately 50 per cent of the total energy consumption of a typical industrialized country, and are the single biggest producers of carbon dioxide emissions.[2] Environmental impact, both in terms of embodied energy (energy used to construct a building) and energy in use, will become *the* major design issue of the next twenty-five years as fossil fuels become scarce and global warming produces noticeable and dramatic climate change.

The response of architects and designers to the ecological crisis so far has been broadly of two sorts. Firstly, there are those who see sophisticated technological solutions as being appropriate and offering the possibility of a new aesthetic generated by an environmental perspective. Many of the resultant projects have questionable ecological credentials on close analysis. Secondly, there is the more radical approach which questions the assumptions made about lifestyle and social form by the designers of normative housing. These projects are more rare but often have an extremely narrow view of architecture, displaying a tendency to strip it of its artistic and creative potential. The examples in this chapter have been chosen to represent approaches which avoid both these pitfalls, but which nevertheless indicate a range of responses to different contexts.

Earlier attempts at autonomous houses, like, for example, the Danish zero energy house of 1975 and the Vale's house in Northamptonshire, England, from the early 1990s, tend to imply a narrow view of domesticity tinged with morality and puritanism. The house that Anthony Hoete designed for his father on the New Zealand island of Motiti, and Skude, Moltke and Jensen's Villa Vision at Taastrup, Denmark, both use a degree of technological sophistication to produce houses which are autonomous and rely, in theory, on no external energy inputs. Both of these houses, in very different ways, integrate a vision of a benign lifestyle with an experimental arrangement of spaces for habitation. Neither suggest any particular settlement pattern if reproduced *en masse* and have an ambivalent relationship to landscape and place.

Bill Dunster's Hope House on the outskirts of London is a suburban model which has implied urban applications due to its compact form. The technology is intelligently pragmatic, utilizing fairly standard components but in inventive combinations and sensitively specified. The aesthetic avoids any esoteric rhetoric, but at the same time does not degenerate into barely disguised developer 'vernacular'. That this approach has broader applications is evidenced by Dunster's recent work for British Housing Associations on large-scale projects with a clear environmental agenda.

All these projects concern themselves with the material nature of the house as the object of environmentally conscious activity. Christopher Day's work in Wales, and that of Samuel Mockbee and the Rural Studio in the United States, extend the ecological agenda into the realm of social ecology: the process of construction, the role of the architect, and the relationship with occupants of the house form part of a broader picture. Day has elaborated his philosophy in two seminal books which explore the social relationships involved in small-scale building work, and he stresses the need for greater participation at all levels of the process. His work is not about the building as object, but as social process, and he puts forward the argument that if this process is healthy, it has enormous healing power at both the personal and collective level.[3] Mockbee's work for the rural poor forms part of a training programme for students of architecture, and emphasizes a strongly practical ethical dimension in a profession that has had a tendency to be highly theoretical about social and political issues.

Scandinavia's commitment to the environmental agenda is clear from the numerous low energy mass housing projects now being produced. One such scheme in Denmark, by Tegnestuen Vandkunsten, built as the result of the Ecohouse 99 competition, could be seen as the application of the principles of Hope House to mass housing in a climate that is more hostile than that of southern England. As is now expected of public housing in Scandinavia, the scheme also encompasses a view of ecology that has social and cultural dimensions: the project has communal facilities, playgroups and leisure areas integrated into the buildings and surrounding landscape.

Finally, Thomas Spiegelhalter's work in the suburb of Rieselfeld provides a model for the transformation of standard contemporary housing typologies into flexible and environmentally sustainable urban dwellings.

project **architect's father's house**

location Motiti Island
New Zealand
date commissioned 1995
architect **Anthony Hoete**

construction architect with family help and specialist sub-contractors
area 100m² (1,076 sq ft)
cost $NZ 65,840 not including labour

The traditional Maori settlement, which has a 1,000-year history, contained houses called *whare* that had individual functions – sleeping, learning, meeting and weaving. These structures were lightweight, low thatched huts comprising one space, normally, with projecting gables to form a porch, and built from locally available materials. With the influx of immigrant Europeans, these building types gradually declined until only the meeting house, or *whare hui*, survived in any numbers. Towards the end of the nineteenth century other materials were introduced into their construction including glass and brick, while pit-sawn timber and corrugated sheeting replaced locally produced elements of construction.

Anthony Hoete's father, Aubrey, wished to return to his small home island of Motiti, which is Maori land with tribal origins, after many years working on the mainland, and so in June 1995 work began on planning this contemporary re-interpretation of the original typology of the *whare*. The only access to Motiti island is by sea or air, and the population of 20 have no cars or services infrastructure, so from the start the concept was, by necessity, of an autonomous house constructed from materials that would either have to be found in the landscape or brought in by boat. The single most important design constraint on the house, therefore, was its isolation – not just physical but cultural and economic (Maori land cannot be bought or sold and sits outside of central government jurisdiction, including planning controls).

The house is sited on open grassland between the sea and an airstrip, its linear plan oriented on the axis of these opposing transport links; with a large centrally pivoting door at either end to recognize both possible means of arrival. There are two principal spaces: the ground floor *whare* for Aubrey Hoete, and a raised room for guests with its own external access stair. Within the *whare* there are only two freestanding forms, a concrete bathroom which incorporates a 1000-litre (220-gallon) rainwater tank, and a suspended cedar table which acts as the kitchen. The south-facing wall is faced in external quality plywood and contains within its varying thickness recesses for beds, a wood burning stove and storage. On the north side, exposed to the sun and prevailing wind, the wall is linear and faced in composite profiled zinc panels into which are inserted two large projecting picture windows. The guest room has both a conventional strip window for the panoramic views of the rocky coastline and a floor-level window which is intended to discourage overlong stays by rendering guests partially visible from the ground – this is, after all, primarily a house intended for solitary living removed from a world that is increasingly dominated by technology and information.

All the water for the house is collected on the roof, which also acts as a helicopter landing pad. Electricity is supplied by both a small wind generator and a photovoltaic panel, while heating is provided by the stove which burns driftwood and has a back boiler to supply hot water. The concrete for the foundations and bathroom contains aggregate from broken up beach pebbles, while all the flooring is made of reclaimed timber from an old hospital. The timbers for the framing and all but one of the other main building components were delivered in one barge load and then moved by tractor to the site. The prefabricated steel component missed this consignment and was flown in later by helicopter in an uncharacteristic act of extravagance. Construction took two years, including an enforced break due to a volcanic eruption on the mainland which coated the entire island in ash.

left The roof is a rainwater collector but also acts as an occasional landing pad for rare environmentally unsound arrivals.

above The materials for construction arrived on a single barge to cut down on transport costs (right), but a late piece of steel-work was flown in as an exception (left).

There is no word for architecture in the Maori language.

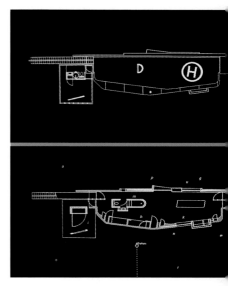

far left The limited privacy of the elevated guest room discourages long stays.

left The house is totally autonomous in use.

above From bottom: ground- and first-floor plans.

below The entrance stair to the guest room is for determined visitors only.

project **Villa Vision**

location Taastrup
Denmark

date commissioned 1993

architect **Flemming Skude, Ivar Moltke and Bertel Jensen**

construction main contractor
area 200m² (2,152 sq ft)
cost undisclosed

Villa Vision was built by the Danish Technological Institute as an exhibition prototype to demonstrate the feasibility of a housing unit existing independently of communal energy and waste systems. It sits within the twentieth-century tradition of houses built solely for exhibition purposes in which the necessary lack of specific site context has generated a geometrical formal arrangement of spaces – as, for example, in Buckminster Fuller's Dymaxion House and Arne Jacobsen's House of the Future, both from 1929. In contrast to Tony Wrench's Round House, or Michael Reynold's inspired Nautilus, this house maintains a belief in technological progress by embracing the implications of lifestyles driven by information technology and electronic communications. Situated in an undistinguished suburb to the west of Copenhagen, Villa Vision's detachment from its surroundings implies a future for the house as a type that encompasses living, working and social interaction in a model not unlike that of Ebenezer Howard's Garden City or Frank Lloyd Wright's Broadacre City.

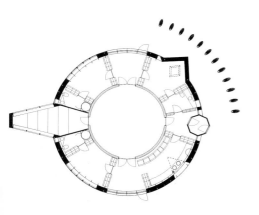

The circular plan comprises a ring of rooms arranged around a central top-lit court. This space has a fully glazed pyramidal roof with automatically operated oilcloth sails to provide shading, its enclosing circular wall of brick acting as a heat sink. The original concept drawings show a living tree growing at the centre of the court, implying that its function was seen as being a true greenhouse, however, in execution this has been replaced by a less convincing sculptural viewing platform. The rooms proper have equal spatial status and are conceived as being flexible in use. Only the architecturally specific television and video room would be difficult to alter, and its form has as much to do with the 20 square metres (215 square feet) of photovoltaic panels on its south-facing roof as the need to reconfigure the traditional function of the living room. The kitchen is made up from small mobile units that allow meals to be prepared and eaten in other parts of the house, including the central court. The radial partition walls between the perimeter rooms are also storage units which can be moved to allow for changing use patterns.

Villa Vision is built on an artificial sand hill, the whole structure being constructed off a super-insulated concrete slab that supports the inner ring of brickwork and the outer ring of two separate timber frames containing 400mm (15 1/2 inches) of insulation. The zinc-clad roof is also structured in timber and has the same thickness of insulation as the floor and walls, creating a building envelope that requires an energy input of roughly 10 per cent of a conventional house of similar size. Hot water is supplied by a solar panel and the system is connected to a heat pump that extracts excess heat and stores it in the earth underneath the house. The photovoltaic array provides electricity for lighting and low energy appliances including the building's own computer aided monitoring systems. Rainwater from the roof is collected but supplemented at present by a municipal supply. Low flush toilets use half a litre (a pint) of water and grey water from the kitchen, shower and basins is filtered and re-used to either flush these toilets or water the garden. The house is not on the public sewage system and black water waste is converted into fertilizer using willow filters and water cascades which form a feature of the garden.

far left The entrance side of the house with the covered area to the right.

left A plan showing the entrance on the right and the TV viewing room on left.

top The kitchen has movable units.

above The interior of the TV room: the roof carries the photovoltaic arrays for electrical generation.

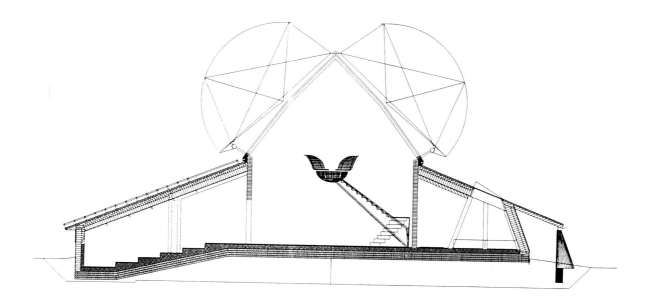

above The inner core of the house acts as a thermal store.

right The house is shown here with its sails closed to reduce solar gain.

project **Hope House**

location East Molesey, Surrey
UK

date commissioned 1995

architect **Bill Dunster**

construction self-build with specialist sub-contractors
area 130m² (1,400 sq ft)
cost £85,000

Although Hope House is a detached house with a highly considered aesthetic, it is in fact a prototype for high-density urban living based on sustainable principles. In opposition to the view that customized, sophisticated technology is the solution to reducing energy demands in domestic architecture, this house utilizes absolutely standard and readily available components, and details which are generic rather than precious. This approach is born out of a carefully considered philosophy: experimental projects which address ecological issues must also engage the practical realities of the building industry, of housing finance, and of the fundamental need to provide solutions to the problem of mass housing.

The site, in spite of its proximity to open water, is restricted and overlooked by adjoining houses. Much of the site is land reclaimed from the river by landfill earlier in the century and is therefore of poor soil quality. The house, carefully sited to maximize solar gain, also preserves the large existing trees and the building line implied by the surrounding properties. In order to minimize its visual impact, the three-storey structure is cut into the ground by approximately 1.5 metres (5 feet), with most of the excavated soil being retained to landscape the garden.

The lowest level of the house is conceived as a flexible multi-purpose space which will at different times in the future perform different functions: an apartment for grandparents, a home office, a retreat for the parents when their children need the rest of the house for themselves, or eventually a separate home for a child who has become independent. The principal floor above is the main living space, directly accessible from the road by a long, gently ascending bridge. The top floor has two bedrooms and a bathroom set under the monopitch of the roof.

All three levels are linked by a large south-facing timber framed conservatory, the top facet of which is designed to incorporate 14 square metres (150 square feet) of photovoltaic panels. A centrally placed spiral stair forms part of the warm air distribution system and its glass block walls shed daylight into the deepest part of the plan, hence minimizing the use of artificial lighting. The ground-floor walls are in insulated cavity brickwork and support a concrete hypocaust first floor containing warm air ducts providing radiant low temperature heating. Above this the house is constructed in insulated softwood framing clad in softwood weather boarding. The external joinery comprises standard units, modified only where the geometry demands it. The main living floor is the only space heated by any means other than the sun, and is thermally insulated from the rest of the house – a deliberate design policy which promotes a more cohesive domestic routine rather than the fragmented life engendered by centrally heated houses. About 30 per cent of the heating load of this space is provided by cooking.

Extensive use has been made of reclaimed materials: re-used boat decking for the bridge, second-hand steel plumbing tube for handrails and bracing rods, and an armour plate glass floor on the internal sun deck from a demolished bank. Specification of other materials has been largely dictated by the drive to reduce embodied energy, with over 85 per cent of the materials, including the bricks, being sourced from within 55 kilometres (35 miles) of the site.

Many of the ideas incorporated in the Hope House are now being reapplied by the architect in a project for the Peabody Housing Trust in the form of 85 rentable zero-energy units in Sutton, a suburb of South London.

below The entrance bridge from the access road leads to the first floor.

right View from the garden. The house is a proto-type for sustainable urban living.

following pages The triple-height sunspace has an internal balcony with a glass floor.

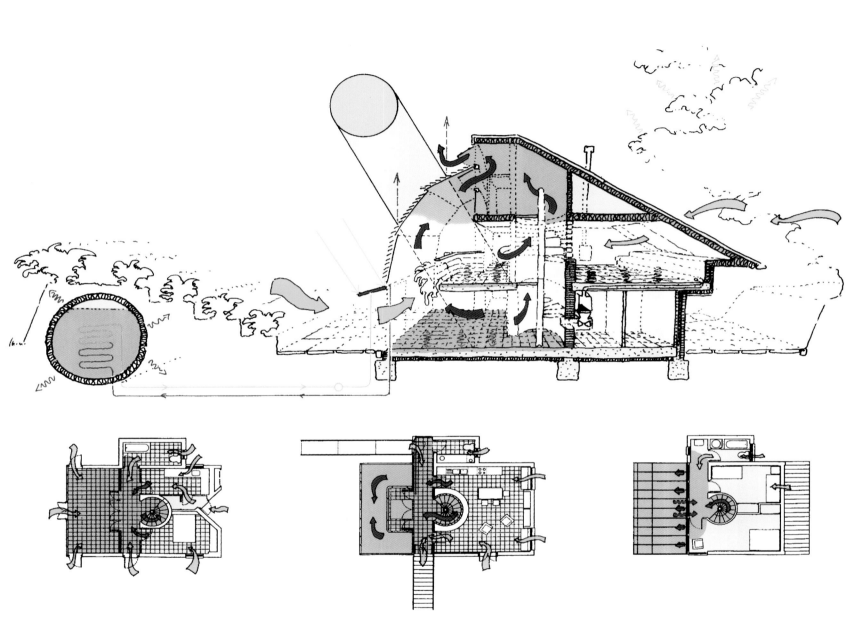

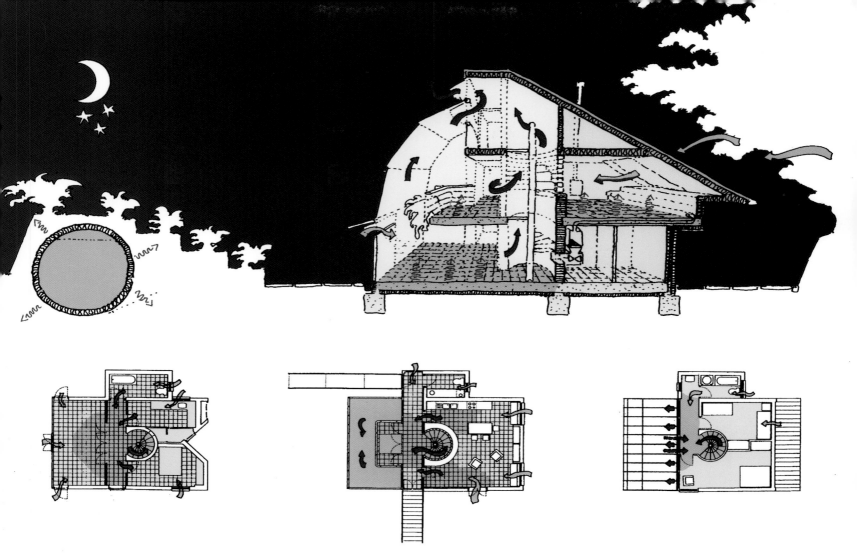

left A section showing thermal performance on a typical summer day. Associated plans show, from left: ground, first and second floors.

above Thermal performance on a typical summer night. The earth mound to the left contains a thermal store.

project **Pen-y-Lyn**

location Crymych
Pembrokeshire
Wales
UK

date of construction 1975–1997

architect Christopher Day

construction self-build
area 215m^2 (2,314 sq ft) including cowshed
approximate cost £10,000 (exclusive of labour)

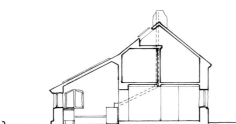

In the preface to *Building with a Heart* (1990) Christopher Day writes, 'I was trained in architectural school to try to like modern architecture – then at its functionalist, rectilinearist peak. Over the years, I became increasingly horrified by the results of such architecture as I began to realize what a harmful influence it had upon people and upon society. I began to wonder: if architecture can be so powerful and destructive, could it not also be beneficial and healing ?'[1] He goes on to describe the process of building various projects as social exercises, including the Nant-y-Cym Steiner School Kindergarten which was completed around in the early 1990s with the help of parents, pupils and teachers.

Day built his first house in West Wales in 1972, but on its completion started the process all over again with Pen-y-Lyn, in order to have more land to work and move towards a self sustaining lifestyle. The site is on the very edge of the heathland at the foot of the Preseli Hills, and on it was the ruin of a traditional Welsh longhouse dating from about 1800. Only three walls of the old house remained and the thick walls of the new house were created by building stone walls on their outside with insulation between the two layers. All the stones used in the building were found on or near the site and moved by hand; this initial work was physically hard and at times stressful. Through this experience, however, Day learnt how to work productively and with a sense of enjoyment – and the knowledge that building could become an artistic experience was then applied to organizing volunteer labour over a period of six years on the Kindergarten Project. The result is a hand-crafted building, available even to financially disadvantaged clients, that would not be possible to achieve with a conventional design process and building contract.

Pen-y-Lyn is, in this sense, a prototype to demonstrate the practical application of Day's philosophy. Most of the components normally bought in for conventional buildings are in this house hand-made: the doors and windows, the staircase, even the door latches. Much use has been made of reclaimed natural material like slate and tiles and these have been detailed on site as part of the actual act of making. When Day does draw detail, he works freehand in pencil and at full size scale to avoid any abstraction of the problem to be solved.

As well as being concerned with social ecology, the house has a number of environmentally conscious features, all created from very simple technology within the scope of the average self-builder. The kitchen is the principle room and a small adjacent south-facing greenhouse provides some supplementary warm air during sunny weather. Above the kitchen a large solar collector provides all the necessary hot water. Cooking is done on a wood burning oven with the exhaust gases passing through a massive stone chimney which acts as a heat sink. The organization of the plan means that all the main living spaces (which, including the bedrooms, only take up 50 per cent of the building volume) get background heat from this chimney. Water comes from a nearby spring and the house has its own anaerobic septic tank. Originally the house was completely autonomous but is now connected to the municipal electricity supply although its actual energy demand is low. The house uses materials of low or zero toxicity and as close to a natural source as possible to reduce embodied energy.

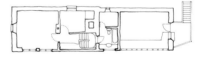

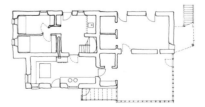

far left bottom The section is compact and utilizes the entire volume of the building.

far left top The south side of the house is designed to maximize solar gain. The roof of the kitchen, to the left, is a solar panel for heating water.

left The studio's balcony acts as a wood store.

above The first-floor studio has views of the Preseli hills.

below From bottom: ground- and first-floor plans. The studio, to the right, has a space underneath for farm animals.

project **Harris house**

location Mason's Bend
Alabama
USA

date completed 1997

architect Samuel Mockbee and the Rural Studio

construction students of the Auburn University School of Architecture
area 60m² (645 sq ft)
cost $30,000

The philosophy that underpins the work of the Rural Studio is that architecture is a social art which needs to be practiced with a sense of moral responsibility. To put this into practice actively, Professor Samuel Mockbee and Professor Dennis Ruth conceived of an initiative whereby students of architecture could, as part of their training programme, jointly design and build new homes for the rural poor in the Deep South. Mockbee, who grew up in northern Mississippi, became increasingly disturbed with the conditions of physical poverty in which one in four of all rural residents of America's Deep South live. In addition, through his teaching at Auburn University School of Architecture in Alabama, Mockbee was concerned to redress the high level of abstraction that all student architects experience in training and instigate an on-going programme in which they would confront real social issues and engage in design and building work as a direct response.

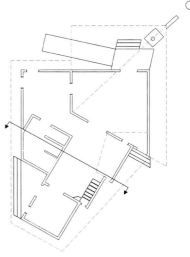

On a regular basis 15 to 20 second-year students relocate in Newbern, Alabama, then together with the Hale County Department of Human Resources identify a family in critical need of new housing and propose an outline design for a replacement home. Each semester, a different group of students modify the design as they build the house in phases collectively. Fifth-year students, remaining in Hale County for up to one year, concentrate on finding funding and resources for these houses and other community-based projects. Since its inception in 1992 the training and building programme has received more than $1.7 million in funds, and has completed five houses as well as a community chapel, a playground, a centre for children suspected of being victims of abuse, and various other smaller projects.

The Harris house was completed in 1997 – designed to a brief which included a very restricted budget, low running costs, and the need to accommodate a couple in which one partner is confined to a wheelchair. The primary space is a high 20 square metres (215 square feet) enclosed porch with a butterfly roof which aids natural ventilation and allows rainwater to be collected in a large cistern (this water is used for toilet flushing and clothes washing). High-level vents control air flow through the house but for additional cooling in summer there is a fan to pull air through the living room. The ancillary spaces are clustered around a centrally located wood burning stove and sit under a simple monopitch roof clad in tin. A small loft, partly over the living room and partially in the porch, provides a sleeping platform for visiting grandchildren. The walls of the house are clad mainly in a combination of tin and salvaged timber, some of it over 100 years old. The external detailing is nevertheless a mosaic of inexpensive found and recycled materials, which reflects the evolutionary design process. The drawings as such merely record the construction after it has occurred and serve only to map the result of this experiment in social ecology. Within the next five years the training programme is planned to expand to areas other than Alabama and to become a multi-disciplinary activity open to students outside Auburn University.

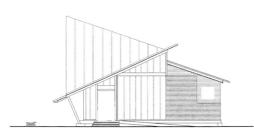

previous page The porch is shown under the distinctive butterfly roof, which collects rainwater for re-use.

far left bottom The kitchen end of the house.

far left top Anderson Harris outside his original house.

left A view of the veranda adjacent to the kitchen, showing details of reclaimed cladding materials.

top The porch has a sleeping platform for visiting grandchildren.

above An elevation of the porch at the end of the house.

right The plan showing the porch on the top right and the kitchen on the bottom left.

project **Ecohouse 99**

location Skejby
Denmark
date completed 1998
architect **Tegnestuen Vandkunsten**

construction design and build based on competition-winning scheme
area 3,650m² (39,288 sq ft)
cost undisclosed

above Model of the competition-winning scheme at Skejby showing the combination of two- and three-storey blocks all with south-facing solar spaces.

far right An axonometric diagram of a typical unit showing the main components of the environmental technology.

In 1963, Denmark agreed to a partition of the Ekkofisk sector of the North Sea which, it subsequently transpired, meant that Norway became the main beneficiary of most of the oil deposits there. Lacking any readily available fossil fuel source, the oil price crisis of the mid-1970s forced the country seriously to review its energy policy, with the result that Denmark now has one of the most advanced environmental programmes within the industrialized world. The Danish Zero Energy house designed by Knud Peter Harboe and Søren Koch in 1975 was an extreme reaction to the environmental crisis and exhibited an overt degree of Protestant fundamentalism in its attitude towards the lifestyle of its inhabitants. However, using less demanding technologies, Denmark has now reduced the average energy consumption of its housing stock by one third through the upgrading of existing units and the building of half a million new ones with higher performance specifications.

Ecohouse 99 came about through a government-backed competition begun in 1996 which aimed to set new environmental standards for social housing. Public or social housing in Denmark is normally provided through housing associations in which tenants have a financial interest, a system which allows greater budget flexibility than under purely state-funded provision. Implicit in the original design brief for four pilot projects in different parts of the country was the idea that previously applied innovations in technology and space planning from one-off experimental projects would be integrated at a larger scale. Funding these innovations on the Skejby scheme has required a 20 per cent increase in budget over the cost of a conventional housing development of the same size, but this will be recovered in energy savings in use.

Tegnestuen Vandkunsten, who have a long history of high quality design in social housing, won agreement to proceed to build projects at Ikast and Skejby under a design-and-build management system in which they were employed by the contractor. Because both the budget and the design were fixed at the end of the competition stage, this did not result in the degraded design standards normally associated with this kind of arrangement. Although the two schemes as built have very different site layouts, they share the same unit plans.

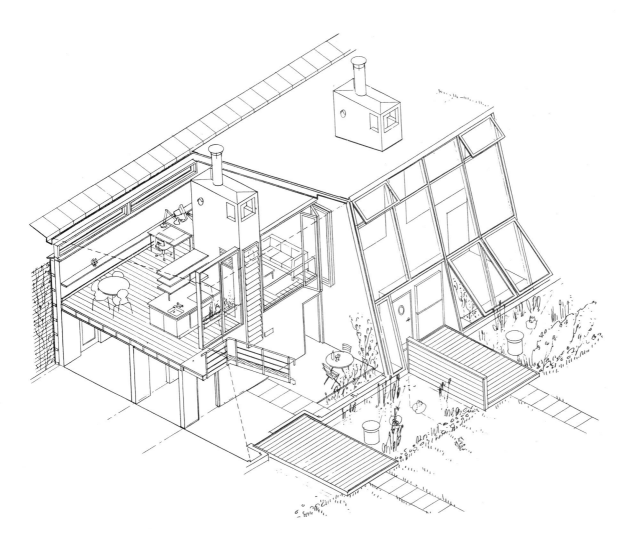

At Skejby, the dwellings are arranged in four terraces of two- and three-storey blocks facing north-south, with the houses accessed via small bridges over a meandering shallow channel that collects rainwater. The two-storey houses have either one or two bedrooms in cell-like spaces on the ground floor, with large open plan living/dining rooms at first-floor level. Linking the two levels on the south side are fully glazed sun spaces which contain the stairs and act as both indoor gardens and entrance halls. A variant on this basic typology are the three-storey blocks which have two-story units over one-storey ground-floor units. In line with current Danish practice, many of the building components are standardized and fabricated off site. To further reduce costs, the finishes are basic by Scandinavian standards. The monopitch roof is asphalt on plywood and has 300mm (12 inches) of insulation, while the north-facing external walls are compressed mineral wool with 200mm (8 inches) of insulation within a timber frame backed by inner walls of recycled concrete which act as heat sinks.

The section is a development of established practice for passive solar heating and regulating the system requires a certain degree of interaction from the inhabitants. The main generator of the plan of each unit is the large central service stack which contains the ventilation and heat recovery systems as well as provision for a wood-burning stove in the living room. Large solar collectors integrated into the solar façade provide hot water for washing.

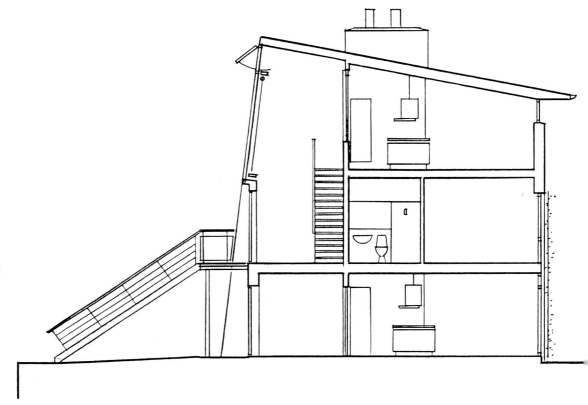

right A section showing a three-storey block comprising a two-storey duplex over a ground-floor apartment.

far right The solar wall has built-in panels for heating water.

far right bottom From left: ground, first and second floors.

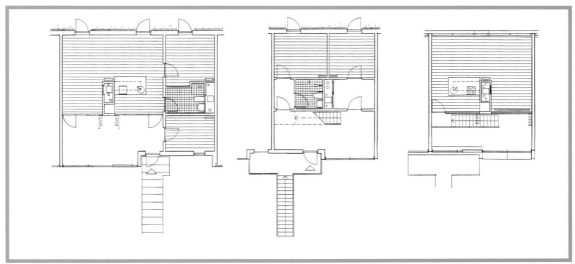

project **solar studio house**

location Rieselfeld
Baden Württemburg
Germany

date commissioned 1996

architect Professor Thomas Spiegelhalter

construction main contractor
area 380m² (4,090 sq ft)
cost DM 684,000

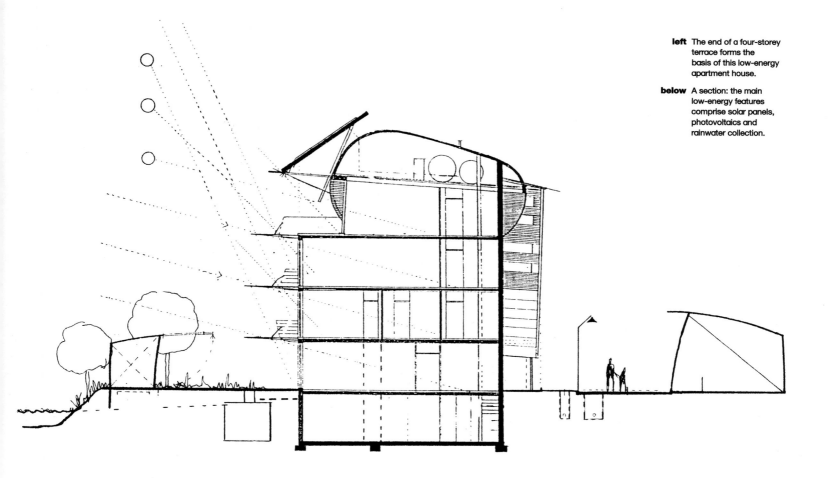

left The end of a four-storey terrace forms the basis of this low-energy apartment house.

below A section: the main low-energy features comprise solar panels, photovoltaics and rainwater collection.

The new suburb of Rieselfeld has been created outside the south-western city of Freiburg as a government-funded model project. The heating demands for these essentially prefabricated medium to high density terraces, are designed to be 30 per cent lower than that achieved under German building standards. The site for the overall development previously formed part of a sewage works and, as with the Emscher Park project (see pp.146–9), the polluted topsoil had to be removed and replaced prior to any building work. Spiegelhalter's design concentrated on the transformation of the shell of a pair of these four-storey units at the end of one of the terraces, providing a model for urban sustainable architecture with energy consumption considerably better than the already efficient neighbouring units. The house is specifically included because it not only provides a rare example of what such an architecture might be like, but also shows future possibilities for transforming existing structures.

The building has numerous unusual characteristics. Firstly, an external staircase on the north-east façade combined with removable internal stairs allows flexible subdivision. For example, the four levels can be used independently to provide small starter apartments. At present, each half of the building has two apartments, one of which has an integrated office space. Secondly, the sophisticated technology of the banks of photovoltaic cells and solar collectors are juxtaposed with carefully composed support structures made of largely recycled materials in an overt attempt to marry technological and artistic considerations. And thirdly, the aesthetic is driven by the concept of transience, as manifested in Freiburg's industrial past and the vestiges of the local but temporary living accommodation of immigrant low-income workers.

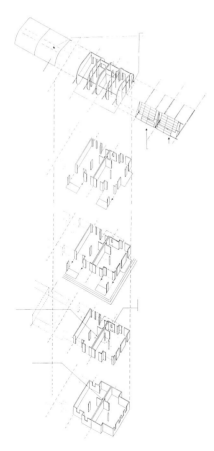

The house boasts several significant environmentally conscious design features. Many materials are recycled, including the steel and timber in the attic roof and removable balcony units, as well as the rainscreen of recycled glazing in the external stairs, which can function as a warm air collector by catching the morning sun. Recycled garage door frames are used as solar screens at high level to shield high summer sun and prevent overheating. Energy-saving features include a projecting solar absorber made of translucent thermal insulation on the east-facing end wall. 120 square metres (394 square feet) of monocrystalline silicate photovoltaic modules provide electricity via an inverter linked to the national grid, normally producing a surplus over that actually used. The building could be electrically autonomous but local legislation forbids this. Specially designed flat plate solar collectors provide hot water and some space heating, and incorporate a combined 500-litre (110-gallon) storage tank in which water for these two functions is separated only by stratification, thus saving space over two tank systems. All the rainwater from the roof is collected in a 10,000-litre (2,200-gallon) tank buried in the garden, and this is used for the low-flush toilets and for irrigating the planters.

These systems combined have resulted in a building that uses approximately one third of the energy of a correspondingly sized group of apartments built to current regulation standards. The thermal solar system has been subsidized by the European THERMIE programme and monitored for performance by the University of Stuttgart. Together with the photovoltaic system, this provides the experimental basis for the proposition that domestic buildings, even in the densely populated and climatically severe Northern Europe, can be energy producers rather than consumers.

far left bottom The arrangement of partitions and internal stairs is flexible.

far left top The add-ons are standard components, such as garage doors, used out of context.

top left Vestiges of the temporary living accommodation in the vicinity.

above The new external stair allows a range of uses and subdivisions.

It is true that I never leave my house, but it is also true that its doors (whose number are infinite) are open day and night to men and animals as well. Anyone may enter. And he will find a house like no other on the face of the earth. (There are those who declare there is a similar one in Egypt, but they lie.) Even my detractors admit there is not one single piece of furniture in the house.

The house is the same size as the world: or rather it is the world.

Jorge Luis Borges: *The House of Asterion* from *Labyrinths*

One-off houses are in a privileged position, by virtue of their particular relationship to architecture's own internal discourse, history and preoccupations. The individual house has been the single most important building type during the past 150 years for architects to test new hypotheses – both in theory through competitions and publications and in practice through built work. It has also been the principal mechanism by which architects have established their careers and promoted their own specific sensibilities. But because architecture is a social art, is reflective of cultural values, and is in part informed by the necessities of function and construction, only rarely do the complex balance of circumstances which surround any particular project allow it to produce what Thomas S. Kuhn would refer to as a new paradigm. Still more problematic is the need to persuade individual clients to fund the testing of such hypotheses and allow themselves to become the subject of the experiment for an indefinite period. In extreme cases, projects are seen as investments by architects seeking to promote a career move.[1]

Two houses in this chapter sidestep this problem. Wendell Burnette and Jørn Utzon have both built houses for themselves and their families, acting as their own general contractor and sub-contracting all aspects of construction under their own management. This working method gives maximum freedom within a fixed budget so that design can evolve as the construction progresses without necessarily involving financial, contractual or emotional implications.[2]

Burnette's own house appears to be influenced by the early work of Schindler, particularly in its overlaying of simple forms of construction with sophisticated ideas, in opposition to the more general tendency to support crude ideas with complex construction. This small house is closer to European space standards than American ones. It is a test bed for the idea that domestic architecture can accommodate both formal and informal elements and that such polarities are not mutually exclusive.

Examined together, Utzon's two houses in Majorca, Can Lis and the recent Can Feliz, form a unity in terms of conception, aesthetics and constructional system. When Sigfried Giedion reissued the fifth edition of *Space, Time, and Architecture* in 1966, he added a chapter headed 'Jørn Utzon and the Third Generation', referring to Utzon as the dominant member of the influential group of architects who began their careers in the early 1950s.[3]

Utzon's personal biography provides a unique link back to the pioneers of the Modern Movement, and his two Majorcan houses represent an exemplary demonstration of the validity of what Giedion called Critical Regionalism. The archetypical forms of Utzon's two houses in the context of the Balearic islands find curious parallels with Burnette's own house in the context of the Sonoran desert.

This idea of the possible existence of archetypes also emerges in a very different way in the Rudin house by Herzog and de Meuron, but the reference is to the generalized indigenous housing forms of Northern Europe. Rather than modify a generic underlying form specific to a particular place, their approach is more abstract and theoretically complex. They have described their work as 'conceptual rather than stylistic' and they reject concepts of perfection and harmony as romantic.[4] The house is conceived on the basis of a pragmatic approach arising out of a reading of the management and construction systems of contemporary industrialized society. The implication of this agenda is that architecture should not locate itself within its own discourse or outside it in other areas of concern, but should occupy the interface between these inner and outer worlds. The manifestations of this position can be clearly seen in the Rudin house, which is an exercise in the possibility of both the ordinary and the extraordinary being coexistent.

An alternative basis for architectural production, used by Steven Holl in the Stretto House in Dallas, is to generate forms by basing their composition on another creative medium – in this case music. This methodology has a higher purpose, stated in the introduction to Holl's book *Intertwining: Projects 1989–95*: 'Our aim is to realize space with strong phenomenal properties while elevating architecture to a level of thought'.[5] Holl's intention has more than one theoretical position to support it: as described, it is a cosmology which sees architecture as a dynamic process whereby we constantly reinvent our relationship to the world of the senses, including our sense of time and space. This mission has an intention rooted in metaphysics and is a foil to what Holl seems to read as the ever more dominant role of materialistic and scientific thinking and the resulting loss of diversity and specificity in local cultural environments.

Crosby Hall, near the former house of William Morris in South-west London, is specifically included because it is experimental by the standards already suggested, and also represents an opposition to Holl's position. Its primary focus is not the future but the past. To enact such projects requires the exact replication of construction techniques, principles of composition and massing, and systems of proportion that have been largely ignored for about 80 years. Carden & Godfrey's Crosby Hall maintains the unavoidable paradox experienced by earlier architects with liberal or socialistic sentiments like Morris, Philip Webb, Norman Shaw and Edwin Lutyens, that although they tried to work within a tradition that sought to liberate the potential creativity of the underprivileged, the actual economic basis of such work is the pure spending power of the beneficiaries of capitalism.

There is a sense in which all these projects do not, as houses, embrace the values of our times – all in some way are about alternatives which imply a shift of emphasis towards, if not a better future, then a culturally richer one. As a clear evocation of the thinking behind the work of Rem Koolhaas and OMA, the Bordeaux house should be seen as a brilliant synthesis of the conditions of modernity, made apparently without reservation. It does not reject the dominant mode of late-twentieth-century technology within the domestic environment. It does not reject our essentially urban condition of life even when located in the country. And it heroically reworks the legacy of the first generation of modernists: Mies van der Rohe (space as an infinitely extendible series of horizontal planes) and Le Corbusier (all five points of architecture are in some form present).

In the three-part division of the section, Koolhaas describes the intermediate living floor as a zone of 'pressure' – an almost invisible room half inside, half outside, and sandwiched between the floating bedroom floor and the cave-like lower level. There are striking parallels with Marshall Berman's 1983 apology for modernity *All That is Solid Melts into Air*, the book's title coming from a passage in the *Communist Manifesto* by Karl Marx.[6] The Bordeaux house confronts us with the necessity to view architecture as an expression of what is, not what might be, in an articulate expression of social realism. The alternative is to engage in the infinitely more difficult and marginal activity of believing that architecture can still be a valid mechanism for exploring what the future needs to become if we are serious about overcoming the significant problems of our time.

project **architect's house**
location Sunnyslope
Phoenix
Arizona
USA
date commissioned 1995
architect **Wendell Burnette**

construction self-build and sub-contracted under architect's direct supervision
area 95m² (1,022 sq ft)
cost $150,000

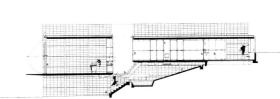

opening pages The view from the road, with the living room over the carport.

previous pages The house sits over the east-west canyon of an old track.

above The one-and-a-half storey height living room has spectacular views.

top The small inner court with a stair up from carport has its own garden and evaporation pool, thereby creating its own microclimate.

right A longitudinal section showing the carport and living room wing to the left, and the bedroom wing to the right.

far right Vertical cantilevered walls are divided by narrow glazed slots. The protected sun deck is to the left.

This compact and modest sized house is set on the edge of the desert, close to a dense neighbourhood of ranch style houses. The site slopes down to a street on its eastern boundary, and to the west, where the slope rises some 6 metres (19 feet 6 inches), are distant views of the Phoenix valley. The linear form of the house sits on the east-west canyon of an old track and the orientation is partly intended to act as a healing device for the man-made scar on the landscape. In response to the relative harshness of the environment, the house has two volumes separated by an internal court which contains a miniature garden and a fully shaded evaporation pool. The entrance to the house is via the carport under the main living space and then an ascent up an *in situ* cast concrete series of stairs and steps located in the court itself which effectively bifurcates the plan.

A single volume one-and-a-half storeys high contains the living and kitchen/dining room and looks east back towards the street. To the west of the court are the studio and two bedrooms with their associated bath or shower rooms. The circulation route in this part of the house is balanced formally by fragmenting the sanitary facilities so that they fit into a 1 metre- (3 foot-) wide zone on the opposing side of the plan. Subdivision of space within this volume is generally by either plywood panels hung from steel tension wires from the ceiling, when parallel to the monolithic external walls, or by glass screens sand blasted to head height, when cutting across the long east-west axis. This arrangement allows the light from both sunrise and sunset to filter deep into the house. The linearity of the overall form is only broken on the south side of the court where one monolithic wall element is slipped in plan to create a shaded sun deck.

The construction of the envelope is based on a series of vertical cantilever walls formed in 200mm- (8 inch-) wide insulated concrete blocks stack-bonded and post-tensioned with steel rods. On the south side of the house these walls are approximately 2.4 metres (8 feet) wide, to give greater shading, while to the north the module is 1.2 metres (4 feet) wide. The 150mm- (6 inch-) wide vertical slots between these monolithic elements are direct glazed, the 6.5mm ($^3/_4$ inch) glass being siliconed into rebates in the blockwork. The floors and roofs are *in situ* cast concrete spanning 5.2 metres (17 feet) between the parallel walls. Burnette devised a system for re-using the shuttering with the help of a water-based release agent and building paper, the plywood being cleaned, sealed and recycled to create the solid internal partitions, their surfaces providing a readable trace of the construction process.

The evaporation pool adjacent to the court and under the studio emits water through a trough down the natural slope of the site, and this helps to create a microclimate which aids cross ventilation in both parts of the house. The roof of the court can be rigged with a suspended clear acrylic plunge pool which links the two roof terraces on top of the house and fills the space below with refracted light.

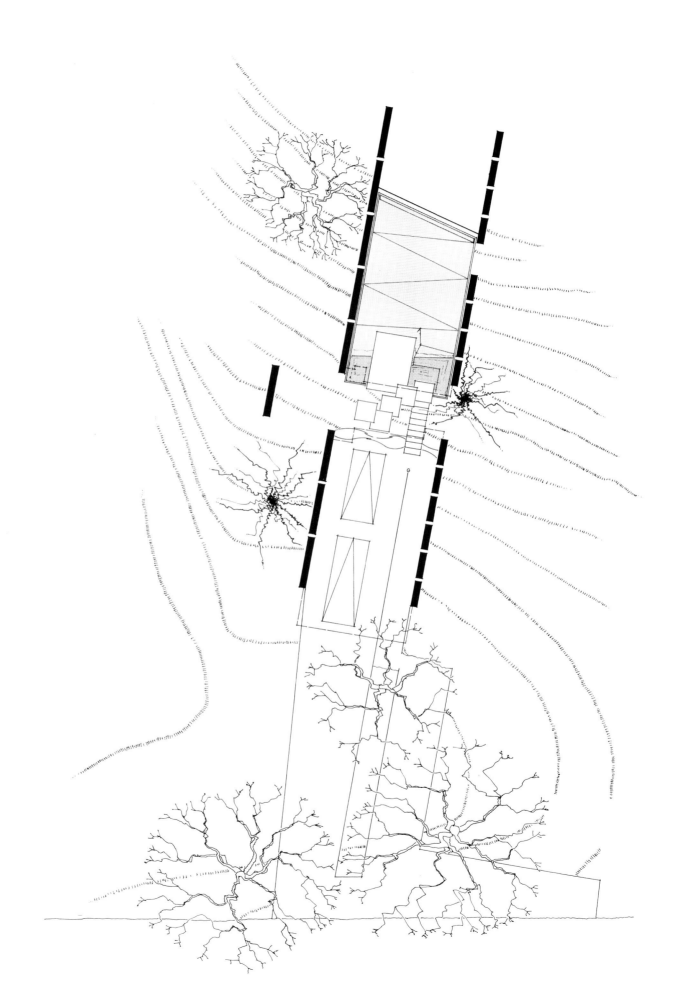

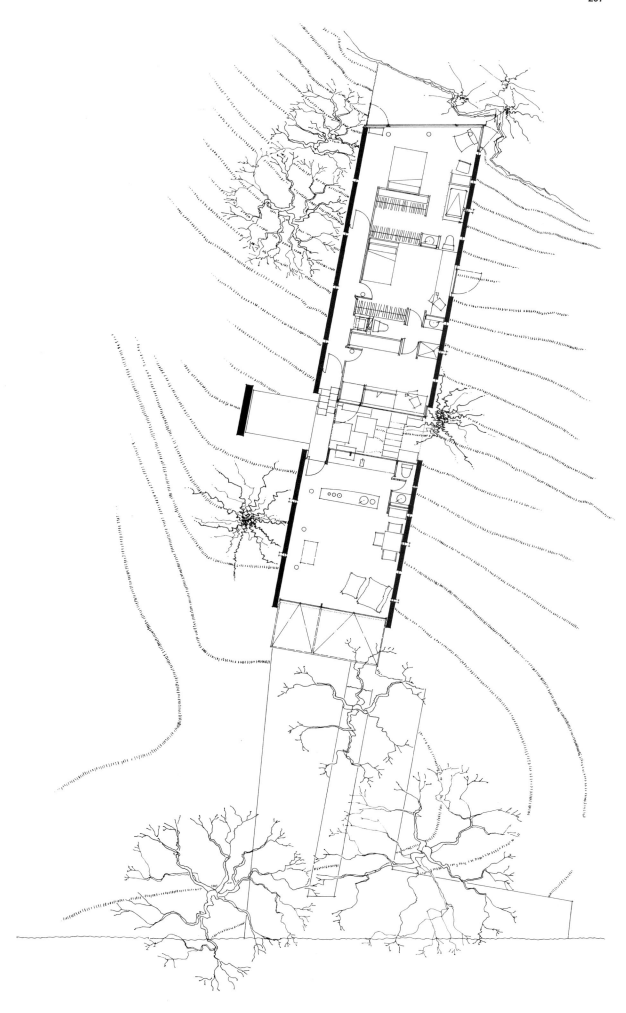

projects **Can Lis and Can Feliz**

location near Porto Petro, Majorca
Spain
date commissioned dates 1971 and 1994
architect Jørn Utzon

construction sub-contracted under architect's direct supervision
area both approximately 150m² (1,615 sq ft) enclosed space
cost not available

These two houses need to be examined together because Can Feliz is an evolution of the earlier and more experimental Can Lis. The formative ideas behind Utzon's first house on Majorca were first tested in an unbuilt project for a house that he planned to build for himself and his family at Bayview, Sydney, soon after he moved to Australia in March 1963 in order to work more intensively with the ongoing design for the Sydney Opera House. In collaboration with the firm Ralph Symonds Ltd, which was making prototypes for the proposed plywood acoustic shells for the two auditoria of the partially completed building, Utzon had mock-ups made of some U-shaped prefabricated plywood roof elements which could span up to 12 metres (39 feet). In the sketches of this project, Utzon shows these units apparently floating over a highly articulated podium of different levels and supported by flank walls.[1] Utzon was never able to realize this house and left Australia in April 1968 following his dispute over the design of the interiors of the Opera House, including the ply shells. However, in 1969 he designed and oversaw the construction of an experimental school project at Herning, Denmark, using prefabricated building elements to achieve extraordinary visual complexity and a variety of forms with a limited range of elements. He termed this design approach 'additive architecture'.[2]

Both Can Lis and Can Feliz are geometrically ordered around a construction system which comprises local sandstone walls or columns supporting closely spaced precast concrete beams, between which span narrow terracotta vaults. The vaulting, together with the patterning of the stone floors, is used in both houses to articulate the spaces and create either a sense of movement or one of containment. In both houses the glazing is set onto the outside of openings in the walls, or rebated directly into the stone, so that no frame is visible from the inside; a device used by Sigurd Lewerentz with whose work Utzon is well acquainted. External joinery is set flush with the stonework, which has deliberately crude flush mortar joints.

Can Lis is set on a terrace next to a 20 metre- (65 foot-) high cliff overlooking the sea on the south-east coast of the island. Four separate pavilions linked by courts are aligned to the edge of the cliff and are accessed from the land side through pine trees. Views of the sea are focused through lens-like stone reveals that act as foils to the otherwise orthogonal planning of each pavilion. The internal accommodation is highly prescriptive in terms of use, with most of the furniture being built-in and formed in stone with highly glazed tiles in very dark blue, sandstone and white arranged in patterns of prismatic geometries.

left Can Lis, here seen from the coast, is a powerful example of what Siegfrid Giedion called 'critical regionalism'.

below A sectional elevation with the access road to the left and the sea to the right, below the cliff.

bottom A plan of the courtyard and four pavilions, from left: courtyard, kitchen/ dining room, living room, bedrooms and guest rooms.

Each of the pavilions conforms to a distinct typology of forms and functions: the kitchen/dining building is located on one side of a terrace flanked by two covered colonnades, while the living room is a double-height volume with a semi-circle of fixed seating at its centre. The third pavilion has two bedrooms situated either side of a court and the fourth, which is a guest suite and study, is an autonomous unit. Movement between the pavilions is through the courts which are themselves conceived as outside rooms to which the internal spaces are subordinate. The overall composition, combined with the limited palette of materials, gives the whole complex an archetypical quality with both art historical and transcultural references. Originally, the house did not have mission tiles on the parapets and had an even more elemental appearance than it has today.

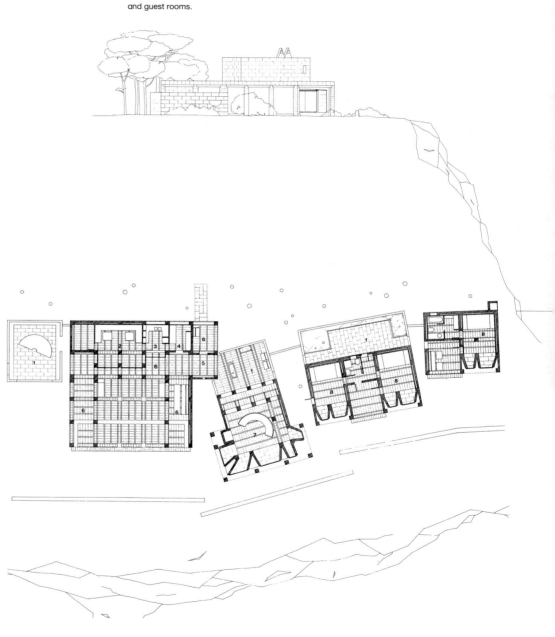

left The living room with built-in furniture: the glass is fixed directly to the external face of the openings in the stonework so that from inside the windows appear unglazed.

above A series of photographs showing the sequential elements of construction of the roofs of both houses.

The tiles on Can Feliz play a more dominant role and are visible on the predominantly pitched roofs, which in combination with the stepped parapets are reminiscent of Utzon's courtyard houses in Helsingør from 1958 with their overt references to ancient Chinese monastic architecture. In Can Feliz, Utzon has abandoned the radical planning of his most esoteric of houses and opted for a more unified massing of form organized around one large central court which overlooks a swimming pool. The house is set on a thickly wooded slope but in sight of the sea. The changes in level in the terrain appear in the split section of the living room and on the cascading terraces with their intricate series of both covered and open spaces. Although the built area is large at between 400–500 metres (1,300–1,600 feet) squared, only a third of this comprises enclosed rooms. Can Feliz was formed through the process of daily design decisions made on site as the building progressed with constant adjustments and corrections. The final drawings in so far as they exist are surveys of decisions already made by a series of far more immediate responses to the particularities of the site, the light and the views.

left Can Feliz is on a remote and peaceful wooded site up in the hills, overlooked by a fourteenth-century castle, in contrast to Can Lis which now has a Club Med as a neighbour.

top right The pool at Can Feliz. Adjacent to it is the place that Utzon most favours for contemplation.

right A plan of Can Feliz: only one third of the built area is made up of enclosed rooms.

This more informal approach is also reflected in the lack of built-in furniture; and although the plan still appears functionally prescriptive, the major spaces are less hierarchical than in Can Lis and consistently orthogonal. The arrangement of spaces has much in common with some of the variants that Utzon illustrated for his proposed Espansiva catalogue of housing designed between 1967 and 1970. This was a modular building system based on historical precedents, particularly from Far Eastern domestic architecture. Utzon's long search to reveal archetypical form and then elaborate particular discoveries as responses to particular places, links his work from the mid-1950s through to the completion of Can Feliz in 1994, by way of the most iconic building of the twentieth century, the Sydney Opera House. Following his resignation from that project he travelled back to Denmark via Hawaii, Mexico and the United States, and from Yucatán he sent a postcard to his former principal assistant Bill Wheatland depicting a Mayan Temple and bearing the message 'The ruins are wonderful so why worry? Sydney Opera House becomes a ruin one day'.[3] Can Feliz already embraces this fate with optimism – its name means 'happy'.

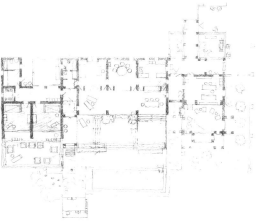

project **Rudin house**

location Leymen
Haut Rhin
France

date commissioned 1997

architect **Herzog & de Meuron**

construction main contractor
area 160m² (1,722 sq ft)
cost 300,000 FF

above and right Superficially conventional, the house appears to be a northern European archetype (above), but closer inspection reveals the house to be on *piloti* with the entry from underneath (right).

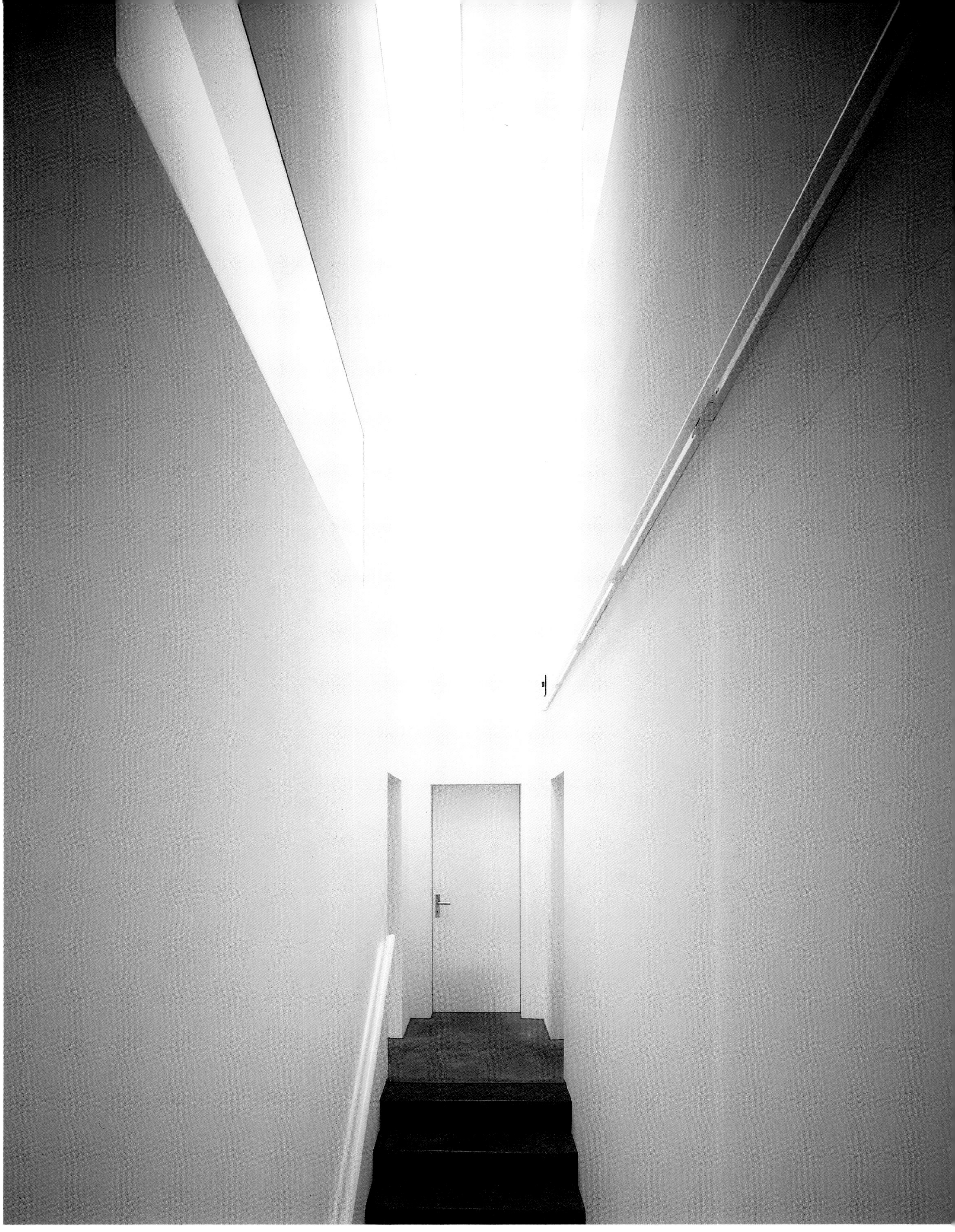

How can this house be experimental? It is an attempt at the transformation of the mythologies of ordinary domestic architecture into the realm of the extraordinary through an intense engagement in architecture's own internal discourses. Roland Barthes, in his essay *Myth Today* (1957), defined myth as the transformation of meaning into form and proposes the following methodology for its exposure as a false consciousness: 'Truth to tell, the best weapon against myth is perhaps to mythify it in its turn, and to produce an *artificial myth*: and this reconstituted myth will in fact be a mythology'.[1] The Rudin house attempts to strip the accepted signs of 'houseness' – their signifying power through irony and inversion – and as such is an exercise in mannerism: the reworking of an established language of forms, compositions and conventions with the aim of exceeding its apparent limitations.

With its roof steeply pitched over a simple rectangular volume, the house refers to an archetypical Northern European model, except that it sits on four columns, one at each corner, and appears to float above the landscape on *piloti* in the manner required by one of Le Corbusier's five principles. Materially, the house appears as if external finishes have been omitted: its external walls of mass *in situ* cast concrete are patterned with a matrix of pour joints, and the roof is finished in felt with prominent joint lines at regular intervals as if detailed as an expensive more permanent covering. The gutters are indented into the roof just above the eaves to allow the basic form to be monolithic with no projections. Internally, the walls are insulated, lined and finished in soft yellow ochre with heavy blue drapes over the windows set in flush ceiling-mounted tracks.

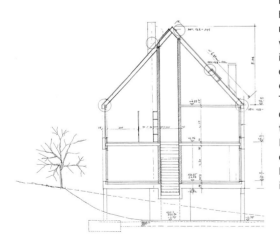

The house sits on a gently sloping site of fruit trees and meadow grass. It has an elevated base, cantilevered out at both gable wall ends. To the east, the direction of approach, this slab forms a shallow pool fed by rainwater from the gutters above, and to the west it provides a terrace overlooking the distant hills. Entry is from underneath via a concrete stair protruding from a door-width slot which is just off the axis of symmetry. This leads to a small entry platform set four steps lower than the living room, which allows an interval in the ascent and gives emphasis to the transition from the compressive experience of the undercroft, to the expansive experience of the living/dining room with its wide low-silled panoramic windows.

Although none of the rooms are spatially exceptional, each has its own distinct characteristic and scale. Again, in another inversion, the bathroom along with the mezzanined master bedroom, has the highest ceiling, thereby disrupting the conventional hierarchies of domestic space. All the principal rooms adjoin the main stair, which is in a top-lit space 1.2 metres (4 feet) wide and 10 metres (33 feet) high protected by, and enclosed within, the surrounding rooms. Although the organization of the house appears to be aimed at minimal circulation on functionalist planning principles, the staircase is the focus of the spatial dynamic of the entire house.

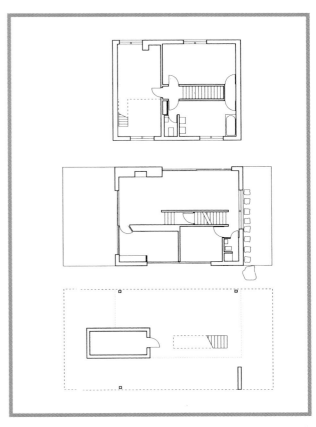

left At one end of the house the projected floor slab forms a shallow pool, at the other a terrace.

above From bottom: ground-, first- and second-floor plans.

project **Stretto House**

location Dallas
Texas
USA

date commissioned 1992

architect Steven Holl Architects

construction main contractor
area 700m² (7,535 sq ft)
cost undisclosed

In the introduction to the book on his own work, *Intertwining* (1996), Steven Holl writes: 'Architecture must remain experimental and open to new ideas and aspirations. In the face of tremendous conservative forces that constantly push it towards the already proven, already built, and already thought, architecture must explore the not-yet felt.'[1] The methodology he used to make his own philosophy manifest in the case of the Stretto House, was to create form as an analogy to music and by employing the laws of geometry and proportion in relation to the specifics of the site itself.

The trajectory of the history of architecture has been a gradual moving away from any underlying concept of universal order, towards either a complete denial of such a possibility, or a subjective and highly individual interpretation of any theory of form. A cursory study of the significant structures of antiquity shows them all to be proportioned to strict geometric principles, and this phenomenon has existed from before Pythagoras to the sixteenth and seventeenth centuries. Rudolph Wittkower has shown that Andrea Palladio's plans, for example, were all based in part on the small integral numbers of the Greek musical scale.[2] In the twentieth century, the composer Iannis Xenakis, while working with Le Corbusier on numerous projects including La Tourette, used his knowledge of music to further develop the Modular system of proportioning.

At the start of the Stretto House project, Holl was involved in the selection of the site, and advised proceeding with one which included a stream and three concrete dams and ponds. The overlapping of the ponds suggested an analogy with the musical concept of 'stretto' which means in this sense the intensification of emotional tension through the overlapping of the instruments as they play their individual pieces. A particular composition was chosen as the most appropriate musical reference – *Music for Strings, Percussion and Celeste* written in 1936 by the radical Hungarian composer Béla Bartók. Its four movements each have a distinct division into two modes of heavy percussion and light strings. The house correspondingly has four sections each comprising a heavy masonry 'space dam' made of ground-faced concrete blocks and an adjoining light steel-framed metal clad roof. The emphasis in the treatment of the floor planes, which visually overlap as they change level, and in the use of cast glass and *in situ* terrazzo, is one of fluidity. Bartók is known to have used the Fibonacci series as a way to structure the significant turning points in the piece – the numbers in the sequence 1, 1, 2, 3, 5, 8, 13, 21, 34 and so on form an unending series in which each number is the sum of the previous two. Successive pairs of numbers further up the scale approach the golden section ratio of 1 to 1.618.

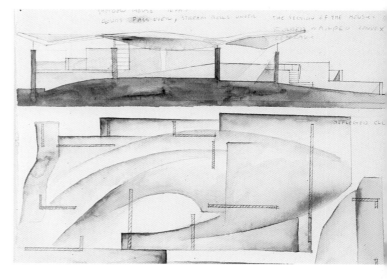

The rooms are organized in a linear sequence leading from the entrance hall, with each successive section of house following the natural contours of the site in a gradual decent. The proportions are based on the golden section ratio and the plan, which is orthogonal, is spatially differentiated from the section which is predominantly curvilinear. The termination of the sequence is an empty room, flooded by one of the existing ponds against which it abuts. The polarities of heavy/light and orthogonal/curvilinear are carried through into the detailing so that the generative ideas do not remain abstract but can be directly experienced as real phenomena.

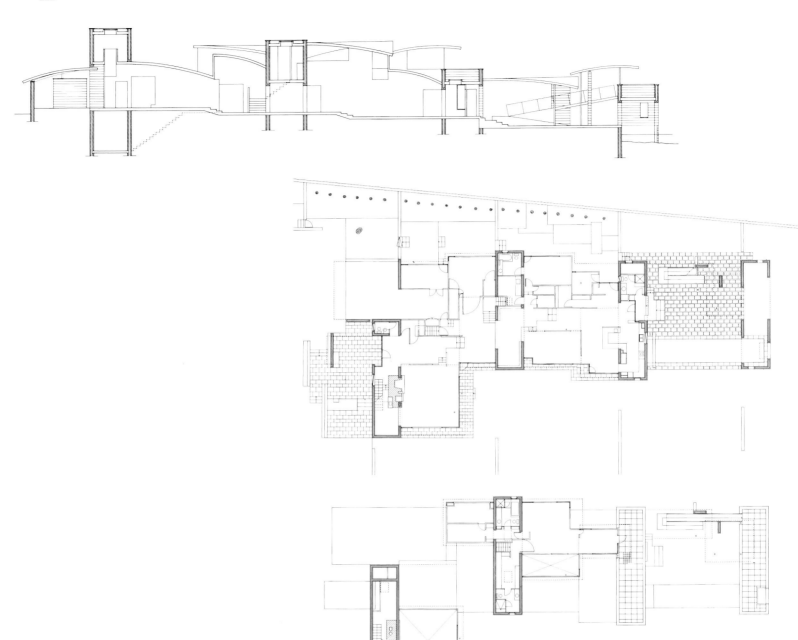

above A section showing the sequence of orthogonal and curvilinear forms.

right From top: ground- and first-floor plans: the entrance is to the left, with the flooded room on the far right.

far right The proportioning system of the house is continued even in the smallest of details, such as the kitchen units.

above The house seen from the end court next to the pool.

right The pool with the flooded room beyond.

far right An isometric diagram shows the organizing principles of the house.

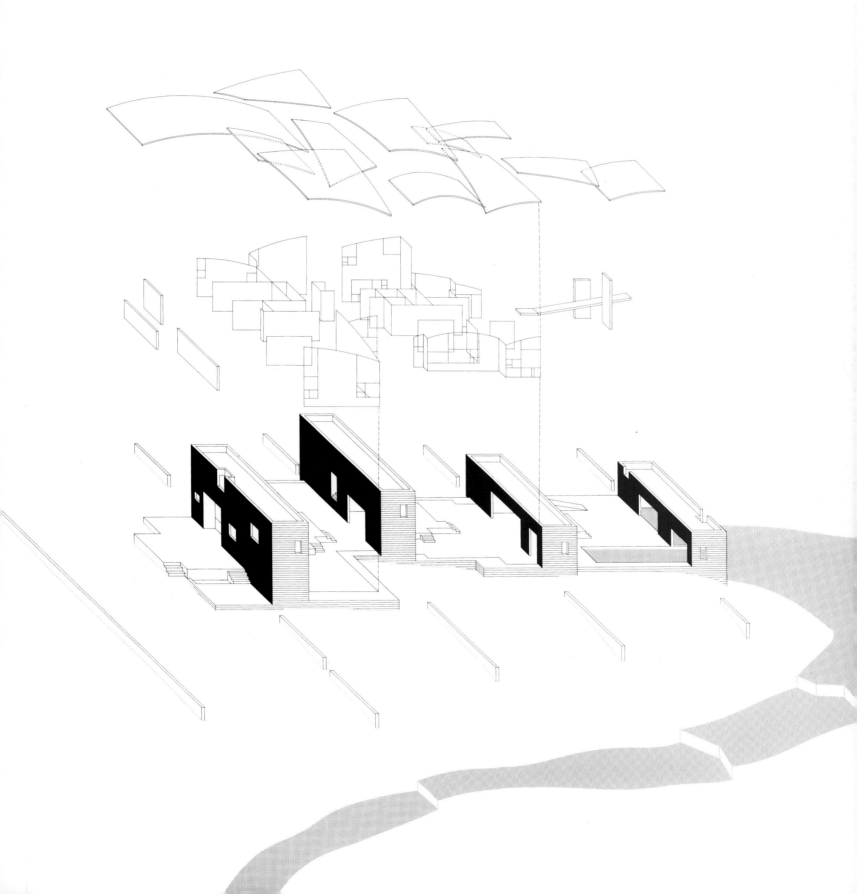

project **Crosby Hall**

location London
UK
date commissioned 1997
architect **Carden & Godfrey Architects**

construction main contractor with specialist nominated sub-contractors
approximate area 3,700m² (39,826 sq ft)
cost £5 million (shell only)

Crosby Hall once formed part of Crosby Place in the City of London, the mediaeval residence of a rich wool merchant. On Sir John Crosby's death in 1475, Crosby Hall in Bishopsgate was a typical mediaeval town house with a great hall, a courtyard and a parlour, but it was unusual because of its size and nearly matched the king's own palace at Eltham in scale. After a complex history including extensive fire damage in 1675, the Hall was finally moved in 1910 to its present site on the Chelsea Embankment overlooking the River Thames and set in a remaining fragment of the garden of a house once inhabited by Sir Thomas More. During the twentieth century various attempts were made to complete the project by creating a quadrangle on the vacant part of the site and to give the Hall a more appropriate context. The Hall itself, rebuilt in brick rather than the original rag stone, was located on the east of the site at right angles to the embankment. In 1925, Walter Godfrey, founder of the present architects' practice, designed the still existing North Wing using an aesthetic heavily influenced by the Tudor style as reinterpreted by the Arts and Crafts movement. In 1955, Carden, Godfrey and Macfadyen added a further building, this time with no attempt at historical referencing, but this has been demolished in order that this recent project could attempt a synthesis of the remaining disparate elements into a coherent whole. The client, the speculator Christopher Moran, wanted to create a London mansion which would provide the setting for his extensive collection of Tudor and Jacobean furniture. Completion of the courtyard required the construction of a fictive history using architectural elements from a narrow and targeted range of English styles.

A new riverfront block of predominantly two storeys forms a main entrance to an inner court; the detailing is essentially Tudor, in hand-made brick with carved stone window surrounds and parapets. The formal composition is only rendered asymmetric from the river by virtue of the elaborate chimney stacks. Godfrey's original North Wing has been remodelled externally, particularly on the attic floor, but his designs for the first and second floor windows have been reproduced elsewhere in order to unify the overall fenestration. The internal elevations of the new sections of the courtyard are more overtly classical in their references and therefore less specifically English.

Crosby Hall does not attempt authenticity in terms of structure and services and the architects make no apologies for this. Behind the solid masonry is an insulated cavity and an inner lining of blockwork. The clay tiled roofs are supported by steel trusses. The floors are *in situ* cast concrete slabs which span unsupported between external walls and allow for the flexible planning of the as yet unbuilt interiors. In the basement are an extensive underground parking area and the vacant volume of a future swimming pool. Awaiting its projected £35 million interior fit-out, Crosby Hall remains an uncompleted experiment in the production of a fictive building history using authentic references, crafts and skills only in so far as they support a visual and tactile experience.

far left Drawing by Russell Taylor showing the Tudor sources of the architectural vocabulary.

top left Riverfront with Crosby Hall at the centre.

top right The colonnade to the inner court is more overtly classical.

above An aerial perspective. The new buildings are bottom left and right.

below A cross section with the courtyard elevation of the colonnade. The original hall is on the left.

project **house near Bordeaux**

location Floirac
Bordeaux
France

date commissioned 1998

architect **OMA/Rem Koolhaas**

construction main contractor
area 500m² (5,382 sq ft) with 100m² (1,076 sq ft) guest suite
cost undisclosed

right The entry court: the house has its own traffic circle.

Entry to this house, which overlooks the city of Bordeaux from a hill, is via a 400 metre- (1,312 foot-) long access road through a lightly wooded and gently sloping site which is part of the garden to an old mansion. The house is built just off the apex of the hill with its entry court and ground floor being partially excavated into the earth: hence on arrival through the enclosing perimeter wall and up the entry ramp, all views of the distant landscape are withheld and an essentially urban environment presented, the size of which is defined largely by the turning radius of a car. The guest suite is a conventionally planned single-storey volume forming the south edge of the court and divided in two in order to accommodate some existing trees. The three-storey volume of the house itself opposite reveals its three-part organization on the court façade.

The lowest level, accessed by an automatically sliding aluminium door, contains the kitchen, dining and media spaces, while deeper into the plan, in cave-like spaces within the hill, are the service rooms and the wine cellar. There are three stairs ascending from this floor: a spiral directly from the media space to the children's bedrooms on the top floor, a grotto-like stair near the front door which leads back up to the open terrace above, and a straight flight off the dining area leading to the main living space on the upper ground floor. In the elevated protecting volume of the bedroom floor, the children's and parents' rooms are separated by an open void which only allows visual connection through semi-obscured glass. The entire volume is contained within a cast concrete box which is supported at only three points: the external wall of the spiral stair to the east, and an asymmetrically loaded beam at the west with both an external and internal column. A roof-mounted steel beam over the spiral stair counteracts the overturning moment of this mass and has an exposed steel tension rod connecting it to the ground in the entry court. The porthole windows are not random but located to focus on particular views, and set at three specific heights: 1.65 metres (5 feet 4 inches), 1.20 metres (4 feet) and 0.75 metres (2 feet 6 inches) to correspond to eye level when standing, sitting in a chair and lying down on a bed.

Between these upper and lower floors is the fully glazed living room with its adjoining covered terrace of travertine marble. The aluminium sheet flooring of this space, with its reflections of the cast concrete ceiling above, extends beyond the line of the glazing to the terrace and the lawn, blurring the distinction between inside and outside. This ambiguity is further enhanced by the north glazed façade which slides back to open up the living room to the lawn and the hill beyond, while simultaneously, by virtue of its position, shielding the terrace.

Linking all three floors is an open 3 x 3.5 metres (10 x 11 feet) elevator platform, supported at its centre by a hydraulic piston and top-lit by an identically sized skylight. Fitted out as a study, this platform, with its elaborate system of sliding or hinged glass balustrades and moving railings, can become part of any of the principal rooms on all three levels of the house. Adjacent to the elevator is a single wall of shelves, 8 metres (26 feet) high, which contains the books and artwork of the wheelchair-bound father of the family.

Using the themes of mobility and inversion, Koolhaas has rendered the owner's disability the normal condition within the house. When the elevator is absent from a particular floor, it becomes dysfunctional to some degree – a state which is at its most extreme on the ground floor, where the wine cellar is isolated beyond the chasm of the hydraulics pit until the arrival of the elevator platform from above.

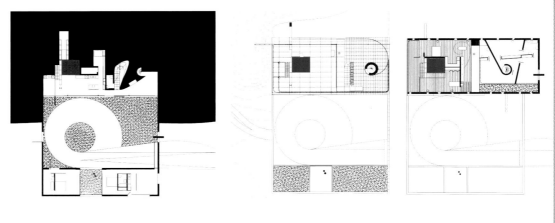

top The living room seen from the garden. The bedroom floor above has only three points of support.

above From left: lower ground floor with entry court and guest wing, upper ground floor and first floor. The red area on each plan denotes the elevator platform.

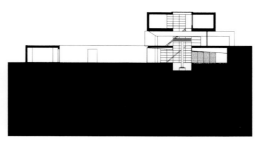

top left The living room with the elevator parked on the bedroom floor above and the wall of shelves to the right.

bottom left The cave-like stair leading from the TV room to the open terrace above.

left Cross section showing the elevator marked in red. Floors become dysfunctional when the elevator is absent.

following pages Three levels of the house seen from the court. The living space occupies the 'zone of pressure' in the middle.

Project credits

apartment block
Innsbruck, Austria
Architects: Kathan-Schranz-Strolz.
Project team: Armin Kathan, Martin
Schranz, Erich Strolz, Helmut Hofer,
Christof Hrdlovics, Ferdinand Reiter,
Sibylle Schwarzmann. Client:
Errichtergemeinschaft Hottinger
au Innsbruck. Main contractor:
Fussenegger und Rummele.
Engineer: Ingo Gehrer. Services:
Huter Vorfertigung. Electrical
consultant: M&S. Structural
consultant: Ingo Gehrer. Lighting,
glazing, flooring, special features:
Armin Kathan.

architect's house
Phoenix, Arizona, USA
Architect, interior designer and
general contractor: Wendell Burnette.
Clients: Wendell and Debra Burnette.
Structural engineers: Caruso Turley,
Scott Consulting Structural Engineers.
Mechanical engineer: Otterbein
Engineering. Electrical engineer:
CA Energy Designs. Landscape
design: Burnette Landscape Design,
Debra Burnette. Furnishings and
storage: Built in by the architect.
Doors and hardware: Custom-made
by the architect. Fixtures: Grohe
and Kohler.

architect's house
Ziegelried, Switzerland
Architect and client: Elemer Zalotay.
Main contractor: Aschwanden
Co. Willbrand.

architect's father's house
Motiti Island, New Zealand
Architect/builder: Anthony Hoete.
Client: Aubrey Hoete. Builder:
Graham Hoete. Main contractor:
Hoete Whanau. Environmental
consultant: Isabelle Adams.

architect's mother's house
Plymouth, UK
Architect: Alex de Rijke. Project team:
Victoria, Ralph and Hugo de Rijke.
Client: Lena de Rijke. Engineering
consultant: Chris Wise. Installation:
BTC Plymouth.

Art house
London, UK
Architect: Brookes, Stacey, Randall.
Project team: Michael Stacey, Nik
Randall (Project Directors), Paul
Voysey (Project Architect), Beverley
Dockray, Emily Bryant, Cody Gaynor,
Nick Vaughn. Client: withheld. Main
Contractor: Delcon Construction Ltd.
Engineers: Michael Baigent, Orla Kelly.
Mechanical and electrical engineer:
Max Fordham and Partners.
Landscape Advisor: Christopher
Bradley-Hole. Planning supervisor:
Hannah Reed. Quantity surveyor:
Dearle & Henderson. Custom-made
items (water spout, fibre optic shower,
circular bath, fitted furniture, bed etc.):
Brookes, Stacey, Randall. Windows:
Velfac. Hi-Fi and IT: Naim. Stone:
Stoneage. Glass: F.A. Firman Ltd.
Blinds: ESB. Joinery: Paul Longpre.
Specialist plasterwork: Atelier Pierre
Bonnefille. Leather floor and boxes:
Bill Amberg. Glass stair: Brookes
Stacy Randall. Door furniture:
Allgood. Wall lights: Kreon UK Ltd.
Skylights: Vitral UK Ltd. Sliding/folding
Doors: HJSJ. Steelwork: Manico
Contracts Ltd.

Aura house
Tokyo, Japan
Architect: F.O.B. Association.
Project team: Katsu Umebayashi
(Principal), Kazuo Kobayashi. Client:
withheld. Structural engineer:
Toshiaki Yamamoto/SD Room.
Main contractor: Kimi Kensetsu.
Services: Kowa Kogyo. Electrical
consultant: Hayama Denki Kogyo.
Tent roof: Taiyo Kogyo. Kitchen:
Shigeru Kogyo. Custom steel sash
windows: Kimi Kensetsu. Concrete
supplier: Tekkin Concrete.

Bo Klok housing
Sweden
Architect: Ahlström Arkitektbyrå.
Client: N/A. Project team: Gun
Ahlström; Inger Olssen (Skanska);
Madeleine Nobs (IKEA). Main
contractor: Skanska AB.
Sub-contractor: Myresjohus AB.

Can Lis and Can Feliz
Majorca, Spain
Architect: Jørn Utzon.

Convent Avenue studios
Tucson, Arizona, USA
Architect: Rick Joy. Project team:
Rick Joy (Principal), Holly Damerell
(Intern Architect), Franz Buhler
(Construction Supervisor). Client:
R.J. Brezer. Structural engineer:
M.R. Behnejad, P.E. Southwest
Structural Engineers, Inc. Mechanical
and plumbing engineer: Roy T.
Otterbein. Walls and foundations:
Quentin Branch, Rammed Earth Solar
Homes, Inc. Carpentry: Franz Buhler.
Adobe restoration and plastering:
Tony Guzman. Floors and showers:
Steve Lambach Electric; Benchmark
Concrete. Plumbing: Bud Brown
Plumbing. Suppliers: Arizona Glass
and Mirror; Able Refrigeration;
Exquisite Floor Design. Furnishings:
Max Gottschaulk (Pretzel chairs,
K bar stool, K dining chairs); Gergo
Bellolli (black leather sling chairs).
Fittings: Rick Joy.

co-operative housing
Hjulby Hegn, Denmark
Architects: Arkitektgruppen Aarhus.
Project team: Lars Due,
Michael Harrebek, Ole Nielsson,
Erling Stadager, Helge Tindal. Client:
Boligforeningen af 1983, Aarhus Nord.
Engineer: Abrahamsen & Nielsen A/S;
Radgivende Ingeniorer. Landscape
architect: Arkitektgruppen i Aarhus
K/S. Architectural assistants:
Per Christensen, Per Feldthaus.

Craven Road house
Toronto, Canada
Architect and interior designer:
Shim-Sutcliffe Architects. Project
team: Brigitte Shim, Howard Sutcliffe
(Principals), Donald Chong. Client:
Robert Hill. Structural engineer:
Onen & Hayda. Specialist consultants:
Radiant City Millworks (custom
windows and millwork). Building:
Ptarmigan Construction.

Crosby Hall
London, UK
Architect: Carden & Godfrey
Architects. Project architect: Russell
Taylor. Client: Christopher Moran.
Structural engineer: Cameron Taylor
Bedford. Quantity surveyor: Kensalls
Ltd. Stonework and carving: Cathedral
Works Organisation (Chichester) Ltd.
Additional carving: Dick Reid. Glazing:
Bernard Becker Studios Ltd. Ironwork:
Charles Normandale. Oak: Henry
Venables Ltd. Bricks: Lamb's Bricks
and Arches. Tiles: Keemer Tiles Ltd.

Double House or Villa KBWW
Utrecht, The Netherlands
Architects: de architectengroep.
rijnboutt ruijssenaars hendriks van
gameren mastenbroek bv: Bjarne
Mastenbroek with Floor Arons and
Michiel Raaphorst
AND: MVRDV: Winy Maas, Jacob van
Rijs, Nathalie de Vries with Mike Booth
and Joost Glissenaar. Client: withheld.
Main contractor: Tiggelman bv,
Spaarndam. Structure: AVT Velp.
Building physics: DGMR, Arnhem.

Ecohouse 99
Skejby, Denmark
Architect: Tegnestuen Vandkunsten.
Main contractor: H. Hoffmann &
Soenner A/S Region Bord (main
structure, brickwork and electrics).
Engineering: Dominia AS. Indoor
climate consultants: Danish Institute of
Biomedicine. Water recycling
consultants: Danish Rootzone
Technique. Carpentry: Egil Rasmussen
A/S. Roofing: Hetag Tagdaekning A/S.
Smith work and plumbing: Fredriks
Smede-og Maskinforretning.
Glazing: FP Alu-glas A/S.
Paintwork: Miljoemaleren.
Hard and soft landscaping:
Anders Andeersens Anlaegsgartneri.
Concrete: A/S Boligbeton. Windows:
Velfac A/S. Doors: Jutlandia Doere
A/S. Folding doors and walls: Flexi
A/S. Kitchen: Befas Koekkener A/S.
Technical control equipment: Saas
Instruments A/S.

Emscher Park housing
Gelsenkirchen, Germany
Architects: Szyszkowitz & Kowalski.
Project team: Gerald Wratschko
(Project Architect); Robert Kropf,
Manfred Suanjak (CAD), Kurt Fandler,
Christian Heim, Zeljka Hajsok-Monic,
Alois Senfter, Elke Schmitter.
General entrepreneur: Peter Bauwens
Bauunternehmung. Clients: Stadt
Gelsenkirchen Philipp Hausbau
GmbH, Heidemann Bau GmbH,
Gemeinnutzige Wohnungsgenossen-
schaft Gelsenkirchen und
Watternscheid EG, Treuhandstelle
GmbH, Ruhr Lippe Wohnungs-
gesellschaft + Landesentwicklungs-
gesellschaft Nordrhein-Westfalen
GmbH; Bau und Grund Immodbilien
GmbH. Structural engineer:
Duro DI Wilhelm Duffel; Di Egon
Herms; Ingenieurburo Di Dieter Lingau;
Sigenieurburo Thomas Kaader.
Service engineer: Concepts
Kommunikations und Gebaudetechnik.
Energy consultant: Ingenieurburo
INCO. Green space planning: Buro
für Orts und Landschaftsplanung.

Kindergarten:
Architects: Szyszkowitz & Kowalski.
Project Team: Gerald Wratschko
(Project Architect), Manfred Suenjak
(CAD), Christian Heim, Kurt Fandler,
Zeljka Hajsok-Momic, Rudolf Manzl.
General entrepreneur: TE_Bau
Bocholt. Client: Stadt Gelsenkirchen.

farmhouse extensions
St Martin an der Raab,
Burgenland, Austria
Design: Walter Pichler. Construction: specialist sub-contractor.

Grania Oi
Findhorn, Scotland
Architect: Nicole Edmonds/EDGE Architecture and Design. Project team: Nicole Edmonds. Client: Auriol de Smidt. Main contractor: Findhorn Foundation. Building consultant: Philip Stewart. Structural Engineer: Bryan Wright of Deeside Structural Design. Barrel/vat tensioning: Joseph Brown & Sons. Builders: Philip Stewart, Peter McKay, Marc Took-Zozoya. Plumbing: Kenny Paterson. Electrical consultant: Northern Lights. Stonework: Stuart Voder. Spiral stair: Philip Stewart, Andy Williams. Plasterwork: Keith Allen. Zinc roof: Philip Steward, Roger Doudna. Doors: Mike Carmell, Peter McKay. Kitchen joinery: Peter McKay & Richard Leigh. Suppliers: Dunedin Builders Merchants (zinc gutters); Joseph Brown & Son (steel tensioning band); Morrison Construction (concrete); System Platon (waterproofing); BI Moll & Klober Tyvek (building paper); Warmcel; Rockwood (insulation); Frenit (bitumen board); Rheinzink & Sogem (zinc); Moray Stone Cutters (sandstone); Hepworth (drainage).

Harris house
Mason's Bend, Alabama, USA
Designers/Builders: Rural Studio, Auburn University – Joe Alcock, David Austin, Cliff Brooks, Catherine Bunn, Bay Chapman, Josh Cooper, Joshua Daniel, Adam Gerndt, JoBeth Gleason, Robert S. Hill IV, Stephen Hoffmann, Charles Hughes, Jeff Johnston, Melissa Kearley, John Keener, Kristen Kepner, Jeffrey Marteski, Jeremy Moffett, Andrew Moore, Justin Patwin, Bryan Pearson, Michael Renauld, Tommy Replogle, John Ritchie, John Schuman, Nathan H. Simmons, Timothy Sliger, Michael Spinello, Robert Sproull, Elizabeth Stallworth, Ian Stewart, Todd Steward, Jon Tate, Melissa Teng, Jimmy D. Turner, John Waters, Samuel Watkins, Bill Whittaker, Jake Wiseman, Heather Wooten. Studio Critics: Richard Hudgens, Charles Jay, Samuel Mockbee, Michael Robinson, D.K. Ruth, Tinka Sack, Jeff Tate, Christian Trask. Client: Anderson Harris.

Hope House
East Molesey, Surrey, UK
Architect: Bill Dunster. Structural engineer: Mark Lovell. Environmental engineer: John White. Clerk of works: Sue Dunster.

house near Bordeaux
Floirac, France
Architect: Office for Metropolitan Architecture. Project team: Rem Koolhaas with Martin van Severen, Julien Monfort, Jeanne Gang, Bill Price, Jeroen Thomas, Yo Yamagata, Chris Dondrop, Erik Schotte, Vincent Costes. Client: withheld. Engineers: Ove Arup & Partners. Fitted furnishing and mobile platform: Maarten van Severen, Raf de Preter. Bookcase: Vincent de Rijk. Coordination and techinical assistance: Michael Regaud. Façade consultant: Robert-Jan van Santen. Hydraulics consultant: Gerard Couillandeau. Interior consultant: Petra Blaisse.

housing and commercial block
Cologne, Germany
Architect and planning: Brandlhuber & Kniess. Project team: Astrid Becker; Arno Brandlhuber; Markus Emde, Bernd Kniess, Andreas Laake. Client: Dr. Annemarie Keller. Glass design: Uwe Schnatz. Structure: Kiklasch. Glazing: Donges. Staircase: Brauckmann. Metalwork: Frobel. Rosengitter: Laboscha. Stone floors: Hentzschel. Wooden floors: Lutze & Törmer. Wooden terrace: Maks. Plasterwork: Mettelsiefen. Tiles: Goldbach. Electrical consultant: Rundholz. Sanitation: Holthausen. Skylight: Konrad.

housing and commercial block
Rathenow, Germany
Architect and interior designer: Architekten Prof. Klaus Sill, Architekt Dipl. Ing. Jochen Keim. Client: Rohwer Ingenieure Rathenow. Construction consultant: Rohwer Ingenieure. Ready-made containers: Fa. D. Rohde. Electrical installation of the containers: Elektro Oesser. Metalwork: Stahlbau Koch. Building construction: Fa. Walter Kunzel. Reinforced concrete sections: Fertigteilwerk. Woodwork and roofing: Weber Bau GmbH. Heating and plumbing: Fa Peetz. Electrical consultant: Frommer Elektrotechnik GmbH.

Kitagata apartments
Gifu Prefecture, Japan
Architect: Kazuyo Sejima & Associates. Client: Gifu Prefecture (Public Housing). General Coordinator: Arata Isozaki. General Contractor: Usami-Gumi. Structural Engineer: Gengo Matsui. Mechanical Engineer: Asano Setsubi. Structure: ORS.

Masgonty house
Saint Pardoux La Rivière, France
Architects: Anne Lacaton and Jean Philippe Vassal. Project team: Sylvain Menaud, Emmanuelle Delage. Client: Mme Masgonty. Main contractor: Brives Construction (skeleton frame, roofing, boarding, insulation). Aluminium works: Miroiterie 2000. Carpentry: Gerard Combeau. Systems: Beneyrol. Reinforced concrete slabs: Sol Charantais.

Master and Slave Unit mobile home
Otterlo
The Netherlands
Designer and all work: Atelier van Lieshout.

Mercaders building
Barcelona, Spain
Architects and interior designers: Enric Miralles, Benedetta Tagliabue. Clients: Enric Miralles, Benedetta Tagliabue. Main contractor: Tierra Y Mar SA. General contractor: Interabarca. Structural system/metal: Esteve Miret, Estmart. Landscape architects: Jardineria Moix, Enric Miralles, Benedetta Tagliabue. Quantity surveyor: Jordi Altes. Structure: R. Brufau. Wood carpenter: J. Figueras.

Nautilus Earthship
Taos, New Mexico, USA
Architect: Michael Reynolds (Principal), Solar Survival International. Client: James Wells.

Open City
Valparaiso, Chile
Members of the Open City co-operative.

Pacemaker
UK
Designers: Birds Portchmouth Russum.

paper log house for disaster relief
Kobe, Japan
Architect: Shigeru Ban. Project team: Shigeru Ban, Takashi Nakagawa, Masao Suzuki, Kitayama Souzou, Kenkuo Sho. Client: Nippon Shinpan. Main contractor: Normura Kougei. Structural engineer: Gengo Matsui; Hoshin Structural Engineering Studio. Sub-contractors: Sanshin Daikin Kisetsu (air-conditioning); Takeomi Industry (plumbing installation); Uemura Denki (electricity).

Pen-y-Lyn
Crymych, Pembrokeshire,
Wales, UK
Architect and all work: Christopher Day.

photographer's retreat
Foxhall, Northamptonshire, UK
Architect: Níall McLaughlin. Clients: Geof Rayner & Gina Glover. Structural engineer: Tony Hayes. Builder: Simon Storey. Furnishing and lighting design: Níall McLaughlin.

Round House
near Newport, Pembrokeshire,
Wales, UK
Architect and all work: Tony Wrench.

Rudin house
Leymen, France
Architect: Herzog & de Meuron Architekten AG. Project team: Jacques Herzog (Partner-in-Charge); Pierre de Meuron; Lukas Bogli (Project Architect). Client: Hanspeter Rudin. Structural engineers: H. P. Frei, Bauingenieur Basel; F. Mannel.

S-house
Okayama Prefecture, Japan
Architect: Kazuyo Sejima and Ryue Nishizawa. Client: withheld. General Contractor: Matsumoto Corporation. Structural engineer: ORS Office. Mechanical engineer: System Design.

solar studio house
Rieselfeld, Germany
Architect and building technology: Prof. Thomas Spiegelhalter. Project team: Spiegelhalter-Schreiber. Clients: Families Schreiber, Mahlstedt, Vrbnak, Stifflers. Civil engineer: Ingenieurbuero Egloff & Rheinberger. Thermal solar system: European Solar Projects. Photovoltaic and thermal solar systems: FEW; LAKRA.

Spiral apartment building
Ramat-Gan, Israel
Architect: Zvi Hecker. Project team: Gil Bernstein, Shmuel Groberman, Rina Hering. Client: Ezra Mualem. Main contractor and structural engineer: Jaakov Hai.

summer house
Risør, Norway
Architect: Carl-Viggo Hølmebakk. Client: withheld. Building statics and civil engineering: Terje Orlien. Main carpenter: Reidar Ornvik. Prefabricated wooden structure: Risør Trevare. Doors and windows: Terje Lindahl. Interior fittings: Aagaards Snekkerverksted. Masonry: Jan Tore Solheim. Zinc roof tinsmith work: Rune Nilsen. Electric installations: Torskeberg elektriske.

Stretto House
Dallas, Texas, USA
Architect: Steven Holl Architects. Project team: Steven Holl (Principal), Adam Yarinsky (Project Architect), Peter Lynch, Bryan Bell, Matthew Karlen, William Wilson, Stephen Cassell, Kent Hikida, Florian Schmidt, Thomas Jenkinson, Lucinda Knox. Client: withheld. Main contractor: Thomas S. Byrne Construction. Consulting architect: Max Levy, Dallas. Landscape consultant: King's Creek Landscaping. Structural consultant: Datum Engineering. Mechanical consultant: Interfield Engineering.

Villa Vision
Taastrup, Denmark
Architects: Flemming Skude, Ivar Moltke, Bertel Jensen. Client: The Danish Institute of Technology. Collaborators: DTI Energi; DTI Traeteknik, Crone & Koch; Statens Byggeforskningsinstitut. Main contractors: Hojgaard & Schultz; Hovedstadens El-teknik A/S. Plumbing and sanitation: Dansk Olie-og Gasteknik. Ventilation: L. C. Service Glass. Roof: P. Jul Hansen. Glazing: Glarmestre Snoer & Sonner A/S. Electrical contractor: NESA A/S; Hovedstadens El-Teknik. Flooring: Tomrer & Byggetek. Painting: V.S. Larsen. Brickwork: Murermester J. E. Haar. Zinc work: Rheinzink DK. Carpets: Texfloor, GL. Sun shades: A/S Chr Fabers Fabriker. Carpentry: L.C. Service. Curtain fabrics: Kvadrat Boligtextiler A/S. Furnishings: Gorm Harkaer; Christian Woetmann; Unicum; Deichmann Planter; Cylindra as; Niels-Ole Zib; Unoform; Erik Jorgensen Mobelfabrik; Getama A/S; 7+7 Futon; Krea A/S; Magnus Olesen A/S; Soren Ulrik Petersen; IKEA.

Endnotes

Introduction

1 Figures taken from the United Nations Annual Bulletin of Housing and Building Statistics for Europe, 1998

2 Kuhn, Thomas S.: *The Structure of Scientific Revolutions*, 2nd edn (University of Chicago Press 1970)

3 Mumford, Lewis: *The City in History* (Martin, Secker, and Warburg 1961)

4 White, Llynn, Jr: *Mediaeval Technology and Social Change* (Oxford University Press 1962)

5 Jones, Roger and Penny, Nicholas: *Raphael* (Book Club Associates and Yale University Press 1983)

6 Hauser, Arnold: *The Social History of Art*, vol 2 (Routledge Kegan Paul 1962)

7 *Visionary Architects* (exhibition catalogue; University of St Thomas, Houston 1968)

8 Diderot, Denis: *A Pictorial Encyclopaedia of Trades and Industry* (reprint Dover Publications, Inc. 1959 and 1987)

9 Vidler, Anthony: *The Writing of the Walls* (Princeton Architectural Press 1987)

10 Davey, Peter: *Arts and Crafts Architecture* (Phaidon 1995). Pugin built over 100 buildings in a very short career. He was married three times and had eight children. On the subject of delegation Pugin once said, 'Clerk, my dear sir, clerk, never employ one, I should kill him in a week.'

11 Muthesius, Hermann: *Das englische Haus*, 3 vols (Wasmuth, Berlin, 1904/5; English edn, Crosby, Lockwood, Staples 1979)

12 Whyte, I. B.: *Bruno Taut and the Architecture of Activism* (Cambridge University Press 1982)

13 *Architecture as a Synthesis of the Arts: Lectures by Rudolf Steiner*, English trans. Christian Thal-Jantzen (Rudolf Steiner Press 1999)

14 El Lissitzky: *Russia: An Architecture for World Revolution* (Lund Humphries 1970)

15 Ford, Edward: *The Details of Modern Architecture*, vol 1 (Massachusetts Institute of Technology 1990)

16 van Duzer, L. and Klienman, K.: *Villa Müller: A Work of Adolf Loos* (Princeton Architectural Press 1994)

17 Benton, Tim: *The Villas of Le Corbusier, 1920–30* (Yale University Press 1987)

18 *Ibid.*

19 Vellay, M. and Frampton, K.: *Pierre Chareau: Architect and Craftsman* (Thames and Hudson 1985)

20 Laura Cohn: *The Door to a Secret Room* (Scolar Press 1999)

21 Barthes, Roland: *Mythologies* English edn (Jonathan Cape 1972)

22 Yorke, F.R.S.: *The Modern House* (Architectural Press 1957)

23 McCoy, Esther: *Case Study Houses*, 1945–62 (Hennessey and Ingalis 1977)

24 Gill, Brendon: *Many Masks – A Life of Frank Lloyd Wright* (Putman 1983)

25 Scully, Vincent: *The Shingle Style Today* (George Braziller 1974)

26 Frank Gehry quoted in *International Architect*, no 2 vol 1 issue 2 (1979)

27 Barthes, Roland: *op cit.*

28 Wigglesworth, Sarah and Till, Jeremy, eds: *Architecture and the Everyday* (Academy Editions, June 1998)

Chapter One

Introduction

1 Bachelard, Gaston: *The Poetics of Space* (Beacon Press 1969)

2 Jung, Carl Gustav: *Memories, Dreams, Reflections* (Random House 1961)

3 Oliver, Paul, ed.: *The Encyclopaedia of Vernacular Architecture of the World*, 3 vols (Cambridge University Press 1997)

Master + Slave Unit mobile home

1 Ballard, J.G.: *The Atrocity Exhibition* (Panther 1979)

2 Barthes, Roland: *Sade, Fourier, Loyola* (Hill & Wang 1976)

photographer's retreat

1 Benjamin, Walter: 'The Work of Art in the Age of Mechanical Reproduction', in *Illuminations* (Collins/Fontana 1973)

Chapter Two

Introduction

1 Vale, Brenda: *A History of the UK Temporary Housing Programme* (E. and F.N. Spon 1995)

2 Levy, Matthys and Salvadori, Mario: *Why Buildings Fall Down* (W. W. Norton and Company 1992)

Bo Klok housing

1 Simmel, Georg: *On Individuality and Social Forms* (University of Chicago Press 1971)

Chapter Three

Introduction

1 United Nations Annual Bulletin of Housing and Building Statistics for Europe, 1998 (*figures for France incomplete)

2 Brand, Stuart: *How Buildings Learn* (Viking Penguin 1994)

Chapter Four

Introduction

1 Goodman, David and Chard, Colin: *European Cities and Technology* (Open University 1999)

2 Roberts, Gerrylynn and Steadman, Philip: *American Cities and Technology* (Open University 1999)

3 Lubbock, Jules: *The Tyranny of Taste* (Yale University Press 1995)

S-house

1 Lao Tzu: *Tao Te Ching* (Penguin 1963)

Craven Road house

1 Bachelard, Gaston: *op cit.*

2 Canetti, Elias: *Auto da Fé* (Picador-Pan 1978)

Convent Avenue studios

1 Scully, Vincent: *Pueblo, Mountain, Village, Dance* (Thames and Hudson 1972)

Chapter Five

Introduction

1 Chandler, T. and Fox, G.: *Three Thousand Years of Urban Growth* (Academic Press 1974)

2 Mungall, Constance and McLaren, Digby J.: *Planet Under Stress* (Oxford University Press 1990)

Spiral apartment building

1 Barzel, Amnon: 'Zvi Hecker's Polyhedral Language', in *Architecture and Urbanism* (Nov 1980)

2 Hecker, Zvi: 'Islamic Patterns, Structures, Aqueducts and Spirals', in *Architecture and Urbanism* (Sept 1987)

Kitigata apartments

1 Marker, Chris: *Sans soleil*, video available from Conoisseur/Academy (Argus Films 1982)

2 interview in *Assemblage* 30

Chapter Six

Introduction

1 Figures from Energy Information Administration, www.eia.doe.gov

2 Figures from the BICEPS Module for Energy Management, BRE. UK. 1997.

3 Day, Christopher: *Places of the Soul* (Aquarian Press 1990)

Pen-y-Lyn

1 Day, Christopher: *Building with a Heart* (Green Books 1990)

Chapter Seven

Introduction

1 Mies van der Rohe, when trying to consolidate his practice work in the US after leaving Germany, is reported to have initially agreed to work for free with Dr Farnsworth, an offer that was later retracted when their relationship deteriorated so that unpaid fees became the subject of legal proceedings. See C. Reed: *Not at Home* (Thames and Hudson 1996)

2 Extreme examples of these fraught situations are legendary. For example in 1938 Alvar Aalto persuaded Harry and Marie Gullichsen to agree to a fundamental replanning of the Villa Mairea in Noormarkku, Finland, after foundations had been dug for an earlier arrangement with which he was dissatisfied. See Richard Weston: *Villa Mairea* (Phaidon 1992)

3 Giedion identified the major design characteristics of projects by this group as being: open ended planning; greater emphasis on the inter-relationship between building and landscape; the forceful use of the horizontal plane as a platform; sculptural tendencies and a strong relationship to the past. See Sigfried Giedion: *Space, Time, and Architecture*, 5th edn (Harvard University Press 1966

4 *Herzog and de Meuron, 1983–93* (El Croquís)

5 Holl, Stephen: *Intertwining: Projects 1989–95* (Princeton University Press 1996)

6 Berman, Marshall: *All That is Solid Melts into Air* (Verso Editions 1983). The title comes from the following passage in the *Communist Manifesto* by Karl Marx: 'All fixed, fast-frozen relations, with their train of ancient and venerable prejudices and opinions, are swept away, all new formed ones become antiquated before they can ossify. All that is solid melts into air, all that is holy is profaned, and men at last are forced to face... the real conditions of their lives, and their relations with their fellow men.'

Can Lis and Can Feliz

1 Drew, Philip: *The Masterpiece: Jørn Utzon – A Secret Life* (Hardie Grant 1999)

2 Utzon, Jørn: articles in *Zodiac*, 14 (1965) and *Arkitektur DK*, 1 (1970)

3 Fromonot, Françoise: *Jørn Utzon: The Sydney Opera House* (Elektra/Gingko 1998)

Rudin house

1 Barthes, Roland: *Mythologies* (Jonathan Cape 1972)

Stretto House

1 Holl, Steven: *op cit.*

2 Wittkower, Rudolf: *Architectural Principles in the Age of Humanism* (Academy Editions 1973)

Biographies

Ahlström Arkitektbyrå AB

Angsstigen 4, 181 41 Lidingö, Sweden

Gun Ahlström studied architecture at the Kungliga Tekniska Högskolan in Stockholm. He worked for Brunnberg & Forshed specializing in municipal housing before opening his own practice in 1993. He believes in supplying affordable accommodation for the general public and worked with IKEA on the Bo Klok development.

Arkitektgruppen Aarhus

Mollegade 9-13, DK-8000 Aarhus c., Denmark

Arkitektgruppen Aarhus has been in business for over 25 years. They have offices in Aarhus and Copenhagen and work in planning, architecture, design, construction, project management and landscape architecture. In recent years they have won over 40 architectural competitions and most of the projects have been built. The current partners are Jorgan Bach, Thomas Carstens, Lars Due, Per Feldthaus, Per Fischer, Michael Harrebek, Ole Nielsson, Erling Stadager and Helge Tindal. The group's built schemes have been awarded major national prizes, most recently the Byggefagenes Kooperative Landssammenslutnings BKL's Byggerpris (1996).

Atelier van Lieshout

Keileweg 26, 3029 BT Rotterdam, The Netherlands

Atelier van Lieshout was founded in 1995 by the Dutch artist Joep van Lieshout when he decided he needed help to construct his large-scale and complex artworks, designs and architecture. The practice now employs 15 individuals comprising artisans and artists; academicians, carpenters, metal workers and construction workers. Van Lieshout was educated at the Academy of Modern Art in Rotterdam, the Atelier 63 in Haarlem and the Villa Arson in Nice. His work won the Mart Stam Award in 1998, and has been the subject of numerous exhibitions throughout Europe and the US. Recent works include the KLM Units G-pier at Schipol Airport, Amsterdam; terrace furniture for the RVU, Hilversum; the Stylos Bookshop, Delft; study cells at the main library in Maastricht and floating sculptures at the Lange Vonder/Twiske Kakoelen, Amsterdam.

b&k
Brandlhuber & Kniess

Lichtstr. 26–28, D-50825 Cologne, Germany

Brandlhuber & Kniess was founded in Cologne in 1998 by Bernd Kniess and Arno Brandlhuber. Both studied architecture and town planning in Darmstadt. Their work has included the Neanderthal Museum, Mettmann (1994–6; with Zamp Kelp and Julius Krauss) and numerous schemes for homes and offices in Germany. Competition entries include the city library in Ulm, the Cologne Science Centre, a sports hall in Finsterwalde, a skyscraper in Frankfurt and the Dusseldorf Messe complex.

Shigeru Ban Architects

5-2-4 Matsubara Ban Bldg, 1FL Setagaya, Tokyo, Japan

Shigeru Ban (b. 1957) was educated at the University of Southern California, Los Angeles and at the Cooper Union School of Architecture in New York. He worked in the studio of Arata Isozaki before establishing his own practice in 1987. He is best-known for his series of paper tube structures, an early example of which is in the Issey Miyake office in Tokyo. Recent work includes a number of homes, such as the House Without Walls and the Furniture House, as well as the JR Tazawako Station. Ban has held exhibitions in Japan and the US and in 1995 won the Mainichi Design Award.

Birds Portchmouth Russum Architects

8 New North Place, London EC2A 4JA, UK

Andrew Birds, Richard Portchmouth and Michael Russum founded BPR in 1989 after winning an open competition for a parking lot in Chichester. All three partners had previously worked for James Stirling, Michael Wilford and Associates and were involved with major schemes including work for the Tate Gallery in London and the Bilbao Transport Interchange in Spain. Prior to this Andrew Birds had worked for Norman Foster and Michael Russum for Ahrends, Burton and Koralek, as well as for Aldo Rossi. Large-scale civic schemes and public projects include the Morecambe Sea Front, the Cardiff Opera House and the British Museum Inner Courtyard, all in the UK. Recent commissions include a restaurant for Somerset House in London and the Plashet Grove School bridge.

Brookes, Stacey, Randall

New Hibernia House
Winchester Walk, London SE1 9AG

Brookes, Stacey, Randall, established in 1987, combine a strong creative approach with an informed use of materials. The practice have gained a growing reputation for quality and efficiency, from research and development to architecture, product and furniture design. Design Council Registered in 1991 by virtue of their consistent high standards of project management and design quality, the firm have won numerous awards including Civic Trust Awards in 1994 and 1995, RIBA Awards in 1993, 1995 and 1997 and the Royal Fine Art Commission/*Sunday Times* Building of the Year Jeux d'Esprit Award in 1995 for the Thames Water Tower in London. Previous projects include the Lloyd Studio at Oxford Brookes University School of Architecture, East Croydon Train Station and the Churchill Centre in Rotterdam.

Wendell Burnette

9830 North 17th Street, Phoenix, Arizona 85020, USA

Wendell Burnette is a self-taught architect who, after spending 11 years in the studio of William Bruder, where he was involved in the Phoenix Library, founded his own company in 1996. His practice specializes in commercial and residential projects. Burnette has won local and national awards and is a guest lecturer at universities and AIA events across North America. He won an Emerging Voices Award from the Architectural League of New York and was the only American in an *Architectural Review* (January 1998) article on six architects considered to 'hold great promise for the coming year and beyond'.

Carden & Godfrey Architects

9 Broad Court, Long Acre, London, WC2E 9JX, UK

Carden & Godfrey, founded in 1946, specialize in all aspects of historic architecture – repairs, alterations, interiors and new construction. The current directors are Ian Steward (Dip. Arch, Dip. Cons (AA), RIBA); Richard Andrews (MA Dip. Arch, RIBA); Ian Angus (Dip. Arch RIBA) and Russell Taylor (D. Arch, Dip. Cons (AA), RIBA, IHBC, FRSA). The architect of Crosby Hall, Russell Taylor, joined the practice in 1988. Completed projects include the extension of the London Library, an office building in Highgate, an apartment block near Marble Arch and a new courtyard façade at the London Oratory. He is currently working on a new education building for the Royal College of Physicians and apartments and houses in Surrey and London.

de architectengroep

Barentzplein 7, 1013 NJ, Amsterdam, The Netherlands

De architectengroep comprises Kees Rijnboutt, Hans Ruijssenaars, Gertjan Hendriks, Dick van Gameren and Bjarne Masterbroek. The firm was founded in 1956, since when they have worked on a variety of projects from office buildings, shopping centres and residences to larger schemes including city halls, libraries and hospitals. Rijnboutt was educated in Delft where he later taught architecture at the Technical University. He is Chief Architect of the Ministry of Housing, Planning and the Environment and since 1995 has been the general architectural consultant of the Hague municipality. Ruijssenaars also trained in Delft, and later became Master of Architecture at the University of Pennsylvannia. He was made Chief Architect of Amsterdam's National Museum in 1995. Hendriks studied at the Academy of Architecture in Amsterdam where he teaches today. He is also a member of the editorial board of *Architectuur/Bouwen*. Van Gameren graduated from the Faculty of Architecture in Delft and worked for Mecanoo and Enric Miralles. Mastenbroek is also from Delft and has also worked for Mecanoo and Miralles. The two collaborate closely and were awarded first prize in the European Competition of 1991.

Christopher Day

Crymych, Pembrokeshire, Wales, UK

Christopher Day has been involved in ecological design projects in the UK, US and Scandinavia. He has also been visiting professor at Queen's University School of Architecture in Belfast. He is now working on the Life Science Trust in East Lothian, Scotland, a study centre based on the scientific work of Goethe. His latest book, *A Haven For Childhood*, was published in 1998.

Bill Dunster

East Molesey, Surrey, UK

Bill Dunster has taught and lectured widely on the subject of urban sustainability. Prior to setting up his own practice he worked with Michael Hopkins and Partners on the New Parliamentary Building in Westminster, London. His offices are now overseeing construction of 76 zero carbon dioxide emission dwellings in Beddington, South London for the Peabody Housing Trust.

DRMM
de rijke marsh morgan architects

1 Clink Street, Bankside, London SE1 9DG, UK

Alex de Rijke studied architecture in Amsterdam at the Royal College of Art. He has worked with Sjoerd Soeters, Rick Mather Architects and Tchaik Chassay Architects. He has taught widely and is a unit master at the Architectural Association and until recently at the Royal College of Art. He is a contributor to the Architecture Foundation Programme. He founded DRMM Architects along with Philip Marsh and Sadie Morgan. Projects include a health club for Curzons Management, a new apartment building for Angel Properties, the Hayward Gallery Mobile Exhibition, the regeneration of Watney Street Market (all in London), a health club in Grayshott, Surrey, a sushi restaurant in Brighton and a proposal for the design of Kingsdale School in London.

Nicole Edmonds/
Edge Architecture and Design

Hillview, 167 Findhorn, Forres IV36 3YL, Moray, Scotland, UK

Nicole Edmonds received a BSC in Architecture in 1982 from the Bartlett School in London. Her Diploma work was recognized by a British Institution Fund award and a nomination for the National Student Prize from the Royal Institute of British Architects. In 1988 Edmonds joined Arup Associates, where she was involved with the Stockley Business Park near Heathrow Airport, the design competition for British Airways Headquarters building and the design of a new grandstand at Goodwood Racecourse. With the aim of bridging the gap between architect and builder Edmonds joined the Findhorn Foundation where she became involved with the construction of ecological timber frame houses. This led to the design of a house made from a recycled whisky vat, which became her first independent project when she opened her own practice, Edge Architecture and Design. Today she works mainly on small residential schemes, including a series of straw bale houses, and renovations.

Flemming Skude, Ivar Moltke and Bertel Jensen

c/o Kunstakademiets Arkitekskole,
Byggeriets Studiearkiv, BSA,
Danneskiold Samsoes Alle 50m 1434
Copenhagen, Denmark

Flemming Skude (b. 1944) and Ivar Moltke (b. 1954) graduated from The Royal Academy of Fine Arts in Copenhagen as architects while Bertel Jensen (b. 1946) is a Bachelor of Science. Whilst Moltke and Jensen are employees at The Danish Institute of Technology, the builder of Villa Vision, Flemming Skude, is an independent architect who has had his own practice since 1978. Whilst his built work comprises mainly smaller houses his company is considered to be innovative in super graphics, design and ecology. He is a well-known architectural critic and philosopher.

F.O.B. Association

34-3 Tanaka Todo, Uji-City,
Kyoto 611-0013, Japan

F.O.B. Association is a collective, collaborative architectural practice with 11 members. The practice was founded in 1996 by Katsu Umebayashi (b. Kyoto 1963). He studied at the Osaka University of Arts and is currently a part-time lecturer at Kyoto Seika University, Kyoto Ritsumeikan University and the Kyoto University of Art and Design. FOBA's major built works include the Organ 1 & 11 complex in Kyoto, the Strata house in Kobe and the Yokokawa House in Tokyo. FOBA received the Tokyo Innovative Housing Award in 1996 (for the Aura house), the Japan Good Design Prize in 1999 (for the Catalyst bar/restaurant), and has been selected for the Venice Biennale 2000.

Zvi Hecker

Oranienburger Strasse 41,
D-10117 Berlin, Germany

Zvi Hecker was born in Poland in 1931. He moved to Israel in 1950 and now has offices in both Tel Aviv and Berlin. He studied architecture at the Krakow Polytechnic and at the Technion, the Israeli Institute of Technology in Haifa, where he received a degree in engineering and architecture in 1955. He set up his architectural practice at first with Eldar Sharon and later with Alfred Neumann, but has been working independently since 1966. Early works include the Club Mediterranée in Arziv and the city centre of Ramat Hasharon. Schemes such as the Spiral apartment house in Ramat-Gan and the Jewish School in Berlin have led to Hecker being considered one of Israel's leading architects and he has recently won much acclaim for the Palmach Museum of History in Tel Aviv and the Holocaust Memorial in Vienna. Hecker represented Israel at the 1991 Venice Biennale, and in 1996 when he curated the 'Architect as Seismograph' exhibition. He won in 1996 the German Critic Prize for Architecture and in 1999 the Rechter Prize for Architecture in Tel Aviv. He has lectured at numerous schools of architecture in Europe and the US and in 1998 was Guest Professor at the Universitat für Angewandte Kunst in Vienna.

Herzog & de Meuron Architekten AG

Rheinschanze 6,
4056 Basle, Switzerland

Jacques Herzog and Pierre de Meuron both studied at the Eidgenossische Technische Hochschule in Zurich and began their partnership in 1978. Along with Harry Gugger and Christine Binswanger, they founded their current practice in 1997. Today they have offices in Basle, London and Munich. Both Herzog and de Meuron are visiting professors at Harvard and are members of the Association of Swiss Architects and of German Architects. Award-winning schemes include the Signal Box and the Engine Depot in Basle. They recently completed Tate Modern in London's Bankside. Their work has been exhibited internationally as well as being the subject of many articles including monographs in *El Croquis* and *A&U* magazine.

Anthony Hoete

119 Avenue Albert,
Brussels 1190, Belgium

Anthony Hoete was born in 1967 on Motiti Island, New Zealand. He studied architecture and engineering at the University of Auckland and later received a M.Arch from the Bartlett School in London. In 1991 he was a member of a group exhibition which was awarded the Venice Prize for Architecture Schools. He has worked with several renowned architects including Stefano di Martino, Nigel Coates, Sauerbruch Hutton and Mecanoo, with whom he collaborated on schemes such as the Chiat Day Advertising office refurbishment, the Hotel Helgoland, Hamburg and the Bilderberg Park Hotel, Rotterdam, as well as on competitions including the Welsh Centre for Literature in Swansea and the masterplan of the Thames Southbank, London. Today his own practice, SLAB, specializes in small-scale domestic and leisure schemes and he also teaches at the Bartlett and the Sint Lucas Schools of Architecture. He edited the first architectural CD-Rom magazine, *Artifice*, and writes for various publications including *Monument Australia* and *Quaderns*.

Steven Holl Architects

435 Hudson Street, 4th Floor,
New York, New York 10014, USA

Steven Holl (b. 1947) is a graduate of the University of Washington. He studied architecture in Rome in 1970 and did post-graduate work at the Architectural Association in London in 1976. In the same year he established Steven Holl Architects in New York. His designs have been the subject of major retrospectives in various museums in the US. Holl won the National AIA Interiors Award for the offices of D. E. Shaw & Co. in New York and the National AIA Honor Award for Excellence in Design for Stretto House in Dallas. In the same year, 1993, Steven Holl Architects submitted the winning design in the competition for the new Museum of Contemporary Art, Helsinki. Among Holl's most recent prizes are the 1996 Progressive Architecture Awards for Excellence in Design for the Hamsun Museum in Bodo, Norway and the Museum of the City in Cassina, Italy. Holl's Ignatius chapel in Seattle won the 1998 National AIA award for Design Excellence. Holl teaches at the Columbia University Graduate School of Architecture and the Pratt Institute in New York, and at the University of Washington in Seattle.

Carl-Viggo Hølmebakk Arkitekt

Sofiesgate 70,
0168 Oslo, Norway

Carl-Viggo Hølmebakk has been a self-employed architect for the last ten years working on small-budget building projects in Norway. He also frequently collaborates with other architectural practices on concepts for larger and more complex schemes whilst teaching at various universities, including the Oslo and Trondheim Schools of Architecture. Hølmebakk is review critic at Helsinki University and at Harvard, and has recently taken part in competitions for the Borgen church and the Filipstad Park and Villa.

Rick Joy Architect

400 South Rubio Avenue,
Tucson, Arizona 85701, USA

Rick Joy studied music performance at the University of Maine, fine art at the Portland School of Art, and architecture at the University of Arizona where he received a B.Arch in 1990. After graduating he joined William Bruder Architect and worked on the Phoenix Central Library. In 1992 he moved to Design and Building Consultants where he was lead designer and project architect for the Axelrod Residence in Tucson. He founded his own practice the following year and is earning international recognition with such schemes as the Tyler residence, Convent Avenue studios and the Palmer/Rose house. His work has been featured in many leading design magazines including, *Architectural Review*, *Domus, GA Houses* and *wallpaper** and has been the recipient of national prizes including the *ID* magazine 1997 Annual Design Award for Convent Avenue studios. Joy lectures at several US universities and is involved with the University of Arizona and Arizona State University as visiting critic for student reviews and seminars.

Kathan-Schranz-Strolz

c/o Holzbox Tirol, Colingasse 3,
A-6020, Innsbruck, Austria

Armin Kathan, Martin Schranz and Erich Strolz began working together in 1993 and have since won awards for New Building in Tirol in 1996, for the Höttingerau house in Innsbruck, and for Innovative Building in Vorarlberg for their living/office space in Vandans. Projects include the Wimberger & Schumacher house in Innsbruck and the LUEF house at Holzbox Tirol. They are currently working on residential projects in Lech. All three partners studied at the University of Innsbruck. Erich Strolz's work has featured in various exhibitions including Innovative Austrian Architecture in 1996. Armin Kathan has worked for architectural firms in Austria, Germany and the US and Martin Schranz, who studied Architecture and Music at the University of Vienna, has worked on several projects in Germany and Austria, and has lectured at the University of Innsbruck.

Anne Lacaton and Jean Philippe Vassal Architects

4 place Pey Berland,
33000 Bordeaux, France

Lacaton and Vassal were born in Saint Pardoux la Rivière, France in 1955 and Casablanca, Morocco in 1954, respectively. They both studied at the Ecole d'Architecture in Bordeaux and hold diplomas in town planning. Since

forming their practice in the early 1990s projects have included residential and renovation schemes, a bar and cafeteria in Vienna, the Arts and Human Sciences Building at the Pierre Mendes-France University and the Palais de Tokyo in Paris. In 1999 they were selected for the Fifth European Architecture Prize at the Mies van der Rohe Foundation and they were recently awarded the Grand Prix for Young Talent by the French Ministry of Culture. Their work has been the subject of numerous exhibitions, most recently in a joint show at the Guggenheim Museum in New York in collaboration with the Musée National d'Art Moderne du Centre Georges Pompidou.

Niall McLaughlin Architect

166 Portobello Road,
London W11 2EB, UK

Niall McLaughlin founded his practice in 1991. He is noted for the extension of the De La Warr Pavilion in Bexhill-on-Sea, England, which was the RIBA competition-winner in 1993. Earlier works include a housing development in Kensington, the refurbishment of the Carmelite Convent and a new chapel in Kensington (which was named one of 'Britain's Modern Wonders' by *The Independent* newspaper) and the Ben Uri Art Gallery in Camden, all London. His work was been exhibited in the touring show of 16 British practices 'Future Visions', and he represented Britain at the Sao Paulo Architecture Biennale in 1997. The following year he was named Young British Architect of the Year by *Building Design*.

Enric Miralles Benedetta Tagliabue Arquitectes Associats

Ptge. Pau 1o bis, Pral,
08002 Barcelona, Spain

As this book was going to press, it was with great sadness that we heard of Enric's death at the tragically early age of 45. Our thoughts go to Benedetta, his children, and all those who enjoyed the warmth of his creative imagination.

Enric Miralles (1955–2000) was an architect and Professor at the School of Architecture in Barcelona and at the Staedelschule in Frankfurt. He founded his own studio in 1984 and in 1993 formed a partnership with Benedetta Tagliabue. Tagliabue graduated from the IUAV in Venice with a thesis on Central Park in New York. She specializes in restoration and is in charge of exhibitions and publications. The practice has been the recipient of numerous prizes in architectural competitions, including the concept for the 'New City of Orestadt' in Copenhagen (1994), the rehabilitation of the Santa Caterina Market in Barcelona (1997), the Cemetery of San Michele, Venice, (1998), the Scottish Parliament building in Edinburgh (1998) and the new headquarters of Natural Gas in Barcelona (1999). Many of these schemes have since been built or are in construction. At the time of Miralles' death, he and Tagliabue were working on many major public works, most notably the Barcelona 2004 Forum of Culture, the School of Architecture in Venice and the Utrecht City Hall. Miralles won many national and international awards, including the Leone d'Oro prize at the 1996 Venice Biennale. He held major retrospectives around the world and taught at several US universities including Harvard, Princeton and Columbia.

MVRDV

Schiehaven 15, 3024 EC Rotterdam,
The Netherlands

The office for architecture and urbanism MVRDV was founded in 1991 by Winy Maas, Jacob van Rijs and Nathalie de Vries, all of whom trained at the Technical University of Delft. The three partners lecture in Europe and the US and have won international acclaim with projects such as the gatekeeper's house at the Hoge Veluwe National Park, the offices of the broadcasting organizations VPRO and RVU in Hilversum, the Double House in Utrecht, and the Dutch Pavilion at the Expo 2000 which was awarded the Belmont Prize Forberg Schnieder Stiftung. They have masterplanned a mediapark in Hilversum, housing in Zoetermeer and the Parklane Airport in Eindhoven. They took part in the 2000 Venice Biennale with the exhibition 'MetaCITY/DATATOWN, KM3/3d City and other MVRDV Projects'. They have shown their work around the world and have been featured in most of the leading architecture and design journals including a monograph published by *El Croquis* (1997).

Office for Metropolitan Architecture

Heer Bokelweg 149, Rotterdam,
The Netherlands 3032 AD

OMA was founded in London in 1975 by Rem Koolhaas, Madelon Vriesendorp, and Elia and Zoe Zenghelis and early work consisted mainly of a number of polemic competition entries. Subsequent to a competition entry for the extension of the Dutch Parliament, OMA was given its first commissions, the IJ plein masterplan in Amsterdam, and the Netherlands Dance Theatre in The Hague. Major schemes to date include the Lille Grand Palais; the masterplan for Eurolille which was executed by Koolhaas in collaboration with Nouvel, de Portzamparc and Shinohara, and the Educatorium at the University of Utrecht. OMA's city planning work encompasses the 1.25 billion Euro development of the new town of Almere in The Netherlands and study projects for the development of the new Seoul International Airport City and the masterplan for Hanoi New Town. OMA is closely linked with the Groszstadt Foundation which was involved in the realization of Koolhaas's book, *SMLXL*. Koolhaas (b. 1944) attended the Architectural Association in London and is currently a professor at Harvard, where he is leading a series of research projects for the Harvard Project in the City, which studies different issues affecting the urban condition.

Walter Pichler

Walter Pichler (b. 1936) studied at the Academy of Applied Arts in Vienna after which he spent a year in Paris where he started his experimentation in the sculpting of plastics. His first exhibition, 'Architecture', in collaboration with Hans Hollein, was held in 1963 at the Galerie Nacht St. Stephen in Vienna. During the following ten years his works, most notably in heavy timbers, metals and man-made products such as concrete, were exhibited throughout Austria and Germany. He believes strongly in the relationship of his sculptures to their surroundings and his first completed buildings at St Martin an der Raab,

Burgenland, to house his creations date from 1972. His reputation as one of Austria's leading artists has grown due to one-man shows at MoMA and the Leo Castelli Gallery in New York, the Whitechapel Gallery in London and the Museum of Israel in Jerusalem. In 1982 he exhibited in the Austrian Pavilion at the Venice Biennale.

Michael Reynolds/ Solar Survival International

PO Box 1041, Taos,
New Mexico 87571, USA

Michael Reynolds graduated from the University of Cincinnati in 1969 with a Bachelor of Architecture degree. He is interested in the development of self-sufficient housing made from recycled materials and founded Solar Survival International, which designs and distributes Earthships. He has worked with Brigham Young University, Utah, on Third World housing in Bolivia, with the Everest Environmental Project to reduce human waste problems in the Himalayas, and on the 'Wheel Kingdom' – a model city for the twenty-first century – in Japan. In 1992 he took part in a European lecture tour and is due to embark on another in 2001.

SANAA Ltd./ Kazuyo Sejima Ryue Nishizawa & Associates

7-A, 2-2-35 Higashi-Shinagawa,
Shinagawa-ku, Tokyo,
140-0002, Japan

Kazuyo Sejima graduated from the Japan Women's University with a M. Arch. degree after which she joined Toyo Ito and Associates. She set up Kazuyo Sejima and Associates six years later and began her collaboration with Ryue Nishizawa (b. Tokyo, 1966) in 1995. He graduated from Yokohama National University with a M. Arch degree and joined Kazuyo Sejima in 1990. He became partner in 1995 and from 1997 has also had his own studio. He is a visiting lecturer at the Yokohama National University and the Nihon University. The practice's major projects include the Museum of Contemporary Art Extension, Sydney; the Stadstheater, Almere, The Netherlands; the regeneration of central Salerno, Italy, and the Museum of Contemporary Art, Kanazawa. Their S & M house series and the Gifu Project have won recognition both nationally and internationally. They were selected in 1998 to design the new Contemporary Art Centre, Rome.

Shim-Sutcliffe Architects

441 Queen Street East,
Toronto, Ontario, Canada M5A IT5

Brigitte Shim and Howard Sutcliffe believe that architecture, furniture design and landscape should be integrated. All their award-winning schemes pay homage to the local environment. Their largest project to date is the Ledbury Park community facility. Their work has appeared in publications such as *Domus*, *L'Architecture d'Aujourd'hui*, *Detail*, *Architectural Review*, *Architectural Record* and *Arquitectura Viva*. Sutcliffe was born in Britain and trained in environmental studies architecture. Shim is a member of the Faculty of Architecture, Landscape and Design at the University of Toronto, and was a visiting professor at Harvard's Graduate School of Design in 1993 and 1996. Their practice has received numerous honours, including five Governor General's Medals and Awards for Architecture along with AIA and *ID* magazine prizes.

Architekten Prof. Klaus Sill

Harkortstrasse 121 22765,
Hamburg, Germany

Prof. Klaus Sill (b. 1955) graduated from the Hochschule für Bildende Künste in Hamburg with a Diploma in Architecture in 1984, and was awarded the student prize by the BDA in Hamburg. He worked in the studio of Otto Steidle and Uwe Kiessler before opening his own practice in 1989 in partnership with Jochen Keim. Since 1999 he has worked independently, and the same year was awarded the Design Chair at the University of Applied Arts in Hamburg. He has participated in numerous design competitions, and specializes in domestic and small-scale public buildings. Prof. Sill's work has been published in most of the main national architecture and design magazines.

Professor Thomas Spiegelhalter

Postfach 5107, 79018 Freiburg,
Germany

Thomas Spiegelhalter began his career as a sculptor. He studied three-dimensional design and architecture in Bremen and at the Hochschule der Künste in Berlin. Today he is a consultant in sustainable architecture, building and object design and has taught at the Carnegie Mellon University, Pittsburgh, since 1999. Spiegelhalter is interested in re-development projects for abandoned industrial architecture and landscapes, in solar low-energy housing and cultural and commercial buildings, and has participated in numerous exhibitions and symposia on experimental solar architecture. Since 1990 he has received over 30 awards in international competitions. Recent schemes include the Solar Houses, Ihringen, the conversion of a pebble bottling plant in Weil am Rhein into a leisure and exhibition centre in 1999, the bridge to the Park of Sense in Laatzen for Expo 2000, and the bridge over the Schelde Kanaal in Belgium. He is currently involved in a research project, 'Sustainable Urban and Lanscape Projects and Solar Design Patterns in Pennsylvania'.

Szyszkowitz & Kowalski Architekten

Elisabethstrasse 52,
Graz, A-8010 Austria

Michael Szyszkowitz and Karla Kowalski have collaborated since 1973 working together in Frankfurt, Munich, Graz and Stuttgart before founding their own studio in 1978 in Graz. They now also have offices in Stuttgart and Braunschweig. Szyszkowitz (b. 1944) trained as an architect at the Technical University in Graz. He worked with Behnisch and Partner and Domenig and Huth before joining Kowalski. Kowalski (b.1941) studied architecture at the Darmstadt Technical University. She trained as a joiner in the early 1960s and also worked for Behnisch and Partners. They have won 22 competitions, most recently the German Architecture Prize (1999). Recent schemes include the UCI Cinema Work in Graz, and housing complexes in Voitsberg and Heidelberg. They are presently working on the prototype of the Dream House – a concept for prefabricated housing – and a business complex on

the Potsdamer Strasse in Berlin. Szyszkowitz and Kowalski are professors at the Technical Universities of Braunschweig and Stuttgart respectively. In 1993 Kowalski was made a member of the Academy of Fine Arts in Berlin.

Tegnestuen Vandkunsten

Badmandsstraede 6,
DK-1407 Copenhagen, Denmark

Tegnestuen Vandkunsten was founded in 1970 by the principal partners, Svend Algren (b. 1937, Landscape Architect PLR, Architect m.a.a/BDA), Jens Thomas Arnfred (b. 1947, Professor, Architect m.a.a), Michael Sten Johnsen (b. 1938, Professor, Architect m.a.a.) and Steffen Kragh (b. 1947, Director, Architect m.a.a./BDA). The practice is a member of both the Professional Architects Council and the Danish Federation of Architects. It specializes in the development of co-operative housing but is involved in all aspects of architecture, from landscape to town planning, and from public and commercial buildings to the interior design of homes and offices. The firm has received over 40 national and international prizes and has worked with numerous municipalities in Denmark on local planning for around 5,000 dwellings, institutions, free areas and industrial buildings. The firm works mainly in Denmark (where they have been the recipient of many awards including the National Arts Foundation Architectural Prize in 1999) but have also worked in Sweden, The Netherlands and Germany.

Jørn Utzon

Jørn Utzon (b. 1918) was educated at the Royal Academy of Arts in Copenhagen. Projects include the Sydney Opera House (1962); the National Assembly Building in Kuwait (1972) and the church at Bagsvaerd (1971). His work has been widely published and is the subject of several monographs. Prizes include the Gold Medal, Royal Academy of Arts, Copenhagen (1945); the Gold Medal, Royal Australian Institute of Architects (1973); the RIBA Gold Medal (1978) and the Alvar Aalto Medal (1982).

Tony Wrench

The Round House,
near Newport, Wales, UK

Tony Wrench plays the tamboura, mandolin, violin and guitar. He has no interest in the past, preferring to concentrate solely on the future. He requests that letters of support for retrospective planning consent for the Round House be addressed to the Welsh National Assembly at Cardiff.

Elemer Zalotay

CH-3054, Schüpfen/Ziegelried,
Switzerland

Elemer Zalotay (b. 1932) studied at the Technical University of Budapest and moved to Switzerland 1973. He considers his greatest achievement to be the publication of his concept for a model town in *Interbuild* magazine, which gave the concept the title 'Corb Plus' and compared it favourably with the town-planning work of Le Corbusier. Without this recognition he feels that he would have never embarked on his life work – the experimental house at Ziegelried which he started in 1978 and which he says will never be completed.

Index of architects and projects

Picture credits